You Can Understand the Old Testament

Its Meaning and Its Message

Second edition

❧

James C. Bangsund

You Can Understand the Old Testament:
Its Meaning and Its Message

Second edition

Cover, graphics, and layout by author

To

my wife Judy

and our children

Naomi, Peter and Sharon

who have been God's greatest sources

of support and encouragement

for many years.

Preface
to the Second Edition

From 1993 through 2006 my wife, Judy, and I taught on the theological faculty of Makumira University College in Tanzania, East Africa. She was campus chaplain and I taught Old Testament and Hebrew.

This book comes out of that experience. It was originally written for the students in my Old Testament classes and, although the present revision has a different audience in view, the original audience of young Tanzanian men and women preparing for the ministry is never far offstage.

The present intended audience is American and would include all serious students of the Bible, whether lay or clergy, including college or seminary students. This second edition was motivated in particular by members of St. Timothy's Lutheran Church in San Jose, California, where I am now on staff. Enough requests were made for the few copies which I had brought back from Tanzania that I thought it was time to reprint. And reprinting gave opportunity for revising, and here we are.

Let me note several characteristics of the book right up front. First, it is written from a Christian perspective. This is not to say that a Jewish reader would find a great deal that is unfamiliar. But the use of the phrase "Old Testament," as distinguished from (though certainly not opposed to) "Hebrew Scriptures," is of itself indication that I believe there is a "New Testament" which must follow. (A discussion of this terminological choice begins on the first page of the first chapter.)

Second, the first edition of the book was written using the resources of the library at Makumira University College around the year 2005. That library is one of the best in Tanzania, but is somewhat limited in terms of recent material. I also use the RSV translation throughout, not so much because of the difficulty of revising but because I still consider it the best English translation.

Third, as already mentioned, the book was originally written for a seminary classroom. For this reason, the reader will find important Hebrew words included in the body of the text in both Hebrew characters as well as in transliteration. That being said, nothing in the book *requires* any understanding of Biblical Hebrew; and, for those who are interested, there is a short overview of Biblical Hebrew, along with a list of important vocabulary, at the end.

There is, in addition, a feature generally lacking in books of this type: a list of verses for memorization at the end of each chapter. Christians who memorize scripture verses often tend to focus heavily upon the New Testament and, while this understandable, I would contend that the Old Testament also has a deep and rich reservoir of texts, the knowledge of which will only enrich one's faith and life. It is, after all, the Bible that Jesus read – and Peter, and Paul, and all the rest. We do well to *know* it well.

James C. Bangsund
San Jose, California
July 2014

Acknowledgments

First Edition

There are many whom I need to thank for their assistance in preparing this book. First, of course, are my students at Makumira University College. The past 13 years of teaching the Exegesis and Theology of the Old Testament class to third year Bachelor of Divinity students, and more recently to Diploma students, have impressed upon me the need for a resource which could serve a number of needs.

First of all, the Exegesis and Theology class covers only a selection of the books of the Old Testament, and thus much remains unexplored. This book gives an overview of the whole Old Testament and can now help fill that gap.

Second, it is hoped that this overview, brief as it is, might be a useful tool in the parish. Parish pastors in Tanzania do not have the luxury of large book allowances or libraries, and it is hoped that a few pages on each of the books of the Old Testament will provide at least a basic foundation for preparation of sermons and Bible studies.

I want in particular to thank the 2005-06 BD3 class and the 2006-07 Diploma 1 class who were the first to go through this material. First readings always reveal weaknesses and shortcomings, and I appreciate the comments and suggestions made by a number of students as the terms progressed. This new edition of the book is a great improvement upon and expansion of the first, due to this student input.

But there have been others, more in the background, who have also contributed much. My wife Judy, chaplain and teacher of homiletics, gave the first reading to all of the material, often within an hour of its coming off the keyboard. I was at times writing just one week ahead of the students, and her critical eye prevented many embarrassments. Once the first edition was finished, I then shared it with four other readers who contributed immensely. The first was Jean Wahlstrom, chaplain at the Masai Girls Lutheran Secondary School in Monduli, Tanzania. Jean read not only as a former Dean of Academic Affairs, but as a teacher of Tanzanian students; thus, she had an eye for rooting out excessive syntactical complexity. Dr. Ronald Eggert, physician, birder, and website builder, and his wife Ingrid, went through the manuscript with a fine tooth comb and revealed to me, among other things, that I have an excessive love of commas! That last sentence has seven, you will note, and I am sure they would cut it to four and the sentence would be improved by it. Rev. Graham Hutchins, Facilitator at Arusha Community Church, read with a theological eye trained by many years of reading and experience. And Beth Elness-Hanson, formerly a volunteer at Masai Girls Lutheran Secondary School and now a theology student at Fuller Theological Seminary, provided perhaps the greatest amount of correction, critique and suggestion. Several pages of additional material are the result of her noting of gaps and deficits.

To all these I am grateful.

James C. Bangsund
Christmas 2006

Second Edition

I want to thank Dr. Nancy Koester of St Paul, Minnesota, who, with a professional eye for detail, noted a goodly number of editorial details in need of attention. This second edition has profited from that close reading, for which I am grateful.

Table of Contents

Abbreviations

Biblical references follow the format suggested by the Society for Biblical Literature (SBL). When the name of the book stands alone, or with chapters but not verses, no abbreviation is used (Genesis; 1 Kings 1; 2 Chronicles 36-37; etc). When verses are included, an abbreviation is used (Gen 1:27; 1 Kgs 2:4; 2 Chr 36:22-23; etc.).

ABD	*Anchor Bible Dictionary*, ed. D. N. Freedman. 6 vols. New York: Doubleday, 1992
ANE	Ancient Near East
ANET	*Ancient Near Eastern Texts Relating to the Old Testament*, 3rd ed. with suppl., ed. J. B. Pritchard, New Jersey: Princeton, 1969.
BHS	*Biblia Hebraica Stuttgartensia*
DH	Deuteronomistic History
IDB	*Interpreter's Dictionary of the Bible*, ed. G. A. Buttrick. 4 vols. Nashville: Abingdon, 1962
ISBE	*International Standard Bible Encyclopedia*, ed. G. W. Bromiley. 4 vols. Grand Rapids: Eerdmans, 1979-1988
LXX	The Septuagint
NASB	New American Standard Bible
NIV	New International Version of the Bible
NRSV	New Revised Standard Version of the Bible
RSV	Revised Standard Version of the Bible

Maps

Lists, Charts, Diagrams

Discussion Blocks

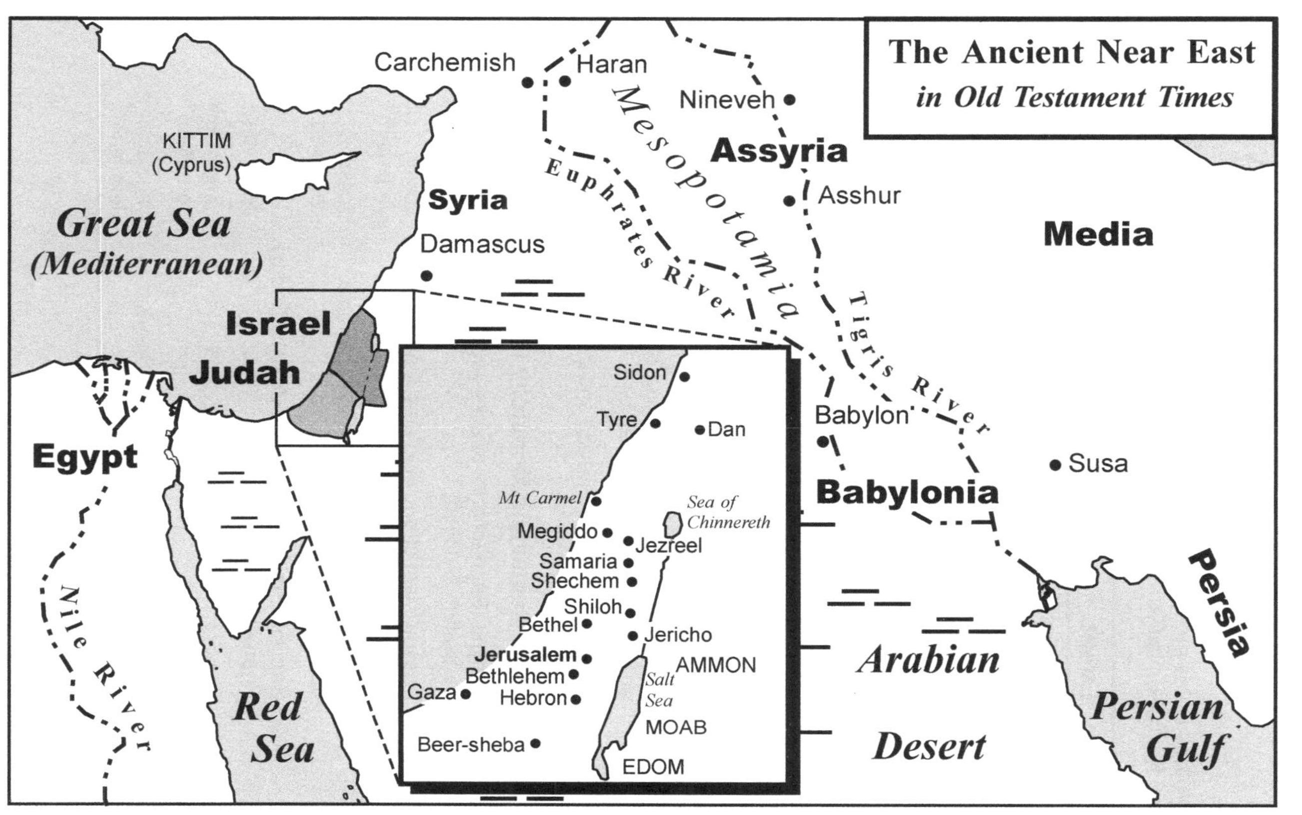

The Ancient Near East
in Old Testament Times
Carchemish
Haran
Nineveh
Mesopotamia
Assyria
Asshur
KITTIM
(Cyprus)
Syria
Euphrates River
Great Sea
(Mediterranean)
Damascus
Media
Tigris River
Israel
Judah
Sidon
Tyre
Dan
Babylon
Egypt
Susa
Mt Carmel
Sea of
Chinnereth
Babylonia
Megiddo
Jezreel
Samaria
Shechem
Shiloh
Persia
Bethel
Jericho
Jerusalem
AMMON
Bethlehem
Salt
Sea
Arabian
Gaza
Hebron
Nile River
Red
Sea
MOAB
Persian
Gulf
Beer-sheba
Desert
EDOM

An Old Testament Chronology

Notes: Dates are B.C. Dates before the Divided Monarchy are approximate.
[U]: King of United Israel, [I]: King of Israel, [J]: King of Judah, [P] = Prophet

Date	Event	Names
1700	Patriarchal period (Genesis 12-50)	Abraham, Sarah, Isaac, Jacob
1350	The Exodus	Moses, Joshua
	United Monarchy (1025-922 B.C.)	
1025	Saul becomes king	Saul[U], Samuel[P]
1000	David becomes king	David [U], Nathan[P]
960	Solomon becomes king	Solomon[U]
	Divided Monarchy (922-724 B.C.)	
922	Civil war splits (united) Israel into Israel (north) and Judah (south)	Rehoboam[J], Jeroboam I [I]
745	Tiglath-Pilesar III becomes king of Assyria and starts expanding his empire	Amos[P], Hosea[P]
722	Assyria (Sargon II) invades and destroys Israel and Samaria	Ahaz[J], 1 Isaiah*[P], Micah[P]
	Remaining Monarchy (715-586 B.C.)	
701	Assyria (Sennacherib) attacks Judah, Jerusalem is saved	Hezekiah[J], 1 Isaiah*(1)[P]
627	Assyria's last strong king dies, Babylon rises, reforms begin in Judah	Josiah[J], Jeremiah[P]
622	Book of the law discovered in the temple during reforms	Josiah[J], Jeremiah[P]
609	Babylon challenges Assyria; Josiah killed by Pharaoh Neco	Josiah[J], Jeremiah[P]
605	Babylon destroys army of Egypt at Carchemish	Jehoiakim[J], Jeremiah[P]
598	Jehoaichim rebels and is killed; Babylon invades & conquers Judah	Jehoiachin[J], Jeremiah[P]

Date	Event	Names
	Exile (597-538 B.C., in Babylon)	
597	First group of Judean exiles is taken to Babylon	Jehoiachin[J], Jeremiah[P]
587	Zedekiah rebels, is blinded and taken to Babylon	Zedekiah[J], Jeremiah[P]
586	Babylon destroys Jerusalem and temple; more exiles are taken	Jeremiah[P], Ezekiel[P]
539	Persia conquers Babylon	2 Isaiah*[P]
	Post-exile (Persian period) (538-333 B.C., in Judea)	
538	Cyrus of Persia allows Jews to return to rebuild	2 Isaiah*[P]
520	Reconstruction of (second) temple begins	Haggai[P], Zechariah[P]
515	Reconstruction of (second) temple completed	3 Isaiah?*[P], Malachi[P]
458	Ezra arrives to encourage the exiles	Ezra, 3 Isaiah?*[P]
445	Nehemiah arrives to rebuild wall of Jerusalem	Nehemiah, 3 Isaiah?*[P]
	Hellenistic Period 333-164 B.C.	Daniel* 165 B.C. ?
	Maccabean period 164-63 B.C.	
	Roman period begins: 63 B.C.	

*See p. 171 for 1 Isaiah, 2 Isaiah, 3 Isaiah. See pp. 5 and 193-198 regarding the dating of Daniel and why Daniel is not here marked as a prophet.

The Old Testament:

-An Overview-

Why is the Old Testament[1] "old"?

Christians call the first 39 books of the Bible the Old Testament. It might be better to call them the "Old Covenant" (as they are called in Swahili), because the idea of *old* and *new* comes from Jer 31:31-34. There we read, "Behold, the days are coming, says the LORD, when I will make a new covenant with the house of Israel and the house of Judah, not like the covenant which I made with their fathers ...."

The first Christians were Jews[2] who recognized Jesus as the ful-

---

[1]I use the term "Old Testament" to refer to the collection of books which is translated from Hebrew and follows the order of the Septuagint. More is said below concerning the relationship of "Old Testament" to "Hebrew Scriptures."

[2]In general, Jews are descendants of Abraham, of course. However the matter is actually more complex than that. According to Genesis, Abraham had two other wives whose children became fathers of Arab tribes. Ishmael was Abraham's son by Hagar (Genesis 16), and after Sarah's death Abraham took Keturah as a wife and had other children who became fathers of other Arab groups (Gen 25:1-6). Thus, it is really the descendants of Abraham *and Sarah* who eventually became a nation named Israel. The Old Testament brings us the history of this family-become-nation, but in a number of ways (which we shall see) it also displays a concern for those outside this nation.

There is a second issue that is important in today's world. The modern state of Israel is not the same as the Israel we find in the Bible. No doubt many, if not most, of the citizens of modern Israel would trace their ancestry back to Abraham. But modern Israel is a secular state which was created by the United Nations in 1947. Thus, we refer to people of the Old Testament as *Israelites*, but the citizens of the modern state of Israel are called *Israelis*. Modern Israel is not a religious state, and most Israelis are not religiously active. The relationship between modern Israel and Palestine has been a complicated and unhappy one, with guilt on both sides. And understanding this relationship can be difficult for us as Christians when we discover that most of the Christians in that part of the world are found among the Palestinians, who trace *their* ancestry back to the earliest Christians of the first century.

fillment of this promise. He was understood to be God's "new covenant," and eventually books were written about him. These books – the four Gospels, the book of Acts, the letters of Paul, etc. – became known as the books of the New Covenant or the New Testament. The original 39 books, Genesis through Malachi, were then called the Old Covenant or Old Testament.[3]

Why do we study the Old Testament?

The first books of the New Testament were not written until about 30 years after Jesus' death and resurrection. Before these new books about Jesus were written, the early Christians had only the Old Testament. Thus, what we call the Old Testament was the Bible for Jesus and for Peter and the other disciples, as well as for Paul and all the rest of the early Christians. We will better understand Jesus and his teachings and his death and resurrection if we understand his Bible; and we will better understand the books written *about* Jesus – the *New* Testament – if we understand their foundation, which is the Old Testament.

And there is another reason for studying the Old Testament. As Christians, we believe that it, too, is God's Word. Like the New Testament, it contains both Law and Gospel. God speaks to us through the Old Testament as well as the New, and thus we need to understand it.

How is the Old Testament organized?

The books of the Old Testament are organized in several different ways by Jews and Christians.

THE HEBREW SCRIPTURES

Jews put the books in a different order than Christians do. They

---

[3]See also page 183, footnote 7. Jews do not call these 39 books the "Old Testament" or "Old Covenant" because they do not agree that Jesus was the fulfillment of Jeremiah's "new covenant" promise. Thus, religious Jews today believe there is still only one covenant, "the covenant which I made with their fathers" (Jer 31:32). They call the 39 books of their scriptures by several names: Torah (which refers only to the first five books), the Hebrew Scriptures, the Hebrew Bible, or *Tanak* (an abbreviation for the Hebrew words "Law, Prophets and Writings"). Muslims, on the other hand, believe that the "original" Old Testament and the Gospels were God's word, but that they have become corrupted.

divide them into:

- **The Law** (Hebrew: *torah,*[4] תּוֹרָה): Genesis, Exodus, Leviticus, Numbers and Deuteronomy (the same as in the Christian Bible)
- **The Prophets** (Hebrew: *nebi'im,* נְבִיאִים): here we find two groups of books in the Hebrew Scriptures:
  - **The "former prophets":** Joshua, Judges (but not Ruth), 1-2 Samuel, 1-2 Kings (but not 1-2 Chronicles). These books are called the "former prophets"[5] because they tell of prophets such as Gad, Nathan, Ahijah, Jehu, Elijah, and Elisha. Their words were collected but not in books bearing their names.
  - **The "latter (classical) prophets":** these books contain the words of Isaiah, Jeremiah, Ezekiel, Hosea, Joel, Amos, Obadiah, Jonah, Micah, Nahum, Habakkuk, Zephaniah, Haggai, Zechariah, Malachi (but not Lamentations or Daniel). The last twelve (Hosea through Malachi) are considered to be a single book because they are short. Thus, in the Hebrew Scriptures, the "latter prophets" are Isaiah, Jeremiah, Ezekiel and The Twelve.
- **The Writings** (Hebrew: *ketubim,* כְּתוּבִים): Psalms, Job, Proverbs, Ruth, Song of Solomon, Ecclesiastes, Lamentations, Esther, Daniel, Ezra-Nehemiah, and 1-2 Chronicles. Note that, in the Hebrew Scriptures, Lamentations and Daniel are found here, and not with the prophets.

This organization developed over time. The Jews first recognized (or "canonized"[6]) the five books of the Law (*torah*) as God's word. "Law" is actually not the most accurate translation of the word *torah*

---

[4]When Hebrew words are mentioned, they will be given in an informal transliterated form. (Technically, תּוֹרָה is transliterated *tôrâ* and the next word (נְבִיאִים) is transliterated n^{e}*ḇî-ʾîm*. For the purposes of this book, however, such formality is not necessary. For more information, see p. 267-271.)

[5]The actual phrase "former prophets" is used in Zech 1:4; 7:7,12.

[6]A canon (note: not "cannon") is a list of books which scholars or other authorities agree belong to a certain collection. For instance, the letters written by the apostle Paul might be called the Pauline canon. Everyone would agree that Romans belongs to that canon, but there would be disagreement about whether the letters to Timothy or Titus were written by Paul. Thus, some would say that they are part of the Pauline canon, and others would not.

(תּוֹרָה), and we should probably speak instead of "instruction" or "guidance." Jews do not understand *torah* in quite the same way that Christians do. Rather than understanding the *torah* as a "law" which shows them their sins (as we read in the book of Romans, for instance), they rejoice in God's gift of *torah* as a sign of his love for them. See, for instance, Ps 19:7-11, or Psalm 119 (especially vv. 44-45).

Later, after these books of instruction or "law" were canonized, the words of the prophets were also recognized as being God's word. The words of some prophets, such as Nathan and Elijah, were not collected into individual books bearing their names. Instead, their words are found in 1-2 Samuel and 1-2 Kings. Jews therefore called 1-2 Samuel and 1-2 Kings the books of the "former prophets" and placed them before the group of "latter" or "writing"[7] prophets such as Isaiah, Jeremiah, Amos, Hosea, etc. This collection of the "former prophets" and the "latter prophets" was then simply called "the Prophets" and forms the second major section of the Hebrew Bible.

At this point, the Jews had "the Law and the Prophets." Jesus often mentions this phrase, and we can even see it represented in the Transfiguration, where Moses (representing the Law) and Elijah (representing the Prophets) appear with Jesus (representing the New Covenant).

After the time of Jesus, the rabbis (teachers of Israel) produced a final list which included a third group of books. This third group of books contained a wide variety of material, and so it was simply called the Writings. It included a lot of poetry, such as the Psalms, but also books like Ruth and Daniel (see the list on p. 3).

THE CHRISTIAN OLD TESTAMENT

Christian tradition generally divides the Old Testament as follows:

Law: Genesis through Deuteronomy (just like the Jews)

History: Joshua, Judges, Ruth, 1-2 Samuel, 1-2 Kings, 1-2 Chronicles, Ezra, Nehemiah, Esther

Poetry: Job, Psalms, Proverbs, Ecclesiastes, Song of Solomon

Prophets: Isaiah, Jeremiah, Lamentations, Ezekiel, Daniel, Hosea,

---

[7]The phrase "writing prophets" is not really correct, since the words of these prophets were usually collected by others; the prophets themselves did not often write (Jeremiah is an exception). The "former" and "latter" prophets are sometimes also called the "pre-classical" and "classical" prophets.

Joel, Amos, Obadiah, Jonah, Micah, Nahum, Habakkuk, Zephaniah, Haggai, Zechariah, Malachi

Here we see several differences between the Hebrew Scriptures and the Christian canon or Old Testament.

- *First*, Christians often call the "former prophets" books of History – and include several books which Jews place in the Writings: Ruth, 1-2 Chronicles, Ezra, Nehemiah and Esther.
- *Second*, the Christian canon places Daniel among the prophets, the Hebrew Scriptures do not. This may mean that Daniel was written rather late, and thus the rabbis placed the book in the Writings. This question of dating is discussed below in the section on Daniel.
- *Third*, the Hebrew Scriptures end with 2 Chronicles and the Christian Old Testament ends with Malachi.

This last point is significant; readers are left with different feelings when they get to the end of each of these "Bibles." For Jews today, the last word of their Bible is Cyrus' proclamation in 2 Chr 36:22-23 that the Jews should return from Babylon to rebuild Jerusalem:

> Whoever is among you of all his people, may the LORD his God be with him! Let him go up!

For Christians, the last words of the Old Testament are those of Mal 4:5 regarding the sending of Elijah:

> Behold, I will send you the prophet Elijah before the great and terrible day of the LORD comes.

Last words are often important words. Because of these two different ways of ending the Bible:

- Jews today often focus upon returning to Jerusalem (each Passover meal, every year throughout the world, concludes with the words, "Next year Jerusalem!")
- Christians hear in the last words of Malachi a promise which pointed to John the Baptist, who came to announce Jesus.

At the time of Jesus, however, the Writings had not yet been canonized. Thus, at the time of Jesus the Hebrew Scriptures ended with Malachi just as the Old Testament does today. This means that, for first century Jews who were waiting for Messiah, the "last word" of the Bible was also this promise that God would first send the prophet Elijah. Thus, the eyes of Judah turned with expectation and hope when John the Baptist arrived and then pointed to Jesus.

THE QUESTION OF THE ROMAN CATHOLIC BIBLE

There is also a second question for Christians to consider: Why do Roman Catholics have more books in their Bible than do Protestants? The lists above (pp. 3 and 4) show 39 books, but the Roman Catholic and Slavonic Bibles have more books than either the Hebrew Scriptures or the Protestant Old Testament. This is because the early church used a Greek translation of the Old Testament called the Septuagint (often abbreviated LXX). Because the Septuagint is written in Greek, it attracted additional Greek books, and so for many years the church had an Old Testament with more books than are found in the Hebrew Scriptures.

In order to better understand this situation, we need to take a closer look at the Septuagint.

THE SEPTUAGINT

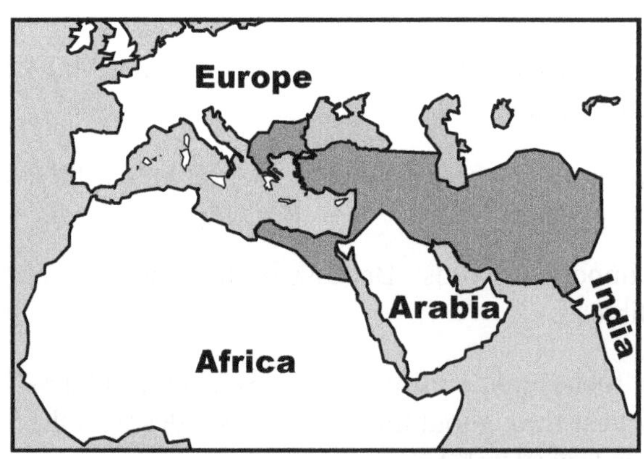

The Empire of Alexander the Great (336-323 B.C.)

About 330 B.C., the young Greek general, Alexander the Great, conquered a large empire which ran from Greece to India. The Greek language became popular throughout the eastern Mediterranean area including northern Africa and the Middle East (thus including Palestine, of course). Because of this, the 39 books of the Hebrew Scriptures were translated into Greek, and this Greek translation became known as the Septuagint.

Then something significant happened. Other books were written – in Greek, not Hebrew. Some of them were closely related to the stories found in the original 39 books of the Hebrew Scriptures. These books had titles such as the Wisdom of Solomon (or Ecclesiasticus – different from Ecclesiastes), the Letter of Jeremiah (different from the prophet Jeremiah), and various additions to the book of Daniel . Other books told about later Jewish history – for instance, the Maccabees. As long as the Hebrew Scriptures were in Hebrew, and these other books were in Greek, there was no confusion. Only the books written in Hebrew were considered by Jews to be God's word.

As Greek became more popular, however, many Jews – and most of the early Christians – began to read the Septuagint instead of the Hebrew Scriptures. The Septuagint became the Bible of the early church. Furthermore, because the Septuagint was written in Greek, it began to attract these other books: Maccabees, Sirach, Psalms of Solomon, etc. These additional books were then added to the Septuagint and were used in the early church, but they were still not considered to be scripture by the Jews.

This continued until the time of the Reformation, when Martin Luther and other reformers decided that it was best to follow the Jewish tradition and eliminate these extra books. However, the Roman Catholic Church decided to keep the additional books, and thus they have them today. We call these other books "deutero-canonical books" (second canon) or sometimes "the Apocrypha." These deutero-canonical books will not be included in the book summaries given below on pages 19 and following. However, they are worth reading in order to learn about the intertestamental period.[8]

Today the Septuagint is important for scholarly work, since we no longer have the original Hebrew Bible. Rather, we have copies of copies of copies of the original texts. If an error was made when the Hebrew text was copied in, say, 500 A.D., that error will not be in the Septuagint, translated in the third century B.C.[9] (The Septuagint has

---

[8]The intertestamental period is the period between the end of the Old Testament and the beginning of the New Testament. Generally, we may think of it as being the period from 400 B.C. to the time of Christ. (The book of Daniel is a special case which will be discussed later.)

[9]One famous examples of this is 1 Sam 10:1, where the scribe copying the Hebrew text accidentally skipped several dozen words. However, this mistake was made after the Septuagint was translated. Thus, the words had already been translated and placed in the Septuagint many years before they were missed by the scribe copying the Hebrew. Thus, the missing words remain in the

picked up copying errors of its own over the centuries, of course).

The Septuagint is also important for New Testament Study. When one sees differences between a text in the Old Testament and the way it is quoted in the New Testament, it is because the New Testament is quoting the Septuagint which often has slight translation differences from the Hebrew.

What are the major concerns of the Old Testament?

The Old Testament tells about God and his relationship with the world before the time of Jesus. It tells how God created the world and its creatures, and how people broke relationship with God. It tells this story in many ways, but primarily with regard to the nation Israel. Israel is often called "God's chosen people," but as we read we discover that God actually *created* Israel rather than *choosing* it. God started with two people (Abraham and Sarah) and from their descendants he created Israel as a new nation among the other nations. And note this: God was

---

Septuagint today and have been recovered. How did the Hebrew scribe miss the words? Quite likely his eye skipped from the first occurrence of the word to its second occurrence. This is called *haplography*. Here is 1 Sam 10:1 with the missing words in italics:

> Then Samuel took a vial of oil and poured it on his head, and kissed him and said, "Has not the LORD anointed you to be prince over *his people Israel? And you shall reign over the people of the LORD and you will save them from the hand of their enemies round about. And this shall be the sign to you that the LORD has anointed you to be prince over* his heritage.

The scribe apparently read the first part of the verse, through the words "anointed you to be prince over" (just before the italics, above) and then turned to copy the text. When he came back to read some more, his eye accidentally went to the second "anointed you to be prince over" phrase (at the end of the italics section above), and he continued his copying with the words "his heritage." Thus, the italicized words were left out of the new Hebrew copy, and today they are still missing in the Hebrew Scriptures. But this haplography did not occur when the Septuagint was translated and copied. Thus, the words have been recovered and are found in modern Bibles.

The opposite of haplography is *dittography*. Dittography occurs when the scribes eye returns to an *earlier* occurrence of a word. In this case, the words in between do not get skipped; rather, they get copied twice. See 2 Sam 6:3 and the RSV/NRSV footnote for an example where the translators use the LXX because the Hebrew accidentally repeats a phrase.

already concerned about *all* nations of the world (see Genesis 11) long before he created Israel (beginning in Genesis 12). The Old Testament is for all of us and about all of us.

Israel's relationship with God showed both great blessing as well as great sin and broken relationships. As Christians, we believe that God created Israel in order to prepare the world for his great healing of this broken relationship. He eventually did this by taking on human flesh and entering the world as a man of Israel: Jesus (the) Christ.[10] The New Testament tells us how this God-man Jesus then lived, and taught, and healed, and suffered and died – and then was raised from the dead to bring forgiveness to the whole world. The Old Testament deals primarily with God preparing his new nation, Israel, to receive this gift.

The Lands of the Old Testament.

In order to understand how God worked with Israel as a nation among other nations, we need to understand where Israel lived. Thus, we need to begin with some maps. Most events in the Bible (both Old and New Testament) took place two to four thousand years ago in what is today the **Middle East**. We shall see below that the location was important then and is still important today.

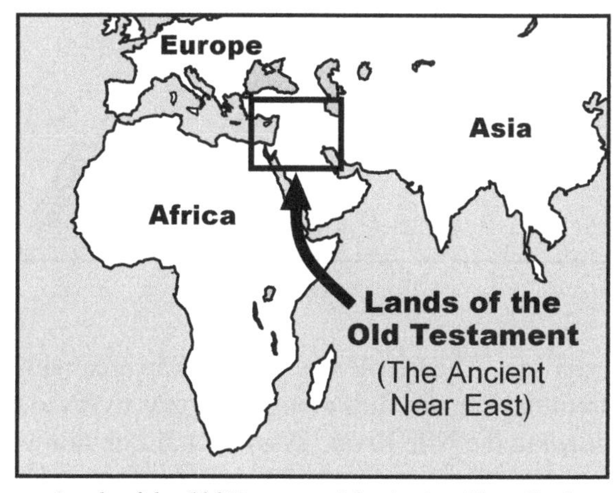

Lands of the Old Testament (*the Ancient Near East*)

As you can see in the first map (*Lands of the Old Testament*), God chose some very centrally located land in which to carry out his relationship with Israel. The lands of the Old Testament were right in the midst

[10]"Christ" is not part of Jesus' name. Rather, it is a Greek word (*christos*, χριστος) which means "Messiah" (*meshiach*, מָשִׁיחַ) or "anointed one." Old Testament kings were anointed (*mashach*, מָשַׁח) by having oil poured over their heads, signifying their installation to office. Thus, "Jesus Christ" really means "Jesus the Messiah" or "Jesus the anointed one."

of Africa, Europe and Asia. This was an ideal location; especially later, in New Testament times, it allowed the news of what God was doing to spread to the rest of the world. When studying this area in biblical times, we call it the **Ancient Near East (ANE)**because we are studying how it was three thousand years ago.

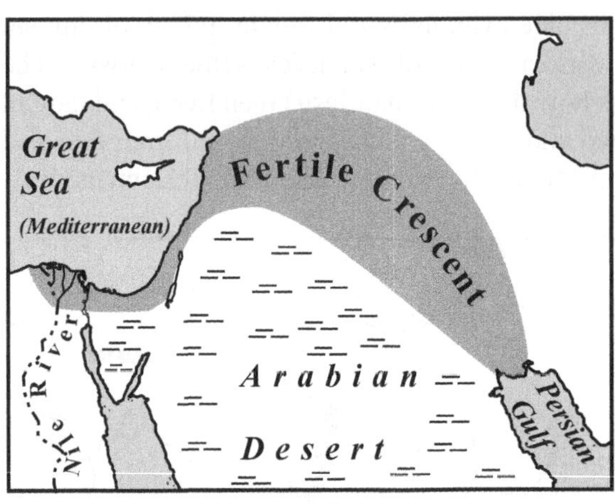

The Fertile Crescent

The next map (*The Fertile Crescent*) gives a more detailed view of the box in the first map. The **Great Sea** (Mediterranean), the **Fertile Crescent** and the **Arabian Desert** are very important. Why? Because water is life! The super powers in the Old Testament were nations which lived on rivers. The Fertile Crescent was an area with water which stretched from the Persian Gulf along two great rivers to the Great Sea and then down to the Nile River. Assyria and Babylon were found along rivers in the Fertile Crescent, and Egypt was found along the Nile. One could not travel in a straight line from the Persian Gulf to the Nile because of the Arabian Desert. Thus, traders and armies followed the Fertile Crescent's rivers and the edge of the Great Sea as they traveled the routes between the Persian Gulf and the Nile.

As you will see in the map on the next page, these areas with good water supplies developed into the leading cultures of the Ancient Near East: Egypt, Assyria and Babylon (and eventually Media and Persia). Actually, these cultures were not nations as we understand nations today; rather, they were collections of cities. Egypt was a collection of large cities along the Nile River, and Assyria and Babylon were groups of cities built along the **Tigris** and **Euphrates Rivers** in what is today Iraq. This area is also called **Mesopotamia** because it lies "between" (meso-) the rivers (-potamia). These two great civilizations – Mesopotamia and Egypt – were in continual competition.

In order to read and understand the Old Testament, you should be familiar with the important place names: **Canaan,** and the "super powers" **Egypt, Assyria and Babylon, Media and Persia**. You should also know the Fertile Crescent, why it is important, and why its eastern part is called Mesopotamia.

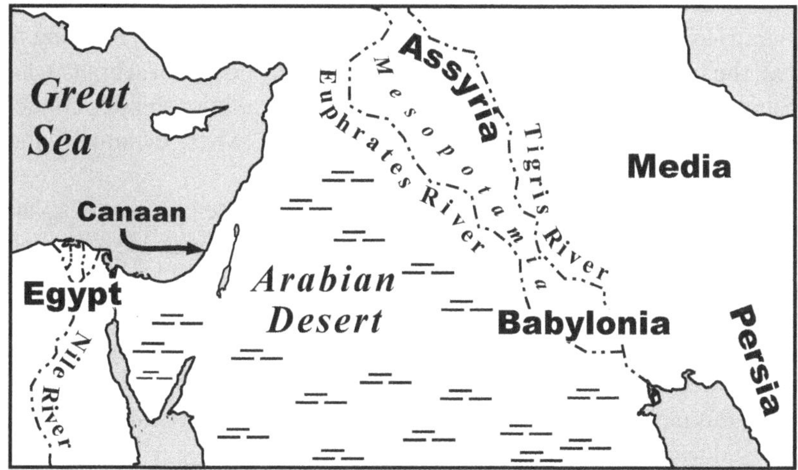

The Ancient Near East

The people of Israel eventually lived in the land of Canaan. Israel was never a superpower, but its location made it very important *to* the super powers. Again, the issue was water. As mentioned above, traders and armies could not travel in a straight line between Mesopotamia and Egypt. They had to remain near water, and so, they followed the Fertile Crescent (see the map on the previous page).

The Fertile Crescent became the major route for trade and war, and Israel sat on the narrow piece that ran along the Great Sea. Whoever controlled this narrow piece of land controlled trade and military travel between Egypt and Mesopotamia. Thus, Israel's location was both a blessing and a curse, and Israel often received unwanted attention, especially from Assyria and Babylon.

The Old Testament story.

The Old Testament story is, in many ways, the story of ancient Israel. It is the story of the movement of God's people back and forth between Mesopotamia and Egypt. Indeed, some of the earliest stories of Genesis seem to have a relationship with Mesopotamia.

Creation and the Patriarchs. Genesis starts with the creation of the world, long before there was a nation of Israel. Genesis 1-11 describes several broken relationships which show the result of people disobeying God.[11] Genesis 12 thus becomes one of the most important chapters in the Bible. There we read how God responded to the human rebellion of Adam and Eve by choosing another man and woman (Abraham and Sarah) to build a new nation. This nation was to become a blessing for "all the families of the earth." Yet as these descendants of Abraham and Sarah began to multiply, the problems of broken relationships continued. The book ends with the whole family in Egypt, where eventually they were made slaves by Pharaoh.

The Exodus and the Judges. In **Egypt**, the descendants of Abraham became a people (though not yet a nation). God chose Moses to lead this new people out of Egypt, and to receive the "Law" (see the discussion of this word on p. 3) at Mt. Sinai.[12] By the time the people reached the promised land of Canaan, they had law, traditions, and a priesthood. The twelve tribes were now ready to become a nation. At first, this new nation of **Israel**[13] was led by **temporary leaders**: Joshua, the Judges, and Samuel.

The first kings of Israel. Eventually the people received a king: Saul. **Saul** was at first a good king, but eventually failed.[14] The next king was **David**. David was Israel's greatest king, and began to reign around the year 1000 B.C. He was generally faithful, and God promised that one of his descendants would always rule as king over Israel. (Jesus was a descendant of David, and Christians see him as the ultimate fulfillment of this promise.) Later, David was remembered as the standard or model for faithfulness, and the other kings were compared to him. David was not a good family manager, however, and power

---

[11]These chapters tell about Adam and Eve, Cain and Abel, Noah and the Flood, and the Tower of Babel. Each of these stories shows an increase of sin in the world. More is said about this in the section on Genesis, below.

[12]Some Biblical writers use the name "Mt Horeb" for Mt Sinai. If you are familiar with source theories of the Pentateuch, it is the Elohist and the Deuteronomist who refer to Mt Horeb.

[13]"Israel" (*yisrael*, יִשְׂרָאֵל) was the new name given to Jacob because, according to Gen 32:28, he had struggled (*sarah*, שָׂרָה) with God and with men. (See p. 26 for more discussion of *sarah*, שָׂרָה.) The name "Israel" may mean either *God strives* or *he (Jacob) strives with God.* This name was then used for the new nation formed by the tribal descendants of his 12 sons.

[14]The failures of Saul are discussed on p. 88.

struggles developed between his sons. **Solomon** finally became king after David but was not faithful, though he was described as wise. Solomon's son **Rehoboam** was not even wise.

The divided kingdom. Rehoboam's arrogance brought **civil war**. In 922 B.C. Israel split into two nations which then continued to fight. The ten northern tribes abandoned Rehoboam and the house of David. They took a northerner, **Jeroboam** (Jeroboam I), as their king, but they kept the name **Israel**. The southern tribes of Judah and Benjamin remained with Rehoboam, and took the name **Judah**.

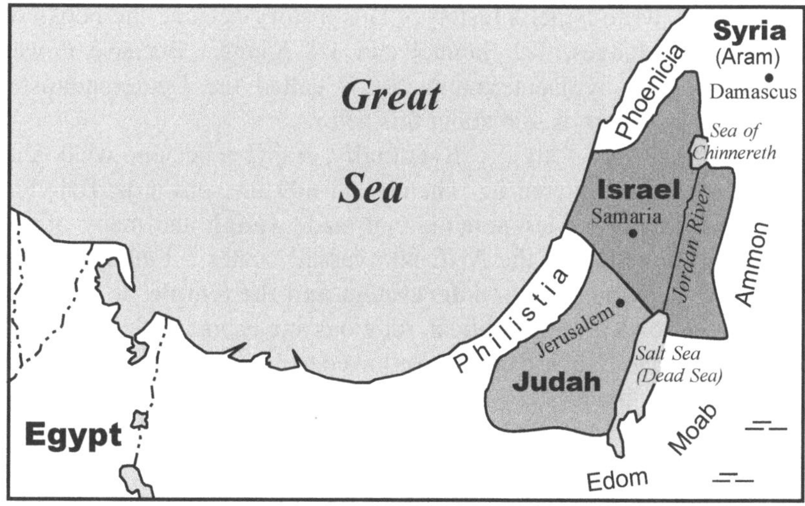

The Kingdoms of Israel and Judah and their Neighbors

The map above shows how the land looked after the civil war. Israel (with its capital **Samaria**) was generally stronger and wealthier than Judah, but the Bible remembers the kings of Judah as being more faithful to God (though not *very* much more faithful!).

You should know the names and locations of the surrounding kingdoms. **Egypt** was the most powerful, but **Syria** (with its capital, Damascus) was also influential. **Philistia**, **Phoenicia**, **Ammon**, **Moab** and **Edom** were not great powers, but were near neighbors and so it is important to know them, too.

After the civil war, and the division of the nation, the remaining history of Israel and Judah was marked by **four major events**:

- ASSYRIAN CONQUEST. In **722 B.C.**, **Assyria** (see map on p. 11) marched from Mesopotamia and destroyed the northern kingdom of Israel and much of Judah to the south. The leadership of **Israel** was taken away and scattered throughout the Assyrian empire. The nation was never restored. Most of the villages of Judah, to the south, were also destroyed, but Jerusalem was spared (as the prophet Isaiah said it would be).

- JOSIAH AND DEUTERONOMY. In **622 B.C., a "book of the law"** was found in the temple during the reforms of Josiah, king of Judah. This was probably an early edition of Deuteronomy, and its discovery led to many other reforms. Deuteronomy also inspired the ministry of the young prophet Jeremiah, and it motivated someone else to write Israel's history. This history became the books of Joshua, Judges, 1-2 Samuel and 1-2 Kings. Because it was influenced by Deuteronomy, it is called the Deuteronomistic History. More is said about this below.
- BABYLONIAN EXILE. Eventually, Assyria became weak and **Babylon** conquered it. Then, from **609 B.C.** onwards, Babylon marched from Mesopotamia and made **Judah** and many of the other countries of the ANE into vassal[15] states. Finally, in **586 B.C.**, Babylon destroyed **Jerusalem and the temple**, as Jeremiah had predicted. The political, religious and economic leaders were all taken to Babylon but were allowed to maintain their culture and religious practices. The Babylonians were more enlightened captors than Assyria had been, and the Jews lived fairly well there.
- RETURN AND RECONSTRUCTION. In 539 B.C., Babylon was defeated by **King Cyrus of Persia** (see the map on p. 11) who, in **538 B.C.**, allowed the Jews to return to **rebuild Jerusalem and its temple**. (As noted on p. 5, above, the words of Cyrus are the last words found in the Hebrew Scriptures.) Most Jews remained behind in Babylon, but several groups returned. After the prophets Haggai and Zechariah encouraged the people, they finished rebuilding the temple in 515 B.C. In the next century, Ezra and Nehemiah led religious reforms and oversaw the completion of the wall around the city.

The prophets. The period of the eighth century B.C. (800-700 B.C.) and the seventh century B.C. (700-600 B.C.) was very difficult for Israel and Judah. God had sent prophets to warn the people and their leaders

---

[15]A vassal is a state or a person who is owned or controlled by someone more powerful, and who therefore must serve them, pay taxes, etc.

about two things in particular:

- IDOLATRY: people had begun to worship not only the Canaanite god Baal, but also the gods and goddesses of many surrounding nations (see the section on ANE gods on pp. 271-275).
- INJUSTICE: the wealthy abused and oppressed those who were weak and the poor in both Israel and Judah.

The prophets also criticized another practice: POLITICAL RELATIONSHIPS WITH FOREIGN NATIONS. This was actually related to the first issue (idolatry) because international treaties and alliances required accepting the gods of the other nations. Furthermore, trusting in such alliances showed a *lack* of trust in the God of Israel.

The prophets therefore brought three kinds of messages:

- WARNING against idolatry and injustice. Ezekiel cried, "Why will you die, O house of Israel? ... turn and live" (Ezek 18:31-32)
- JUDGMENT when the warnings were ignored. Jeremiah said: "Prepare yourself baggage for exile" (Jer 46:19).
- HOPE after the judgment. While the people were in Babylon, God told Isaiah to, "Comfort, comfort my people" (Isa 40:1).

Then, as mentioned above, when the people had returned to Judah from Babylon, several prophets spoke words to encourage the rebuilding of the temple and moral reform.

That, in brief, is "The Old Testament Story." More is given in the chapters ahead, of course, but even there we can only give an introduction and survey of the grand drama which makes up the Old Testament. After reading this book, students of scripture who want to dig deeper will need to engage in three more tasks which are different but related:

- EXEGESIS: This is the detailed examination of the text, preferably in its original language. One investigates matters such as date, historical setting, and purpose of writing. One watches how a given text relates to what comes before and after it, and one tries to observe the rhetorical moves of the author. Grammatical issues of gender and number, tenses of verbs, and unusual vocabulary are noted. The goal is to understand as well as possible what the text meant to its original hearers, and to do so at a basic level which is free of cultural and theological bias. That, at least, is the goal. We can never completely free ourselves from our own background and presuppositions, of course, but we can at least be aware that we do carry such bias and try to minimize its effect.

- HERMENEUTICS: Here we move from the basic understanding of the texts provided by exegesis to an interpretation. One might say that we now move from "What does the text say?" to "What does it mean?" At this point, our own background, presuppositions, and theology will have more effect. To some extent this is good. One of the goals of hermeneutics is to interpret a text in light of the theology and meaning of the rest of scripture. But, again, we must also be aware of, and try to fight, our tendency to bend the meaning of text in order to make it say what we already believe.

- THEOLOGY AND THEOLOGIES: When we collect our hermeneutical work – our interpretations of many texts – we can then work on theology. The theology of a text is a summation of what it says about God and about our relationship with God. We can speak of the theology of a verse of scripture, but more often we speak of the theology of an author (for instance, Jeremiah or Paul) or of a book (such as Deuteronomy) or of a group of books (the Pentateuch, or perhaps the first four books of the Pentateuch).

  And we need to realize that the Old Testament (and indeed the whole Bible) contains more than one theology. These theologies will sometimes challenge and contest one another in ways which provide healthy and necessary tensions[16] in scripture. The interplay of these tensions can then itself be discussed in theological terms.

The three tasks mentioned above bring us beyond the goals of this book – though at times we may touch upon one or another of them. For instance, each of the book discussions below will include a short section on the "Message" of the book.

Before continuing to the Old Testament books themselves, you should be sure you know the following:

- Why is the Old Testament "old"?
- How it is organized (for Jews and for Christians)?
- What is the Septuagint, and why is it important?
- What is a canon?

---

[16]A "tension" can be thought of as two truths which challenge and perhaps even conflict with each other, and yet both are necessary and both are true.

- What is the Old Testament about, generally?
- What is the Old Testament story? Be able to tell it from beginning to end.
- What nations and cities are important? Know the maps (including important rivers and bodies of water).
- What dates are important? Be sure to know the dates listed below:

SOME BASIC DATES[17]

1700 B.C.	Abraham and Sarah (date is very approximate)
1350 B.C.	the Exodus under Moses (date is very approximate)
1000 B.C.	David became king
922 B.C.	Civil war splits Israel into Israel (north) and Judah (south)
722 B.C.	Assyria invades and destroys Israel (north) and its capital Samaria; leadership is scattered throughout Assyrian empire
622 B.C.	"Book of the law" is discovered in the temple during the reign of Josiah
586 B.C.	Babylonian invasion and destruction of Judah, Jerusalem, and the temple; leadership is exiled to Babylon
538 B.C.	Cyrus of Persia allows the Jews to return to rebuild Jerusalem and the temple
515 B.C.	Reconstruction of the (second) temple is completed

[17]Dating of events in the Old Testament is often difficult. One problem is that the Jewish calendar is lunar, and does not simply run January through December (see p. 278). Thus, books written about the Old Testament may give dates which are one year apart. For instance, the fall of Samaria may be dated 722 or 721 B.C., the discovery of the "book of the law" may be 622 or 621 B.C., etc.

The Pentateuch
(The five books of the Law)
-An Overview-

Jews consider the first five books of the Old Testament to be the most important. They were canonized first (see p. 3, above), and they contain all the laws, or instructions,[1] followed by observant Jews[2] even today. (Today, however, there is no temple and no sacrifice). Since these first five books were originally written on five scrolls, they are called the Pentateuch (*penta* = five, *teuchos* = scroll).

Christians also consider these books to be extremely important. This is not because of the details of the law but rather because of other foundations which are found there. In addition to the giving of the law (especially the Ten Commandments), the Pentateuch introduces Creation and humanity's Fall into sin, the stories of the early patriarchs,[3] God's delivering Israel from slavery in Egypt, and Israel's arrival at the edge of the promised land of Canaan. More is said about these "beginnings" in the "Message" section on p. 21.

Authorship: Did Moses write the Pentateuch? Some evidence seems to indicate that he did. The Jews have always called these books "the books of Moses." And Jesus several times refers to "Moses," "the book of Moses," or "the law of Moses." On the other hand, some parts of the Pentateuch seem not to have been written by Moses.[4] Although

---

[1]See p. 3 regarding the meaning of *torah* as "instruction or guidance" rather than merely "law."

[2]An "observant" Jew is a religious Jew who tries to follow all the laws of the *torah* and the traditions of the rabbis.

[3]The patriarchs of Israel were Abraham, Isaac, Jacob, and Jacob's 12 sons who became heads of the twelve tribes. The matriarchs of Israel were their wives, Sarah, Rebekah, Rachel and Leah, and so on.

[4]There are notes which were added later such as "At that time the Canaanites were in the land"(Gen 12:6; 13:7) or the description of Moses' death at the end of Deuteronomy. There are places where material seems to come

this question of authorship is very interesting, it can also get in the way of our understanding. It can consume our attention and our energy and prevent us from hearing what the Bible itself is saying. Therefore, in this book we will not spend a great deal of time on this question. You may believe the Pentateuch was written by Moses, or you may consider it to be the result of several authors and sources and editors; the important thing is not to get lost in arguments about such matters and instead to listen to what Scripture is saying.

The question of Deuteronomy: Leaving aside the question of authorship, it is still important to recognize that the Pentateuch has two very different parts. The major story is found in the first four books, Genesis through Numbers. This story includes the Creation and Fall, the stories of the patriarchs, the deliverance from Egypt, and the giving of *torah*. Then there is the book of Deuteronomy, which tells the story again. Therefore it is called Deuteronomy (*deuteros* = two, *nomos* = law), or "the second telling of the law." The first four books (Genesis through Numbers) read like a *story*; Deuteronomy, on the other hand, reads like a *sermon* by Moses.

The difference is so great that some have suggested that we do not have a Pentateuch (five books), but rather a *Tetra*teuch (four books) plus Deuteronomy. The theologies of these two pieces – the "tetrateuch" and Deuteronomy – are also somewhat different. Furthermore, the theology of Deuteronomy is then found also in Joshua, Judges, 1-2 Samuel and 1-2 Kings. Those six books are therefore called the Deuteronomistic History, and some would place Deuteronomy with them. More is said about that in the discussion of those books beginning on p. 63.

Sinai material: Finally, even Genesis through Numbers has two major pieces. The main story, from creation through Abraham and Moses to arrival in the Promised Land, is found in Genesis, Exodus 1-19 and Numbers 10-36. The material is primarily narrative; that is, it is in the form of a story. On the other hand, Exodus 20 through Numbers 9 (actually through Num 10:10) is all about Sinai. It is heavily legal, including not only the giving of the Ten Commandments but also a great deal of detailed law code material which may have been added later.

---

from more than one source, such as when two different explanations are given for the name Beer-sheba (Gen 21:31 and 26:33) or when the call of Moses is given twice (Exodus 3 and Exodus 6). And in general, Moses appears in the third person (*Moses, he, him*) rather than the first person (*I, me* as, for instance, is found in the book of Nehemiah).

Thus, the Pentateuch seems to have a complex history.

The Pentateuch as a whole. When did Israel first have and read the whole Pentateuch? The various parts of the Pentateuch were probably carried to Babylon when the leadership was taken into exile around the year 600 B.C. There, the pieces were put together, perhaps by a scribe like Ezra. Ezra is suggested because he was among those who later returned from Babylon to Jerusalem in the fifth century B.C. (see the Old Testament Chronology on p. xv.) Nehemiah 8 describes the moment when Ezra stood before the people and read "the book of the law." This may have been around 440 B.C., and was perhaps the world's first public reading of the Pentateuch. It was a dramatic moment. "All the people wept when they heard the words of the law" (Neh 8:9), because these "words of the law" – this Pentateuch – would become the text which defined and guided them for all time to come.

Outline:

- **I. Creation and Fall (Genesis 1-11)**
- **II. Patriarchs (Genesis 12-50)**
  - A. Abraham (and Isaac*) (Genesis 12-25)
  - B. Jacob (and Isaac*) (Genesis 26-36)
  - C. Joseph (and his brothers) (Genesis 37-50)
- **III. Moses (Exodus through Numbers)**
  - A. Deliverance from Egypt (Exodus 1-19)
  - B. The giving of the Law at Sinai (Exodus 20-Numbers 9)
  - C. Traveling toward the Promised Land (Numbers 10-36)
- **IV. Moses' final sermon (Deuteronomy)**

* There are only a few stories of Isaac, and they are mixed in with the stories of Abraham (his father) and Jacob (his son).

Message

The Pentateuch is the foundation for the rest of the Old Testament, and therefore for the rest of the Bible. In it we read of beginnings:

- The beginning of the world
- The beginning of people
- The beginning of sin and God's plan to save people from sin
- The beginning of Israel
- The beginning of the Law (instruction, guidance), and

- The beginning of the cult:[5] priests, sacrifice, the temple, etc.

The Pentateuch tells us that God is the source of everything, and that we (humanity as a whole) have rebelled against God. However, it also tells us that God desires to create, to love and to save; that is his nature. He did not simply punish or destroy the rebels; rather, he started with the patriarchs and gave them descendants, land and blessing. He created a people named Israel so that they could become a blessing to the world. Part of that blessing was the *torah*, the guidance and instruction which we usually call "the Law (of Moses)."

In many ways, Israel and these blessings pointed ahead to the day when God would enter the world in human form as Jesus the Christ,[6] Jesus the Messiah. On that day, God's promise to Abraham would be fulfilled – his promise that through Abraham's descendants "all the families of the earth will be blessed" (Gen 12:3).

---

[5]When we speak of Israel's "cult" we mean its formal religious structures and practices: the priests and Levites, the tabernacle or temple, Israel's sacrificial and other worship practices, etc. See p. 46 for more detail.

[6]See footnote 10 on p. 9 for a discussion of the title "the Christ."

Genesis

❧

Overview

Genesis is the first book of the Pentateuch.[1] It has two major sections:

I. The Prehistory (Genesis 1-11)
II. The Patriarchs (Genesis 12-50)

Prehistory (*Genesis 1-11*). The first eleven chapters are called "prehistory" because they describe events which we cannot date and so cannot be placed in history. The stories of creation, or Adam and Eve, or any of the other episodes in these chapters are timeless, or outside time; they are thus "before history." Many people consider them to be historical, nonetheless. Others consider these stories to be like parables: stories which teach us truth, but which did not happen historically. Again, either of these opinions still allows us to hear what the Bible is teaching, and that is what is important. Fighting over opinions on creation, Adam and Eve, the Flood, etc., only prevents us hearing what God wants us to learn from his Word.

In Genesis 3-11, we read four stories of the Fall into sin (see the diagram on the next page). Each story shows people trying to "become like God." And there is a pattern: In each story there is **sin**, then God's **judgment**, then an act of **mercy** from God. For instance, in the second story the sin is murder, the punishment is Cain's being sent away, and the act of mercy is the mark God puts on Cain. Sin then spreads further and God's judgment is a flood.[2] Yet he grants mercy by having Noah build an

---

[1]For an overview of the Pentateuch, see pp. 19-22, above.

[2]In this case, the spread of sin is shown in the strange story of Gen 6:1-4, in which "the sons of God" take the "daughters of men" for wives. Who are these "sons of God"? More is said of them on p. 134 in the section on Job. At present, it is enough to note that Genesis 6 is showing the increase of sin in the world through an improper mixing of the human and the divine.

ark and later makes a covenant with Noah and the world. However, the fourth story (Tower of Babel) ends without an act of mercy.

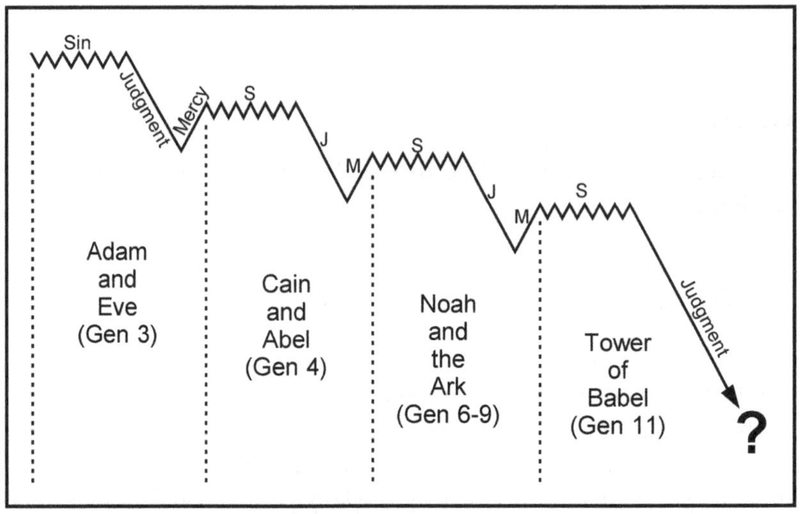

The Structure of Genesis 2-11

Why is the pattern broken here? (Note the question mark at the lower right side of the diagram indicating no act of mercy.) Many think that the great act of mercy for the fourth story – and really, for all four stories – is found in Genesis 12. In Gen 12:1-3, God calls Abraham,[3] and promises him land and descendants, and that he and his descendants would become a blessing for "all the families of the earth."

Genesis 12-50. The rest of Genesis tells us about the family and descendants of Abraham. Abraham is not mentioned in ancient literature outside the Bible (for instance, in material from Mesopotamia or Egypt), and the Bible does not give us any dates. So it is difficult to know when Abraham lived. Some would say he lived around 1700 B.C., however, and that date is sufficient for our study. In Genesis we read that God made a promise and a covenant with Abraham, and that these were then passed on to his descendants.

The Promise to Abraham. At the end of Genesis 11, Terah, the father of Abraham, takes his family from Ur and settles in Haran. In Genesis 12, God calls Abraham to take his family and go to Canaan.

---

[3]Actually, his name was Abram until God gave him the name Abraham in Genesis 17.

God promises Abraham land, descendants and blessing, and that through him all the nations of the world would be blessed. This is therefore a promise not merely for Abraham or for his descendants but for the whole world. The rest of Pentateuch, and indeed the rest of the Old Testament, brings us the beginnings of how this is to take place.

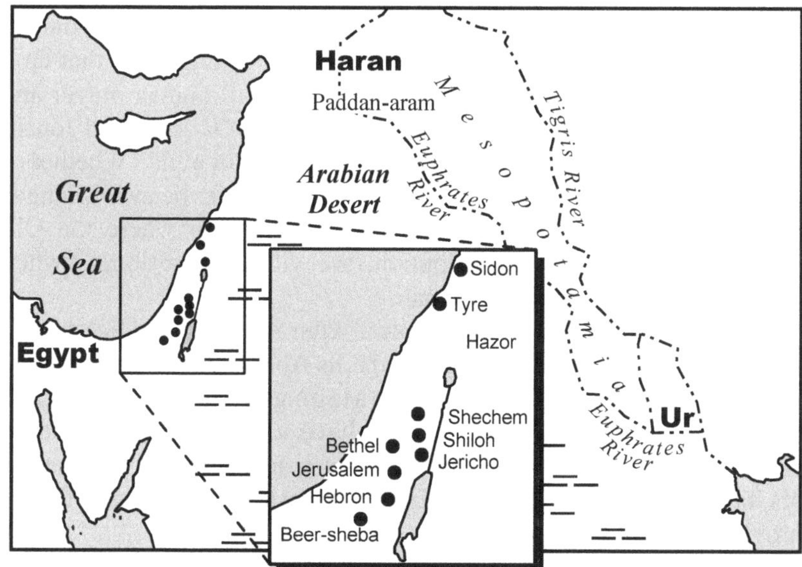

The Lands of Genesis (Inset: the Land of Canaan)

The Covenant with Abraham (Genesis 15 and 17). In Genesis 15, Abraham complains to God. God had promised to make his descendants into a great nation, but he still had no child. Thus, his servant Eleazar was going to become his heir. God says no; rather "your own son shall be your heir" (Gen 15:4).God then makes a covenant with him, saying, "To your descendants I give this land, from the river of Egypt to the great river, the river Euphrates" (Gen 15:18). Sarah is not mentioned in Genesis 15, and so in Genesis 16 she and Abraham consider the possibility that perhaps God intends Hagar to be the mother of the covenant promise.[4]

Sarah therefore follows the custom of that day for wives who were unable to bear children. She gives her maid Hagar to Abraham to bear a child on her behalf. Hagar becomes pregnant, Ishmael is born, and Abraham rejoices. However, in Genesis 17 God repeats the covenant

[4]Martin Luther also notes this in his commentary on Galatians (4:22-23).

promise, and this time it becomes clear that Sarah, not Hagar, is to become the mother of the covenant. Yet, in spite of this, a great blessing and promise are also given to Ishmael and his descendants (Gen 17:20). God has not forgotten them!

Genesis 18 prepares Abraham and the reader for the destruction of Sodom and Gomorrah (Genesis 19). It also gives an early hint of incarnation, since God appears in human form with two angels. And the chapter introduces a new and very thought-provoking idea: that God might be willing to change his mind in the face of human prayer and even argument. We will see more of this idea in Exodus and Jonah, where it is even suggested that God might "repent of evil." Whether or not God actually ever repents of anything, or whether he even changes his mind, this is an area of thought and reflection where the Old Testament brings a major contribution. We will say more about it when we get to Exodus 3-4, 32 and Jonah.

Genesis 22 is a disturbing chapter. After Abraham and Sarah have waited long for the birth of Isaac, God tells Abraham to sacrifice Isaac. The story is generally understood to be a testing of Abraham's faith (and that of Isaac, one would think!). Some have suggested that this should be called "child abuse," but this criticism is too strong.[5] Abraham is obedient, but the story also suggests he senses that God will finally provide an alternative sacrifice.[6]

Strife. The stories of Abraham and Sarah and Hagar, of Isaac and Rebekah, and of Jacob and his wives Leah and Rachel, are not happy stories. God indeed blesses them greatly, but there is much competition and strife in these families. In fact, the name Sarah is spelled exactly the same as the Hebrew verb *to strive*. Both are *sarah*[7] (שָׂרָה). And Gen

---

[5]See, for instance, T. E. Fretheim, "God, Abraham and the Abuse of Isaac" in *Word & World* Vol. XV, No. 1 (Winter 1995), 49-57. Also the Harvard Divinity School interview of artist Bernard Greenwald by Wendy McDowell at http://www.hds.harvard.edu/news-events/articles/2011/02/07/akedah-conversation-with-the-artist.

[6]Gen 22:5 contains cohortative Hebrew verb forms which may be translated: "Let us go ... let us worship ... let us return again to you." And when Abraham responds to Isaac's question in Gen 22:7, he literally says "God will see to it – the lamb for burnt offering, my son."

[7](See p. 3 footnote 4 regarding this simplified form of transliteration.) Some suggest that *sarah* (שָׂרָה) simply means "princess" – a feminine form of "prince" (*sar*, שַׂר). However this is certainly too tame for a book as intense as Genesis. In Gen 17:5, Abram is renamed Abraham, and the reader is told why.

32:28 (where Jacob wrestles with the "man"[8]) tells us that the name Israel is also built on this verb. If so, then "Israel" means either *God strives* or *he* (*Jacob*) *strives with God.* This mysterious story of wrestling comes just before the final chapters of Jacob's strife with Esau. Indeed, there is no real reconciliation with Esau in Genesis 33 (in spite of what is said in many commentaries and study Bibles). The chapter merely concludes with one final deception (Gen 33:14-17).

The last chapters of Genesis (37-50) stand almost alone as a separate story or *novella*, but they also contain much strife. They tell of Joseph and his brothers who sell Joseph to traders going to Egypt. But Joseph succeeds in Egypt. He is wise, he interprets dreams, and eventually he becomes second only to Pharaoh. By the end of the story the family of Jacob has moved down to Egypt because of a famine in Canaan. There they find food and favor because of Joseph.

Genesis begins with a Fall and contains much strife after that. Perhaps it is significant that the story, which began with a garden, now ends in a grave. The last verse of the book of Genesis reads:

> So Joseph died, being a hundred and ten years old; and they embalmed him, and he was put in a coffin in Egypt.

Outline

I. **Prehistory** (Genesis 1-11)
   A. Creation (Genesis 1-2)
   B. Adam and Eve and the Fall (Genesis 2-3)
   C. Cain and Abel, the descendants of Adam (Genesis 4-5)
   D. Noah and the Ark, and the descendants of Noah (table of nations) (Genesis 6-10)
   E. The Tower of Babel (Genesis 11)

II. **Patriarchs** (Genesis 12-50)
   A. Abraham (and Isaac) (Genesis 12-25)

But when Sarai is renamed Sarah in Gen 17:15, no reason is given; the reader is left to figure it out. Surely the fact that this renaming occurs just after Sarah's strife with Hagar in Genesis 16 (and before their strife in Genesis 21) is significant. The fact that Sarai's new name Sarah is spelled exactly the same as the Hebrew verb "to strive" (*sarah*, שָׂרָה) would not be missed by a Hebrew reader. And Genesis is certainly filled with strife!

[8]The story does not mention an "angel." Only Hos 12:4 mentions an "angel" in this encounter. The Hebrew word for "angel" is *mal'ak* (מַלְאָךְ) and is often just translated "messenger" (for instance, Gen 32:3,6).

B. Jacob (and Isaac) (Genesis 26-36)
C. Joseph (and his brothers) (Genesis 37-50)

Message

Genesis tells us that God created everything, and that "he saw that it was very good." Thus, at the very beginning of the Bible we are told that the physical world is good. This is quite different from certain ancient Greek philosophies (and some modern misinformed Christian opinions) which suggest that the physical world is inferior or even bad, and that only spiritual things are truly good. Genesis, and indeed the whole Bible, affirms that the creation is good.

At the same time, it clearly shows that there is a distinction between the Creator and his creation. God is external to the creation, and the creation itself is not divine. Furthermore, human beings are not gods and they should not try to "become like God" (as noted above). This is one of the points of the stories of Genesis 3-11 (including the mysterious "sons of God" story, p. 23, footnote 2).

Genesis also shows that men and women are equal. See, for instance, Gen 1:27 where "image of God" is parallel to "male and female."[9] Note also the order of creation, in the final form of Genesis 1-2. Taken as a whole, the story moves from lower forms (plants, birds and fish) to higher ones (land animals, the man, and finally the woman). Then there is the creation of the woman herself. Translators of Gen 2:21-23 have traditionally said God used a "rib" from Adam. But the word in Hebrew is *tsela'* (צֵלָע) and it would be better to translate it "side" not "rib."[10] Here God "splits the Adam," making one side of the male-female creature (Gen 1:27) into Adam and the other into Eve.

But Genesis then tells us that humanity rebelled against God. The rest of the book brings us the story of a troubled and dysfunctional family in which there is competitive striving, deception and anger. Near the end, Joseph's eleven brothers even sell him into Egypt. God's intention to bless and save is finally achieved, however. This is seen first in

---

[9]Read the discussion of chiasm on p. 126 to see how this works.

[10]Aside from the two occurrences in Gen 2:21,22, the word *tsela'* is found 38 more times (for instance, Exod 25:12,14; 1 Kgs 6:5,8,15,16,34). In these cases, the word is translated "side," but never "rib."

his well-known promise and covenant to Abraham,[11] and finally in the less well-known *inclusio*[12] found at the beginning and end of Genesis.

The Genesis *inclusio* works in the following way. The story of the Fall comes at the beginning of Genesis (Genesis 3), and shows people seeking to "become like God" by disobediently taking from the forbidden tree of the knowledge of Good and Evil. After that, the rest of Genesis tells stories of people who knew the good but did the evil. At the end of Genesis, these themes reappear: in Gen 50:19-20, Joseph stands over his terrified brothers and says:

"Fear not"	That's God-language!
"am I in the place of God?"	That's a very interesting question at this point, since throughout Genesis people have been putting themselves in the place of God. This was what Adam and Eve tried to do. Cain also did it with respect to Abel (life belongs to God). Will Joseph do the same now?
"you meant evil against me"	This has been the problem throughout Genesis, ever since the man and the woman ate from the tree of the knowledge of good and evil![13] People know good but do evil.
"but God meant it for good"	This, on the other hand, is what God has been doing in the background all the way through Genesis.

God, after all, is the only one who both knows the good and does the

---

[11]Some would actually see the first indication of God's intent to save in Gen 3:15, where God says to the snake, "I will put enmity between you and the woman, and between your offspring and hers; he will strike your head, and you will strike his heel." This has been called the *proto-evangelion*, the first Gospel. Traditional Christian interpretation has said that this refers to Satan striking Christ's heel in the Crucifixion, but Christ striking Satan's head in Resurrection victory. A wound to the head is much more serious than a wound to the heel, and in this case was fatal.

[12]An *inclusio* is like a frame or bracket. A story has an *inclusio* when important events are mentioned at the beginning, and then are mentioned at the end again. Sometimes an *inclusio* helps make the point of a story clear.

[13]The Hebrew words are exactly the same in both cases: *tob* (טוֹב) and *ra'* (רַע) for "good" and "evil."

good. God is God and we are not; this is the first lesson of Genesis. And the second is like it: we should not *try to become* like God. And there is a third lesson: in spite of humanity's sin and rebellion, God's intentions toward us are for the good. God intends to save and restore. He does this throughout Genesis, beginning with the provision of clothing for fallen Adam and Eve (Gen 3:21). This continues through the saving of Noah (and thus of humanity as a whole), and then in the saving of the family of Jacob (as well as all of Egypt) from famine through the wisdom of Joseph. Here, again, the Old Testament points ahead to God's ultimate intent: to save the world through the sending of his Son.

Some important texts: Creation (Genesis 1-2), Fall (Genesis 3), Call of Abraham (Gen 12:1-3), Sacrifice of Isaac (Genesis 22); Jacob wrestles (Gen 32:24-32); Joseph before his brothers (Gen 50:15-21)

Verses for memory: Gen 1:1, 27; 2:24; 3:14-15; 12:1-3; 50:19-20

Exodus

❧

Overview

Exodus is the second book of the Pentateuch[1]. Like Genesis, Exodus also has two major sections. In addition, Exodus has an important bridge or "hinge" in the middle: Exodus 19. This chapter contains an important event which causes the action to swing like a door on a hinge from the first section to the second one:

- RESCUE: God's Redeemed People (Exodus 1-18)
- THE HINGE (Exodus 19)
- RESPONSE: God's Responsible People (Exodus 20-40)

The first major section (Rescue) tells about God bringing the people of Israel out of Egypt; chapter 19 (the "hinge") contains God's statement to them when they arrive at Mt. Sinai (discussed below). The second major section (Response) then deals with the giving of the Law on Mt. Sinai, and the design and building of the ark of the covenant and the tabernacle tent. This Response section also describes a major failure and rebellion, when the people make a golden calf to worship.

RESCUE (Exodus 1-18)

The appearance of the angel of the LORD in the theophany[2] of the burning bush, the plagues on Egypt, and the parting and crossing of the

---

[1]For an overview of the Pentateuch, see pages 19-22

[2]A theophany is an appearance of God to human beings. Theophany is not the same as incarnation, but it can point in the direction of that possibility. One of the Bible's first theophanies is God's appearance to Abraham in Genesis 18. Another is the scene of Jacob wrestling with the "man" in Gen 32:24-30. The burning bush (Exodus 3-4) may be the most dramatic theophany in the Bible (though see also Exod 24:8-11 and Ezekiel 1). Some biblical writers are very cautious about this idea, and refer only to an appearance of "the angel of the LORD" rather than of God himself.

"Red" Sea (actually "Reed Sea"[3]) are well known, of course. But the *reason* they happen is actually found in *Genesis*.

The Genesis connections. Exod 1:1 begins with words taken directly from Gen 46:8: "Now these are the names of the descendants of Israel, who came into Egypt." Why is this connection with Genesis important? We find out in Exod 2:24-25, where God sees the suffering of the Israelites in Egypt and "remember[s] his covenant with Abraham, Isaac and Jacob." That covenant was made in Genesis, not in Exodus; this is important. The promises which God makes in Genesis (*to* the patriarchs and *for* the whole world) become the reason for his activity in Exodus. And there are other Genesis connections which show that God's concern is for the whole world, not just Israel.[4]

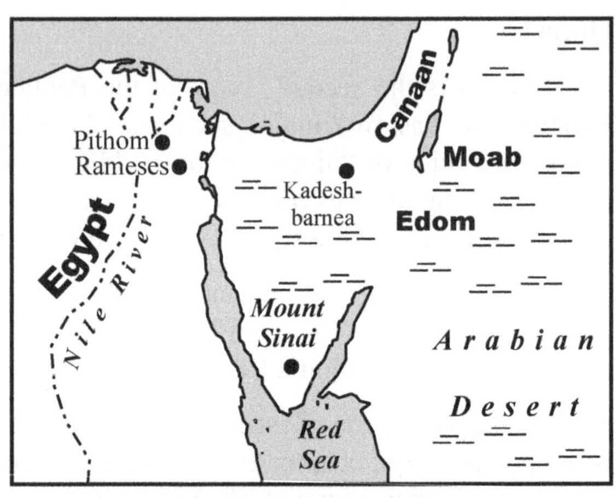

The Lands of the Exodus

---

[3]The Hebrew word is *suph* (סוּף), which means "reeds" or "water grasses," not "red." The same word is found in Exod 2:3, where baby Moses is put in a basket and placed "among the reeds (*suph*) by the bank of the Nile."

[4]The language of Exodus shows this universal concern several times with connections to the (universal) creation and Noah stories. **Exod 1:7** uses language from Gen 1:28 when it says that the Israelites were "fruitful and ... multiplied" and that "the land (literally 'the earth,') was filled with them." **Exod 2:2** says that when Moses was born, his mother "saw that he/it was good." The words "he" and "it" are the same in Hebrew, and so this statement reminds the reader of the six times in Genesis 1 that God created and "saw that it was good." **Exod 2:3-5** says that when Moses' mother hid him, she hid him in a *tebah* (תֵּבָה). What is a *tebah*? Most translations say "basket," but actually it is the same word that is used for Noah's ark in Genesis 6-9. God saved the world through Noah and his ark; now he is going to save Israel (and the world, again) through Moses and *his* "ark." And we will see another connection with Genesis and Noah in Exodus 32, discussed on p. 41, below.

Another interesting feature in the early chapters of Exodus is that women, not men, play major roles in God's plan to save Israel.[5] And when God finally does calls a man – Moses, in Exodus 3 and 6 – this man is very reluctant to go. But God is patient with Moses, and we may be amazed to discover how much God listens to him. God responds to his concerns and objections, and even changes his own plans in these chapters. We learn that God takes people seriously; he values our relationship with him so much that he even allows argument.

Irony.[6] There are several uses of irony in the opening chapters of Exodus. All of Pharaoh's attempts to destroy Israel produce results opposite to his intention:

(1) *The "people" Israel.* Pharaoh wants to *destroy* the people of Israel, but he becomes the first person to *call* them a people[7] (Exod 1:9).
(2) *Death of sons.* Pharaoh's command to kill the *sons of Israel* leads to the death of the *sons of Egypt* and even of his own son.
(3) *Fear.* Pharaoh feared the *male* population, but it was *women* who

---

[5]**Exod 1:17-21** tells of the faith of the midwives, and how God approves of their deception as they save the male babies of the Israelites. In **Exod 2:1-10**, Moses' mother and sister save *him* – and thus Israel. And in **Exod 4:24-26** his wife Zipporah does so again. The last event is most mysterious. Why does God want to kill Moses?! Actually, the only name mentioned in the text is that of Zipporah. (The Hebrew of Exod 4:25 just says "*his* feet," not "Moses' feet.") Possibly Moses had not circumcised his son. Or perhaps Moses himself had not been circumcised. Whatever the case, Zipporah knew what to do. There are also two important literary considerations. First, this story comes just before Moses' meeting with Pharaoh. Its mysterious darkness and conflict are similar to that of Jacob's wrestling in Gen 32:24-32, which also comes before an important meeting. Second, if this story is really about God attacking Moses' first-born son (and not Moses), then there is a literary link between verses Exod 4:23 (Pharaoh's son) and Exod 4:24 (Moses' son).

[6]Irony is when the result of an action is the opposite of what was intended. Irony also occurs when there is a (sometimes deliberate) difference between the literal meaning of something that is said and the intended meaning. It would be ironic, for instance, if a man built a wall to protect himself, and then the wall fell on him and killed him.

[7]In this context, "people" (Hebrew '*am*, עַם) essentially means "nation." We read that Pharaoh "said to his people('*am*), "Behold, the people ('*am*) of Israel...." This puts the people ('*am*) of Israel on the same level as the people Egypt. Thus, ironically, it is Pharaoh himself who first elevates Israel from being merely a family to a nation.

outwitted him (see footnote 5).

(4) *Obedience*. Pharaoh commanded that Israel's baby boys be thrown into the river, and Moses' mother indeed obeys and puts him into the river – in a basket to save him!

(5) *Water*. Pharaoh tries to use water (of the Nile) to destroy Israel, and in the end it is water (of the Reed Sea[8]) which destroys his army.

(6) *God with them*. Pharaoh's sarcastic "The LORD be with you, if ever I let you and your little ones go!" is indeed what happens. The LORD was with them as they went.

The divine name Yahweh. God values his relationship with Moses and Israel so much that he tells Moses his name. In Exod 3:14-15, we read:

> God said to Moses, "I AM WHO I AM." And he said, "Say this to the people of Israel, 'I AM has sent me to you.'" God also said to Moses, "Say this to the people of Israel, 'The LORD, the God of your fathers, the God of Abraham, the God of Isaac, and the God of Jacob,[9] has sent me to you': this is my name for ever, and thus I am to be remembered throughout all generations.

The name which God gave to Moses was probably *Yahweh*. We do not know for sure, because the rabbis believed that the name was too holy to pronounce. Thus, to keep people from trying to pronounce the name, they removed its vowels, leaving only the consonants *YHWH* (יהוה).[10] In English Bibles, this holy name is usually translated "the LORD." Note the unusual use of capital letters: "the LORD" not "the Lord." Most important: the name *Yahweh* is based on the Hebrew verb "to be" (*hayah*, הָיָה) and thus even God's name is a promise to "be with" Moses

---

[8]For "Reed Sea" instead of "Red Sea," see p. 32 footnote 3.

[9]Jesus quotes these words in his dispute with the Sadducees regarding the resurrection of the dead (Mk 12:26-27 || Mt 22:32; Lk 20:37-38).

[10]In addition, they then took the vowels from the Hebrew word *adonay* (אֲדֹנָי, which means "lord") and added them to *YHWH* (יהוה) to remind people to say *adonay* instead of *Yahweh* when they see the holy name. Thus, in the Bible we see יְהוָה, which is not pronounceable. Those who *do* try to pronounce this spelling will say "Yehowah" or "Jehovah." But "Jehovah" is not God's name. It is simply a mispronunciation of an impossible spelling.

and Israel. This is not merely to claim that God "exists."[11] Rather, the divine name is a promise of presence ("I will be with you," Exod 3:12).

Appearances before Pharaoh. In Exodus 5, Moses and Aaron appear before Pharaoh for the first time. Moses says more than God told him to say (compare Exod 5:3 to Exod 3:18). Perhaps he hopes to impress Pharaoh, but this is a mistake. Moses and Aaron return defeated from this first meeting, and so God renews his call in Exodus 6.[12] When Moses returns to Pharaoh, in Exodus 7 and the following chapters, there is an important and significant play on two Hebrew words. The verb *abad* (עָבַד) can mean "to work or serve" or it can mean "to worship." The noun *abodah* (עֲבוֹדָה) can mean "work or service" or it can mean "worship." The major question in these chapters is, "Will Israel serve (*abad*) Pharaoh or will they worship (*abad*) God?" Whose *abodah* (service or worship) will they perform?

Hardening of Pharaoh's heart. In Exod 4:21 (cf. 7:3), God says "I will harden [Pharaoh's] heart, so that he will not let the people go." This seems unfair, and we need to study the situation. Note that these words (in both Exod 4:21 and 7:3) are predictions. God does not harden Pharaoh's heart in these verses, but announces that he *will* do so. But when? And why?

As we read, we find that it is *Pharaoh* who first hardens his *own* heart (or his heart becomes hard). This happens six times (Exod 7:13,14,22; 8:15,19,32) before *God* hardens Pharaoh's heart for the first time in Exod 9:12. Thus, it seems that God finally hardens Pharaoh's heart as a punishment for Pharaoh first hardening his own heart many times (against Moses and against God). After God hardens Pharaoh's heart, we read that Pharaoh hardens his own heart twice more (Exod 9:34,35); after that, God's punishment arrives in full. We read of him hardening Pharaoh's heart five more times in Exod 10:1,20,27; 11:10; 14:8. But it was Pharaoh who had begun the whole process earlier by hardening his own heart the first time in Exod 7:13. In the end, it became a case of "let the punishment fit the crime."

---

[11]The Septuagint (page 6) does move in the direction of "existence" when it translates the "I AM" of Exod 3:14 as ὁ ὤν. In doing so, however, it loses this sense of "promise of presence" found in the Hebrew.

[12]For those who are interested in sources, it may be that originally Exodus 3 and Exodus 6 were two accounts of the same event. But now Exodus 6, by appearing later, gives us the effect of a renewed call which encourages Moses after his disastrous first encounter with Pharaoh.

Passover. The Passover and the Feast of Unleavened Bread in Exodus 12 are a part of the final plague (the killing of the firstborn). These two events, Passover and Unleavened Bread, may have a complex history. As they stand now, however, they provide instructions for worship. Read Exodus 12 carefully and you will see that it is aimed at future generations and their Passover celebrations. Note, for instance, the detailed description in Exod 12:11 concerning even how they should dress in order to remind themselves of their hasty escape from Egypt. And the question asked by the children in Exod 12:26, "What do you mean by this service (*abodah*)?" has grown to four questions in the modern Passover service.

THE HINGE (Exodus 19)

After the Rescue (the escape from Egypt described above), Israel gathers before God at Mt. Sinai. Exodus 19 describes this encounter in which they learn how they now should respond to God. Through Moses, God tells the people, "You have seen what I did to the Egyptians, and how I bore you on eagles' wings[13] and brought you to myself" (Exod 19:4). Thus, they are to become God's own "possession" (*segullah*, סְגֻלָּה[14]) among all peoples, and they will be a nation of priests (Exod 19:5-6). If Israel is going to become a "nation of priests," then surely the congregation is to be the rest of the nations of the world. This is a programmatic statement. We should at this point remember the original programmatic promise to Abraham that "all peoples on earth will be blessed through you" (Gen 12:3). 1 Pet 2:9 later picks up this Exodus 19 text and applies it to the New Testament people of God:

> But you are a chosen race, a royal priesthood, a holy nation, God's own people, that you may declare the wonderful deeds of him who called you out of darkness into his marvelous light.

---

[13]The *eagles' wings* probably represent God's mighty acts, such as the plagues. The phrase does not refer to God himself carrying them, since (1) the word is *eagles'* (i.e., many eagles) not *eagle's* (one eagle), and (2) the *eagles' wings* have been used to bring the people *to* God at Sinai.

[14]The Hebrew word *segullah* means a king's special treasure. It occurs eight times in the Old Testament, and six of those times it is used to describe Israel. For the secular meaning, see 1 Chr 29:3 and Eccl 2:8.

RESPONSE (Exodus 20-40)

In the first half of Exodus (chapters 1-18) God *rescued* his people. Now, in the second half, the people are to *respond* and be obedient to God's covenant. In particular, they are to obey the Law, given on Mt. Sinai to Moses. But note: this obedience is to be a response to what God has done first. We often forget that even the Ten Commandments begin with gospel, good news: "I am the LORD your God, *who brought you out of the land of Egypt, out of the house of bondage*" (Exod 20:2) Only after this reminder of what God has first done for them do we then read: "You shall have no other gods before me."

Now Israel has two covenants: the Abrahamic covenant and the Mosaic covenant.[15] The Ten Commandments (Exodus 20) are understood by most people to be the central feature of the giving of the law. Their style is "apodictic" (simple statements of "You shall ...; you shall not ...."). But there are other features in this section as well. For instance, Exodus 21-23 contains a group of "casuistic" (case) laws ("If or when *A* happens, then you should do *B*."). These three chapters are sometimes called the "Book of the Covenant" and may contain laws from both before and after the time of Moses. In Exod 23:14-17, we read of three annual pilgrimage feasts:

Feasts and Festivals

Exod 23:14-17 (also Exod 34:22-23; Leviticus 23; Num 28:16-29:40; Deut 16:1-17) tells of three major annual feasts at which every male Israelite was expected to "appear before the LORD":

- **Passover and Unleavened Bread.** These two celebrations are described in detail in Exodus 12. Originally, they may have been separate but they were celebrated together in the first month, called Nisan or Abib (March/April).[16] The blood of a lamb was put on the door posts and lintel so that the "destroyer" would "pass over;" and unleavened bread was prepared to remind the people of their hasty departure from Egypt. (Today, Passover is celebrated by families in homes.)

[15] In Genesis 9, there was also the covenant with Noah, known as the Noahic covenant. Since the Noahic covenant was given before God called Abraham, it is considered to be with all humanity and not just with Israel.

[16] See page 278 for an explanation of the Hebrew calendar.

- **Weeks/Pentecost.**[17] This feast was held in the middle of the summer, between barley and wheat harvests. It included the waving of two leavened loaves of bread before God.
- **Ingathering/Booths**. This feast was held in the seventh month, called Tishri or Ethanim (September/October). The month began with a major night of celebration.[18] The **Day of Atonement** (p. 44, below) fell on the tenth day of the month. Then, beginning on the fifteenth day of the month, as part of the harvest celebration, the people lived in booths for seven days to remember the time their ancestors spent in "booths" as they left Egypt and traveled through the wilderness.[19]

The pattern provided a chronological symmetry to the year. On the first month, the Passover observations began on the 10th day with the selection of the lamb (Exod 12:3), followed by Unleavened bread on days 15-21. Six months later (that is, in the seventh month), the same pattern was followed. The Day of Atonement fell on the 10th day, followed by Booths on days 15-21.

In addition to these three annual feasts, there were:

- The **Sabbath Day**. This was the seventh day of every week. It was a holy day on which no work was to be performed (Exod 20:8-11; Deut 5:12-15).
- The **Sabbatical Year**. This came every seventh year, and the people were to release all Israelite slaves at that time (Exod 21:2-6; Deut 15:12-18). Furthermore, they were also to give the land a sabbath rest; there was to be no planting of crops or tending of vineyards (Exod 23:10-11; Lev 25:2-7).
- The **Year of Jubilee**. This came after seven groups of seven years, that is, every fiftieth year. On this year also, they were to free Israelite slaves and give the land a year of rest. In addition, land which had been sold was to be returned to its original owner (Lev 25:8-55; 27:16-24). The reason: "The land shall not be sold in perpetuity, for the land is mine; for you are strangers and sojourners with me" (Lev 25:23).

---

[17]The word "Pentecost" comes from the Septuagint, where Lev 23:16 mentions "fifty" (*pentēkonta*, πεντήκοντα) days.

[18]Lighting of fires, dancing, pouring of water and prayer for rain (cf Zech 14:16-17). This was split into three feasts during second temple period.

[19]Each of these traditions may have a long history of development behind it. Here, we are merely concerned with the way these traditions are now described in the Pentateuch.

After the Law is given in Exodus 20-24, attention turns to the tabernacle,[20] the ark of the covenant and the priests' clothing. In Exodus 25-31 these are described and then they are made in Exodus 35-40. Between these two sections, however, there is a major crisis. While Moses is on the mountain, the people make a golden calf (Exodus 32-34). God's "wrath burns hot" against the people, and he says he will destroy them and start again with Moses; but Moses convinces God to change his mind.

When Moses returns to the people, he destroys the calf and has the Levites kill 3,000 people as a punishment. This event was always later remembered as a major apostasy. (More is said of all this in "Message" section, below.) However, Exodus ends on a good note. The ark and the tabernacle are finally built, and in the last verses we read that "the glory of the LORD filled the tabernacle" and "throughout all their journeys the cloud of the LORD was upon the tabernacle by day, and fire was in it by night."

Outline

- **I. Rescue: God's Redeemed People (The Exodus from Egypt)** (Exodus 1-18)
  - A. God's People: their oppression (Exodus 1)
  - B. God's Deliverer: Moses (Exod 2:1-7:6)
  - C. God's Deliverance: The Exodus (Exod 7:7-15:21)
  - D. God's Provision in the Wilderness (and the People's Complaints) (Exod 15:22-18:27)
- **II. The Hinge: Sinai Arrival and Preparation** (Exodus 19)
- **III. Response: God's Responsible People (The Mosaic Covenant)** (Exodus 20-40)

---

[20]A "tent of meeting" is also mentioned, especially in Exodus, Leviticus and Numbers. Usually it just refers to the tabernacle tent, which was set up in the middle of the camp (Num 3:23,29,35,38). In Exod 33:7-11, however, the "tent of meeting" is a small tent which Moses himself could carry and set up outside the camp for private meetings with God. (Num 12:4 may also show the tent of meeting outside the camp). Since the large tabernacle tent was not built and set up until Exodus 40, the smaller tent in Exod 33:7-11 may simply be an earlier tent. Later it was not used and the phrase "tent of meeting" was then applied to the larger tabernacle tent. The two phrases ("tabernacle" and "tent of meeting") are combined in Exod 39:32,40, throughout Exodus 40 and also in Numbers 3 and 4.

A. Words of the Covenant: the Law (Exodus 20-24)
B. Design of the Ark and Tabernacle (Exodus 25-31)
C. Breaking and Renewal of the Covenant: the Golden Calf (Exodus 32-34)
D. Building the Ark and Tabernacle (Exodus 35-40)

Message

Exodus shows us that God is faithful to his promises. In Exodus, God begins to act when he remembers[21] his covenant with Abraham, Isaac and Jacob (Exod 2:24-25). We also learn that it is God's nature to reveal himself (burning bush) and to save (the Exodus itself). In all this, God desires that Israel and Pharaoh will come to "know that I am the LORD." Israel learns this through deliverance; Pharaoh learns through judgment. This is always the choice that lies before people confronted by God.

The Exodus event is as central to the Old Testament and for the Jews as Jesus' Resurrection is to the New Testament and for Christians. Exodus gives us language which greatly influences the New Testament; for instance, words such as redeem, deliver, save, mighty acts, etc., are first found in Exodus. The priests and Levites, the ark and the tabernacle all begin in Exodus. Moses becomes Matthew's paradigm (pattern) for the way he describes Jesus.[22] For instance:

Exodus (Moses)	***Matthew (Jesus)***
Manna in wilderness	Feeding of 5,000
Mt. Sinai	Sermon on the mount
The Law	The Gospel

At the same time, Exodus, like Genesis, also shows us the people's ungrateful rebellion in the face of God's great mercy and generosity. Almost immediately after leaving Egypt, the people begin to complain. And then there is the golden calf incident of Exodus 32. When Aaron makes the calf, the people cry, "These are your gods, O Israel, who brought you up out of the land of Egypt" (Exod 32:4).

---

[21]Does God forget? Exodus is not raising that question here. Rather, God's response to Israel's suffering is seen as faithfulness to his covenant. His faithful response is described as "remembering" (or honoring) his covenant.

[22]Finally, of course, Matthew shows that Jesus' authority is even greater than that of Moses or the Law. For in Matthew Jesus says six times, "You have heard that it was said..., but I say to you...." See also Heb 3:1-5.

The use of plural language ("your *gods*"), when there is only one calf, points ahead to Jeroboam's apostasy in 1 Kgs 12:28, where the same words are found. Exodus does this intentionally to show the reader how serious the sin is. At this point God threatens to destroy the people and start again with Moses. Here we have another parallel with Genesis,[23] where God made a second start with Noah. This time, God changes his mind (RSV says he repents![24]) only when Moses pleads with him (Exod 32.11-14; cf. also Num 14:11-35).

After Moses destroys the golden calf, he tells the Levites, "Thus says the LORD, ... go ... throughout the camp and slay every man his brother, ... his companion, and ... his neighbor" (Exod 32:27). Is this genocide really God's will? Indeed, Moses says "thus says the LORD;" but God did not say this to Moses when he was up on the mountain (read Exod 32:7-14 carefully). Furthermore, there are other places where Moses adds words to what God tells him to say.[25] Finally, in the very next verse (Exod 32:28) we read that "the sons of Levi did according to the *word of Moses*" – not "the word of the LORD." Does this indicate that the genocide was really Moses' idea, and not God's? The reader is left to decide. We will see the people's ungratefulness again in Numbers. But we will also see more of the grace and mercy of God – who never gives up on his troublesome people.

Some important texts: Call of Moses (Exodus 3 and 6); Passover (Exodus 12); Ten Commandments (Exod 20:1-17; also Deut 5:6-21); Book of the Covenant (Exodus 21-23); Golden Calf (Exodus 32-34)

Verses for memory: Exod 2:23-25; 3:14-15; 19:4-6; 20:1-3; 34:6-7

---

[23]Remember the Genesis connections mentioned above on p. 32.

[24]If so, this is the first time in the Bible that anyone repents. See also T. Fretheim, *Exodus* (Louisville: John Knox Press, 1991) 38. There is more discussion of the "repentance of God" on p. 228 in the section on Jonah.

[25]He did this when he and Aaron went before Pharaoh in Exodus 5, p. 35, above. For another possible example, see Exod 19:15, where Moses says "do not go near a woman." God did not tell him to say this in Exod 19:10-13.

The famous Baal of Peor rebellion of Numbers 25 provides another example: in verse 4 God tells Moses to hang "all the chiefs of the people" in the sun. But in the next verse, instead of punishing the leaders, Moses tells each leader to "slay his men." The plague which follows is stopped only when Phineas slays two people who were children of "chiefs of the people" (actually "heads of fathers' houses," vv. 14-15).

Leviticus

❧

Overview

Leviticus is the heart of the *torah*. It is the middle of the five "books of Moses," and it contains the core of the legal and cultic[1] material. However, Jews have not followed its detailed sacrificial system since the temple was destroyed in 70 A.D.[2] The book has two large sections:

- General priestly material in Leviticus 1-16 and
- The Holiness Code in Leviticus 17-26.

These two large sections are followed by a final chapter (27) on vows.

PRIESTLY MATERIAL (*Leviticus 1-16*)

Priests are central to Leviticus. The heart of Leviticus is chapters 8-10 where Aaron and his sons are consecrated to the priesthood. Since this consecration involved a variety of offerings, we first find those offerings described in chapters 1-7.

And since the work of the priests was to guarantee the purity of the nation of Israel, chapters 11-16 come after the consecration and deal with purity regulations. However, in spite of these regulations, the nation did sin. Thus, this section of Priestly material ends with the Day of Atonement (ch. 16):

---

[1]When we speak of Israel's "cult" we mean its formal religious structures and practices: the priests and Levites, the tabernacle or temple, Israel's sacrificial and other worship practices, etc. See p. 46 for more detail.

[2] Observant Jews (p. 19, footnote 2) today follow the dietary and other laws of *torah*, but they do not perform any of the sacrifices. And they will not do so unless the temple is built again. Modern Judaism has rabbis (teachers), but it no longer has priests.

Sacrifices and offerings (chapters 1-7)
Consecration of priests (chapters 8-10)
Purity regulations (and Day of Atonement) (chapters 11-16)

Purification and Reparation offerings. Leviticus 1-7 describes "sin" and "guilt" offerings. These words are somewhat misleading. The purpose of the "sin" offering was to cleanse or purify the sanctuary and the various cultic objects; thus, it is better to call it a "purification offering." The "guilt" offering was for those who sinned unknowingly concerning holy things or who had sinned against a neighbor. In such cases, a situation had to be "repaired," and so the offering is best called a "reparation" offering.

Purity Regulations. The purity regulations of Leviticus 11-16 are concerned with clean and unclean animals (ch. 11), childbirth (ch. 12), "leprosy"[3] (ch. 13-14) and bodily (genital) discharges (ch. 15). Issues of purity and impurity are found in all cultures. They are not concerned with dirt, cleanliness or physical contamination. Rather, they are related to custom and taboos. Following some of the Leviticus purity regulations may lead to a healthier life, but that is not their primary purpose. Israel's concern for purity was primarily so that nothing would defile the sanctuary (that is, the tabernacle tent or the temple), since the sanctuary represented the presence of God in their midst.[4] Because of this

[3]"Leprosy" is actually not the right word to use, since leprosy as we know it today was unknown in Old Testament times. The Hebrew word is *tsara'at* (צָרַעַת). When the Old Testament speaks of "leprosy" on the skin, it means a non-contagious skin disease such as leukoderma (vitiligo) or psoriasis. Leviticus also speaks of "leprosy" in clothing (Lev 13:47ff) and houses (Lev 14:34ff), and probably means some kind of mildew or fungus.

[4]This is particularly clear in Lev 11:29-38, where clothing, earthen vessels or food become unclean if a "swarming thing" like a lizard falls upon it or into it, and yet a cistern holding water will not become unclean. Certainly if the issue were physical contamination, the cistern of water would also become

concern, the last chapter of the purity regulations (Leviticus 16) deals with the Day of Atonement and the purification of the sanctuary. On the **Day of Atonement**, the priests made atonement[5] for the sins of the nation. A bull was offered on behalf of the high priest, and two goats on behalf of the people. One of the goats was sacrificed to the LORD and the other was sent into the wilderness, symbolically carrying away the sins of the nation.[6] The Day of Atonement was also the only day during the year when the High Priest (alone) entered the Most Holy Place (called the Holy of Holies in many translations, see p. 46).

The purity regulations are not the end of the book of Leviticus, however. The largest section of the book, the Holiness Code (Leviticus 17-26), now follows.

HOLINESS CODE (*Leviticus 17-26*)

Several times in Leviticus we read the phrase "you shall be holy because I, the LORD your God, am holy" (Lev 19:2; cf. 11:44, 45; 20:7, 26; 21:8). Leviticus 17-26 contains regulations which sought to ensure this holiness, and so this section is often called the "Holiness Code." Holiness was also discussed in the first part of the book (Leviticus 1-16), but there is a difference. The first part of the book (Leviticus 1-16) emphasizes the holiness of the temple, the priests and the Nazirites.[7] The second part (Leviticus 17-26, that is, the Holiness Code) expands this concern to include the whole land and all the people. Impurity in the first part of Leviticus has to do with rituals, and so rituals can be

---

unclean. But this is not the case here. The real concern is found in verse 44: "For I am the LORD your God; consecrate yourselves therefore, and be holy, for I am holy. You shall not defile yourselves with any swarming thing that crawls upon the earth."

[5]Atonement means at-one-ment – that is, making people "at one" with God.

[6]The second goat is sent into the wilderness to Azazel (Lev 16:8,10,26). Earlier in Israel's history, people may have believed that "Azazel" was a wilderness demon. Here, however, that sense is now gone, and Azazel simply represents a distant and desolate place to which the sins of the people are sent.

[7]Nazirites were men or women who made a special promise or vow before God. In some cases, the vow was made by the parents of the Nazirite. During the period of consecration, Nazirites could not eat grapes or grape products (including wine). They were not to cut their hair, and could not have contact with a dead body. Samson is the most well known Nazirite, but Samuel may also have been one. See Num 6:1-21; Judg 13:1-7.

used to atone for the impurity. In the second part of Leviticus, however, impurity has to do with violations of the covenant, not rituals, and offenders must be expelled ("cut off from the people"). The Holiness Code deals especially with matters of slaughtering animals, sexual relationships, ethical social relationships, offerings and festivals. For instance, this is where we find the Sabbatical Year (Lev 25:1-7) and the Year of Jubilee (Lev 25:8-55; cf. Lev 27:16-24). See p. 38 for descriptions of these years.

The Holiness Code then ends with a series of blessings for obedience (Lev 26:3-13) and curses for disobedience (Lev 26:14-39). This pattern is also seen in Deuteronomy, and is typical of a covenant document. The curses sound harsh to us, but God's true desire and purpose are found in vv. 11-13:

> I will make my abode among you, and my soul shall not abhor you. And I will walk among you, and will be your God, and you shall be my people. I am the LORD your God, who brought you forth out of the land of Egypt, that you should not be their slaves; and I have broken the bars of your yoke and made you walk erect.

And at the end of all the curses, we find that even they were for a purpose: so that land might have its sabbaths (Lev 26:34-35, 43) which had been missed. And when all is said and done, we read that God will not abandon or "abhor" his people, but will remember the covenant with their ancestors "that I might be their God" (Lev 26:44-45).

Vows (Leviticus 27). The book concludes with chapter 27 which deals with the making of vows and offerings related to vows.

Outline

I. **Sacrifices** (burnt offerings; grain, peace, purification and reparation offerings (Leviticus 1-7)
   A. Instructions for the people (Lev 1:1-6:7)
   B. Instructions for the priests (Lev 6:8-7:36)
   C. Summary (Lev 7:37-38)

II. **Consecration of Priests** (Leviticus 8-10)

III. **Purity Regulations** (Leviticus 11-16)
   A. Individual purity regulations (Leviticus 11-15)
   B. The Atonement ritual (Leviticus 16)

IV. **Laws of Holiness** (Holiness Code) (Leviticus 17-26)

V. **Vows and votive offerings** (Leviticus 27)

The Cult: an Overview

The word "cult" has several meanings.[8] In Old Testament theology it means the formal structures of the religion of Israel: the temple, the priesthood, the sacrifices and worship practices.

The Temple. The people of Israel did not worship inside the temple. Only the priests entered the temple, with the male population of Israel gathering in the court outside three times each year for special feast days (see "Worship Practices," p. 48).

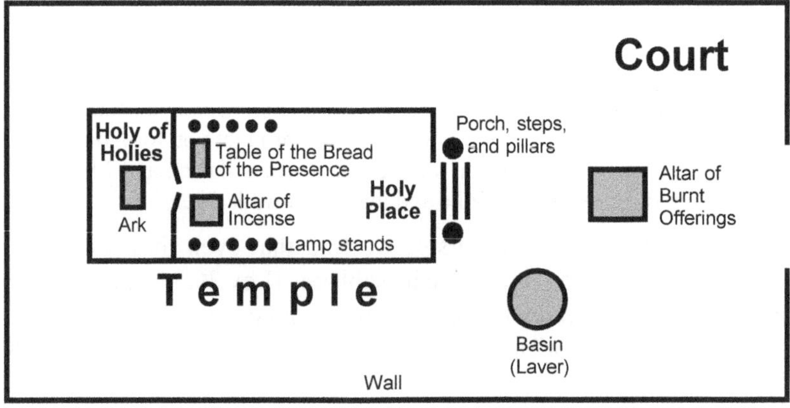

Simplified Plan of the Temple. *The exact locations of the lamp stands, table(s) of the Bread of the Presence and the basin outside the temple are not certain.*

The altar for burnt offerings was outside the temple. Inside the temple (in the "Holy Place") there was only a small altar for incense along with lamp stands and a table (or tables) for the Bread of the Presence (see "Worship Practices," below). In the very front (at the left in the picture above), behind doors, was the "Holy of Holies" or "Most Holy Place," where the Ark of the Covenant was kept. Only the High Priest entered the Most Holy

[8]One popular meaning of "cult," which we are not using here, is a non-Christian or pseudo-Christian religious group. Such groups have unorthodox beliefs and they often aggressively seek new members. Examples would be the Jehovah's Witnesses, the Mormons (Church of Jesus Christ of the Latter Day Saints), Christian Science, Scientology and Hare Krishna. Again, this is not the way we are using the word "cult" in this book.

Place, and he did so only once each year, on the Day of Atonement (p. 44).

The temple itself was a mixed blessing. In some ways, it was a foreign addition to the faith of Israel. In Israel's early history, there had always been holy places where Israel worshiped (e.g., Bethel, Sinai, Shechem). Later, the Pentateuch describes the tabernacle, a moveable tent which gave a dynamic image of God and his people being on the move, traveling, literally "tenting" (for that's what the verb meant) in this world.

But the temple was different. It was not a dynamic image, but rather was an immoveable stone building. This made the idea of "place" more rigid, less flexible, less dynamic. And there were other ways in which the temple was a mixed blessing. On the one hand, it gave Israel's religion a fixed center, a sense of stability. On the other hand, Solomon built it right next to his palace and enclosed both with a single wall, thus using the temple as a symbol of political legitimacy.

Finally, the people began to take the temple for granted. They assumed that its presence was a guarantee of God's approval and protection even when they were not loyal to God. See Jeremiah's famous temple sermon (Jeremiah 7-8), in which he preaches against the false security of the temple.

The Priests and Levites. Exod 19:22-24 shows that Israel already had ***priests*** when the people arrived at Mt Sinai. But it is in the *torah* that their offices are defined. According to Exodus, Moses and Aaron were of the tribe of Levi, and Aaron's descendants became the priests of Israel.

The duties of the priests were:

- ADVISING (determining and interpreting the will of the LORD),[9]
- TEACHING (ensuring proper worship of God), and
- SACRIFICE (mediating between God and the people, atoning for sin).

---

[9]In determining God's will, the priests used the "lot" (variously called Urim and Thummim (twice just Urim), the ephod, or even the "ark"). No one knows what the Urim and Thummim looked like or how they were used, but when they were used they gave a "Yes" or "No" (or "heads or tails") answer. Examples: Num 27:21; 1 Sam 14:41; 23:6-12; 30:7-8. They are not mentioned after the time of David, which may indicate that the voice of the prophets became more important at that time.

The rest of the tribe of Levi – the ***Levites*** – were originally assigned the duties of transporting and caring for the tabernacle tent, the ark of the covenant and other worship items. However, after the ark was captured by the Philistines and later returned (1 Samuel 4 and 7), the Levites no longer had this responsibility. Eventually, they wandered through the land seeking private employment as chaplains. David later brought them to Jerusalem and made them into singers and leaders of worship.[10]

Worship Practices.

The priests. *Daily* (see Exod 29:38-46; Lev 6:8-18; 24:1-4; Num 28:1-8), the ashes on the sacrificial altar (outside the temple) were removed, and a one year old male lamb was offered as a burnt offering, along with cereal and drink offerings. The priest then entered the temple, trimmed the lamps and offered incense on the incense altar. Then they went back outside, where a cereal offering of wheat cakes cooked on a griddle was offered. The whole process was repeated in the evening.

On the Sabbath (Lev 24:5-9, Num 28:9-10), the same routine was followed, except two additional lambs were offered. In addition, inside the sanctuary the twelve loaves of Bread of the Presence[11] were replaced with new loaves.

Each new moon there was blowing of trumpets and offering of additional sacrifices (Num 10:10). *The Day of Atonement* (Leviticus 16) has already been mentioned above (p. 44).

The people. Three times each year, all male Israelites gathered for the feasts of Passover and Unleavened Bread, Weeks (Pentecost), and Ingathering and Booths (Exod 23:14-17). See pp. 37-38 for a discussion of these feast days.

Sacrifices. Sacrifices were made for several reasons: (1) to win God's favor, (2) to purify the sanctuary and its cultic

---

[10]This description is the simplest, but things may have been more complicated. It is possible that the Levites were originally a religious class different from the tribe of Levi, and that the two names were later confused. There are also 13 somewhat puzzling reference to "Levitical priests" generally in Deuteronomic material (Deuteronomy, Joshua, Jeremiah, Ezekiel and Chronicles).

[11]The Bread of the Presence, sometimes called "showbread," represented the covenant.

objects,[12] (3) to bring atonement between people and God. There were several types of sacrifices – burnt offerings, cereal offerings, peace offerings, "sin" (purification) offerings, and "guilt" (or reparation) offerings. You can read about them in detail in G. A. Anderson "Sacrifice and Sacrificial Offerings (OT)" in *ABD* 5:870-886.

Message

Holiness is more than "being good." In the Bible, especially in the Old Testament, holiness is both being set apart *from* and being set apart *for*. People and objects are set apart *from* common or secular purposes, and they are set apart *for* use by God. This was true of the priests, of the temple and altar, and ultimately of the people of God as a whole.

But there is also the sense that God's people should live in ways which reflect and represent the God they worship. Several times in Leviticus, God says "you shall be holy because I am holy" (see *Holiness Code*, p. 44, above). The people of Israel often did not live this way, of course. Therefore, one important message of Leviticus was that even when the people sinned – even when God sent them into exile – God would not forget his covenant with them:

> When they are in the land of their enemies, I will not spurn them, neither will I abhor them so as to destroy them utterly and break my covenant with them; for I am the LORD their God; but I will for their sake remember the covenant with their forefathers, whom I brought forth out of the land of Egypt in the sight of the nations, that I might be their God: I am the LORD (Lev 26:44-45).

There was still hope of atonement and reconciliation.

So what does Leviticus have to say to us today? The detailed directions for sacrifices have little to say to us in the Christian context. Christians do not sacrifice in this way. Anders Nygren has said it well:

> Very early an interpretation pushed its way into the church according to which the primary function of the ministry ought to be that of a sacrificing priesthood, men who by virtue of their ordination were in a position to present an efficacious and purifying sacrifice. ... It is wholly false. In other religions there is a place for sacrificing

[12]This was very important because God is holy and the relationship with him was to be guarded.

> priests; indeed, there the offering of sacrifices is central in the priest's duties. But in the congregation of Christ there is no longer any place for such. The gospel signifies the great revolution in the religious world. The sacrifice which reconciles us to God is not our act, but God's. ... Christ is the new covenant's only high priest, the offering brought by him is the sole, but also the eternally efficacious, sacrifice. ... with Christ the time of the high priest has come to an end. For when Christ offered himself he did it "once for all" (Heb. 7:27; 9:28). Here there is no place for a new offering. Here there is no longer any place for a sacrificing priesthood.[13]

Other themes from Leviticus do still speak to us, however. Like Israel, which was redeemed from Egypt, we who have been redeemed in Christ should reflect in our lives the fact that we are a holy people; for we bear Christ's holiness.

As observed by Nygren, above, the book of Hebrews picks up many of the themes from Leviticus, and shows that Jesus Christ is the one complete, sufficient and final atoning sacrifice. And Heb 13:11-12 notes a very interesting parallel between the "sin offering" of Leviticus and the death of Christ. The writer refers to Lev 16:27 (the Day of Atonement) and notes that

> the bodies of those animals whose blood is brought into the sanctuary by the high priest as a sacrifice for sin are burned outside the camp. So Jesus also suffered outside the gate in order to sanctify the people through his own blood.

Some important texts: Day of Atonement (Leviticus 16); Holiness Code (Leviticus 17-26); Jubilee (Lev 25:8-55)

Verses for memory: Lev 16:27; 19:2; Heb 13:11-12

---

[13]Anders Nygren, *The Gospel of God*, trans. L. J. Trinterud (London: SCM Press, 1951) 21ff.

Numbers

❧

Overview

Numbers contains some of the most well known stories in the entire Old Testament (see "Some important texts," below). But it must also be read in the context of the whole Pentateuch, for there are many connections with what has gone before. The English title of the book is "Numbers" because of two places (Numbers 1-4 and Numbers 26) where a census is taken of the people of Israel as they move from Egypt to the promised land of Canaan.

The Hebrew title of the book is "In-the-Wilderness." It is taken from the first verse of the book, and this title gives a better description of what the book is really about: the experiences of the people of Israel as they traveled through the wilderness on their way to Canaan.

The book of Numbers can be divided into two unequal sections:[1]

- Chapters 1-26 in which the people are unfaithful to God, and
- Chapters 27-36 in which they are faithful

Each of these two sections is framed by an *inclusio*:[2]

- A pair of censuses frames the first section (chapters 1-26)
- A pair of requests from the daughters of Zelophehad frames chapters 27-36

See the illustration on the next page.

---

[1]The book can also be divided into three sections:
- Camping at Sinai (Num 1:1-10:10),
- Camping at Kadesh (Num 10:11-20:13) and
- Traveling from Kadesh to the edge of Moab (Num 20:14-36:13).

[2]An *inclusio* is a literary frame around a text. See p. 29 footnote 12.

Numbers 1-26

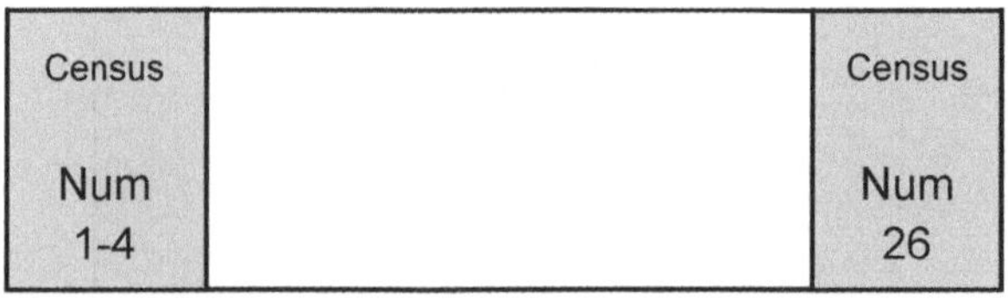

Census Num 1-4		Census Num 26

Numbers 27-36

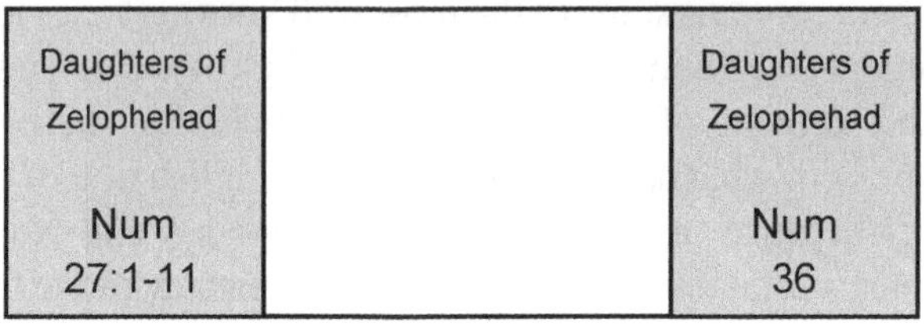

Daughters of Zelophehad Num 27:1-11		Daughters of Zelophehad Num 36

In addition, each half has a section of preparation for travel and a section of moving toward the promised land (see the outline on p. 54). Throughout the book, there is also a continual movement back and forth between Law and Narrative (or Story): (Law: 1:1-10:10; Narrative: 10:11-14:45; Law: 15; Narrative: 16-17, etc. to the end of the book).[3]

NUMBERS 1-26

In the first part of the book (Numbers 1-26), after the first census,

---

[3]*Some thoughts on Biblical Criticism.* When we say "criticism" in this sense, we simply mean study or analysis; in this sense, "criticism" is not a negative thing. Note that I have just done a literary "criticism" of Numbers in two ways. First, I described how two censuses form an *inclusio*, and I noted that the book has two sections. Those are structural observations. Second, I talked about "Law" and "Narrative" (or "Story"). "Law" and "narrative" are kinds or "genres" of literature: legal material is different from story. And there are other ways to discuss the material. We could consider what the writer wants the words to do to the reader (reader-response criticism). We could study the sources of material used by the editors (source criticism). We could talk about phrases that come out of certain situations in life which were well-known to ancient Jewish readers, though perhaps not to us (form criticism). All of these kinds of "biblical criticism" are helpful as we try to understand the text. For further reading, see John Barton, *Reading the Old Testament* (Philadelphia: Westminster Press, 1984).

we read of the unfaithfulness of the people. Again and again they complain against God who has been faithful to them (see Numbers 11-14, 16-17). In the midst of this unfaithfulness and rebellion, God at one point threatens to destroy the people and start again with Moses (Num 14:11-35, cf the golden calf incident of Exodus 32). Once again, Moses pleads with God and God again relents. But God declares that none of those who came out of Egypt (except Caleb and Joshua) will live to see the land of Canaan (Num 14:20-24, 30). All will die in the wilderness and only the next generation will see the promised land. Even Moses fails. He goes beyond the command of God when he strikes the rock to get water at Meribah (Num 20:2-13).[4] He had been told only to "*tell* the rock to yield its water," not to strike it;[5] thus, he also is told that he will not enter the land with the next generation.

Near the end of this first section, we find two famous texts:

- Balaam the Son of Beor (and his famous talking donkey) (Numbers 22-24) and
- The Apostasy at Peor (Baal of Peor) (Numbers 25).

The second event is similar to the golden calf incident of Exodus 32-34. This first section of the book of Numbers then concludes with the second census (Numbers 26, see diagram on p. 52). This census notes that none of those from the first census was still alive. As God had said, all died in the wilderness except Caleb and Joshua (Num 26:64-65).

NUMBERS 27-36

As noted above, the second part of the book (Numbers 27-36) is also framed by an *inclusio*. At the beginning (Num 27:1-11), the daughters of Zelophehad come to Moses and ask that *torah* be changed to

---

[4]The "waters of Meribah" are mentioned several times in the Old Testament as a place of rebellion (Exod 17:7; Num 20:13,24; 27:14; Deut 33:8; Pss 81:7; 95:8; 106:32). In Exod 17:1-7 we read of "the faultfinding of the children of Israel" but here in Numbers 20 it is Moses who is described as the guilty party.

[5]Emphasis added. We have noted that Moses sometimes said more than God told him to say. See p. 35 regarding his first appearance before Pharaoh; see also p. 41 regarding the genocide at the hands of the Levites (especially footnote 25 on that page). Here he *does* more than God tells him to do.

allow them to inherit land. Moses appeals to God and the change is allowed. At the end of this section (Numbers 36), a further request is made concerning this matter and it, too, is permitted. Between these two events, this second section of the book deals with a change of leadership. Because of Moses' disobedience in the water-from-the-rock incident (above), Joshua is chosen as a new leader in Num 27:12-14. From this point onward, the people are described as faithful to God as they prepare for travel and begin to move into the promised land.

Outline

I. **The first generation: unfaithful** (Numbers 1-26)
   A. The first numbering (Numbers 1-4)
   B. Preparing for the journey (laws, offerings, dedication of Levites, Passover) (Numbers 5-9)
   C. Travel through the wilderness – and apostasy at Peor (Numbers 10-25)
   D. The second numbering (Numbers 26)

II. **The next generation: faithful** (Numbers 27-36)
   A. Daughters of Zelophehad – first request (Num 27:1-11)
   B. Joshua chosen as new leader (Num 27:12-23)
   C. Preparing for the journey (festivals, offerings and laws) (Numbers 28-30)
   D. Moving into the land (Numbers 31-35)
   E. Daughters of Zelophehad – second request (Numbers 36)

Message

Major Themes. As mentioned above, the book of Numbers continually moves back and forth between narrative and law. Early readers would recognize this as being similar to ancient treaty-covenants between nations. These treaty-covenants had sections of narrative which described the favor granted by the powerful nation. After these sections came legal requirements for the weaker nation to follow. Therefore, one major theme of the book of Numbers is that God had granted favor to Israel by bringing them out of Egypt. Now, they were to live in obedience to God as his people.

Another major theme of Numbers, however, is that the people were *not* faithful to God. As was the case in Exodus, the people rebel and complain again and again even though God has just rescued them from slavery in Egypt. Even after God gives them a great victory over the Canaanites (Num 21:1-3), the people immediately begin to complain until God sends "fiery serpents" which cause them to repent (Num 21:4-9).[6] The apostasy at Peor (Baal of Peor, Numbers 25) comes right after God has made Balaam bless Israel! Yet in the end God remains faithful in spite of their rebellion, and his presence is shown by pillars of cloud and fire which continually move before them (Num 9:15-16).

Intercession. The importance of intercession is seen in several places. As noted above, Moses must again stand between the people and the wrath of God as he did after the golden calf incident in Exodus. He bases his prayer upon the *chesed* (חֶסֶד, covenant loyalty and faithfulness) of God, and God again relents. In both cases – in Exodus as well as here – the point is not that God becomes angry or merely that he changes his mind (a mystery in itself). Rather, we are shown that God takes prayer seriously and responds to us in relationship. This is seen also in the requests of the daughters of Zelophehad in which Moses goes before God on their behalf and God responds positively.

Two interesting texts. Finally, two very interesting sets of texts need some comment. **Numbers 22-24** describes Balak trying to hire the prophet Balaam to curse Israel. In these chapters, God blesses and protects Israel, and Balaam is shown to be a faithful person. Yet there are some unanswered questions about Balaam. It is not clear why God becomes angry in Num 22:22 (cf Num 22:20-21), and other texts say that Balaam did not act faithfully toward Israel (Num 31:8,16; Deut 23:4-5; 2 Pet 2:15; Rev 2:14). So perhaps we do not know the whole story of Balaam. These other texts may be aware of Balaam stories or traditions which are not found in the Bible.

The second text, **Num 5:11-31**, is sometimes called The Ordeal. The story sounds primitive, barbaric and abusive of women. Indeed, we would never follow this ritual in our churches today! At the same time, we must realize that jealous husbands sometimes kill innocent wives, and this ritual at least forced a jealous husband to bring his wife to the priest. At that point, the situation became semi-public and perhaps some

[6]When the people repent, God has Moses make a bronze serpent and put it on a pole. Anyone looking at the bronze serpent after being bitten would live. In John 3:14-15, Jesus uses this as a sign of the Cross.

discussion and mediation could take place. It was not a perfect solution; but perhaps it was better than what would have happened without the ritual. In this sense, we might look upon this situation the same way Jesus looked upon the law of divorce in Mark 10:5-9 (parallel Matt 19:8): it was given because of human "hardness of heart," and was not God's intent "from the beginning."

Some important texts: The Ordeal (Num 5:11-31); Benediction of Aaron (Num 6:22-27); Manna and quails (Numbers 11); Spies sent to Canaan (Numbers 13); Water from the rock (Numbers 20); Bronze serpent (Numbers 21); Balaam (Numbers 22-24); Apostasy at Baal-Peor (Numbers 25)

Verses for memory: Num 6:22-27; 21:9

Deuteronomy

❧

Overview

"Deuteronomy" means "second law," and indeed the book brings us a second account of the giving of the law.[1] But the book is also important because it became the foundation for many other books.

The (re)discovery of Deuteronomy. During the reforms of King Josiah in 622 B.C., a "book of the law" was discovered in the temple (2 Kgs 22:8). It was probably an early version of Deuteronomy (perhaps Deut 4:44-28:68). This discovery had a very dramatic effect, because this "book of the law" was received and recognized as the written word of God.

Certainly the people were aware of other stories and texts which had been saved (no doubt in the temple, too). But these other stories and texts were not yet considered to be inspired in the same way. When this "book of the law" was discovered at the time of Josiah, however, it was recognized as something different. It was understood to be an authoritative written word from God.

Perhaps this was because of the series of blessings and curses found near the end (Deuteronomy 27-28). For Josiah and many others, the curses explained why things had become so bad for Judah: it was because they had ignored and broken the Mosaic Covenant. This understanding inspired further reforms. The reason this "book of the law" is thought to have been an early version of Deuteronomy is because, after its discovery, the reforms of Josiah (2 Kings 23:4-24) follow instructions which are found in Deuteronomy (see, for instance, Deut 7:5,25; 16:2-8; 18:10-12).

The influence of Deuteronomy. This "book of the law," containing the Mosaic Covenant, also inspired the young prophet Jeremiah. Jeremiah at one point became an "evangelist of the covenant" through-

---

[1]The first account is found in Exodus through Numbers, of course.

out Judah.[2] Furthermore, this early version of Deuteronomy also seems to have inspired a historian who began to write the history of Israel. We call his writings the "Deuteronomistic History" because their theology is that of Deuteronomy. These writings are now the books of Joshua, Judges, 1-2 Samuel and 1-2 Kings.[3] Perhaps Deuteronomy was originally the first book of this Deuteronomistic History; remember what was said about the possibility of a Tetrateuch on p. 20.

The unique style of Deuteronomy. The first four books of the Pentateuch are generally a narrative, but much of Deuteronomy (though not all of it) comes to us as a farewell sermon by Moses at Moab.[4] God had said that Moses could not go with the people into the land of Canaan because of his earlier sin (Num 27:12-14). Thus, in this sermon he gives the people his last words, words of guidance for the new life that lies ahead of them. He begins with a review of the giving of the Ten Commandments, but there is much more after that. Deuteronomy is primarily a book of ethical exhortation (encouragement to live properly). Again and again, the people are told: "Remember how God saved you when you were slaves in Egypt, therefore ...."[5] The word "*therefore*" is

---

[2]See Jeremiah 11. Later, when Jeremiah saw how superficial the actions of the people were, he realized that even this rediscovery of the Mosaic covenant was not enough. At that point, he began to speak of the need for a New Covenant (Jer 31:31-34). For more information, see the chapter on Jeremiah, pp. 178-184.

[3]The Deuteronomistic History did not include Ruth or 1-2 Chronicles. The Hebrew Scriptures include these later books in The Writings (see p. 3).

[4]When I say that much of Deuteronomy is a farewell sermon, I am talking about its "form." (See p. 52, footnote 3.) A form is more than style or genre. A form is a group or pattern of words that makes us think of a certain situation in life – like a leader saying goodbye for the last time to his people. Other well known biblical forms are the "messenger formula" ("Hear the word of the king; thus says the king") which the prophets modified and used, or the "annunciation" formula ("Behold, you are with child, and shall bear a son; you shall call his name *X*; and he shall do *Y*;" see Gen 16:11-12; Judg 13:3-5; 1 Chr 22:9-10). Thus, "form criticism" is another way of studying, critiquing or "criticizing" the Bible.

[5]The "you" of Deuteronomy is sometimes singular and sometimes plural – and sometimes changes within a single verse! (In Deut 4:29, for instance, the first "you" is plural and the others are singular.) Earlier scholars saw this as an indication of sources, but now it is thought that this may just be a matter of style. This is also seen in other ANE documents, and so may not be significant.

very important here. It shows that the words which come before it ("God has done *this* for you") are the reason and foundation for the commands which come after it ("you should do *this*").

Yet Deuteronomy is more than a sermon. It generally follows the pattern of an ancient treaty-covenant,[6] especially in the way it concludes with a series of blessings and curses.[7] Here, again, we are talking about form. Ancient treaties between a powerful and a weaker nation often followed this pattern. They mentioned what the powerful nation had done for the weaker one and what the weaker one was thus obligated to do in response. And they included curses in case the weaker nation did not fulfill its obligations. If Deuteronomy is following this kind of pattern, then the message of this pattern is: "Remember what God has done for you; therefore obey and be blessed and live."

It is also possible that Deuteronomy functioned as a "loyalty oath" to the LORD. And Deuteronomy may have originated in Samaria, not Jerusalem. It may then have been brought south when Assyria destroyed Samaria in 722 B.C., during the reign of Hezekiah in Jerusalem. Note that Hezekiah, like Josiah, also undertook reforms (2 Kgs 18:3-6). Were the reforms of Hezekiah also inspired by Deuteronomy? If so, then perhaps Deuteronomy functioned as a loyalty oath to Yahweh – an alternative and a challenge to the loyalty oaths which the kings of Israel and Judah had to swear to Assyria. Deuteronomy may be saying, "Remain faithful to the LORD even when you stand before the king of Assyria."

Outline

I. **Introduction:** Deuteronomy 1-4 (1:1-4:43)
  A. Moses reviews what God has done (Deuteronomy 1-3)
  B. Moses exhorts the people to "listen to the statutes and ordinances ... that you may live" (Deut 4:1-40)
  C. Moses sets aside the cities of refuge (Deut 4:41-43)

II. **The Law of Moses:** Deuteronomy 5-26 (4:44-26:19)
  A. Editor's introduction (Deut 4:44-49)
  B. The Ten Commandments (Deuteronomy 5)
  C. Other "statutes and ordinances" (Deuteronomy 6-26)

---

[6]This may also be true for the book of Numbers, as mentioned on p. 54.

[7]Deuteronomy 27-28; see also Deut 11:26-29 and Leviticus 26.

III. The covenant (perhaps "loyalty oath") at Moab: Deuteronomy 27-28
- A. The ceremony (Deuteronomy 27)
- B. Blessings and curses (Deuteronomy 28)

IV. Moses' final words: Deuteronomy 29-32 (29:1-32:47)
- A. Exhortation to obey (Deuteronomy 29-30)
- B. Other exhortations and final matters (Deuteronomy 31 [31:1-29])
- C. Song of Moses[8] (Deuteronomy 32 [31:30-32:47])

V. The death of Moses: Deuteronomy 33-34 (32:48-34:12)
- A. Moses goes to Mt Nebo (Deut 32:48-52)
- B. The blessing of Moses (Deuteronomy 33)
- C. The death of Moses (Deuteronomy 34)

Message

Theological authority. The New Testament frequently quotes Deuteronomy. Jesus especially does so, and uses it all three times in his answers to Satan's temptations in Matthew 4 and Luke 4. And when Jesus was asked what is "the great commandment" (Matt 22:35-40), he quotes Deut 6:5: "you shall love the LORD your God with all your heart, and with all your soul, and with all your might."[9]

Leadership. Deuteronomy is concerned about new leadership. Moses is about to die, and Joshua will soon lead the people. Strong promises that God will be with Joshua are found in Deuteronomy 1-3 and Deuteronomy 31, just before and just after the central portions of the book. (Similar promises are then found at the beginning of the book of Joshua.)

Monotheism and centralization of worship. Deuteronomy insists that the people of Israel be monotheistic and worship no other gods (Deut 6:4,13-15; 8:19-20; 11:16-17, 28 and many other places). Those who worshiped in local shrines faced a particular danger as they met their Canaanite neighbors who were worshiping Baal. There was a great temptation to become syncretistic.[10] For this reason, Deuteronomy seeks

---

[8]This is different from the "Song of Moses" found in Exodus 15.

[9]The "second" which is "like it" is Lev 19:18, "you shall love your neighbor as yourself."

[10]Syncretism is the mixing together of two or more religions or systems of belief. Here, the danger was mixing the worship of Yahweh and Baal.

to centralize worship in one location. People are not to worship in the high places[11] or shrines of Canaan. Instead, when they enter the land of Canaan, they are to worship in "the place which the LORD your God will choose" (Deut 12:5, 11, 14, 18, 21 and in sixteen other places). Readers at the time of Hezekiah or Josiah would understand this to mean Jerusalem. In the later chapters (Deuteronomy 27-28), Moses calls the people to make a covenant at Moab. This may be a "loyalty oath" rather than a covenant, as mentioned above (p. 59). This would especially encourage readers at the time of Hezekiah and Josiah (in the eighth and seventh centuries B.C.) when the king of Assyria was demanding loyalty oaths from those he had conquered. Deuteronomy tells people of all times and places that they should be loyal to God alone.

Obedience as a response. Both Deuteronomy and the later Deuteronomistic History insist that the proper response of God's people is obedience. Obedience brings blessing and life, whereas disobedience brings curse and death (Deut 10:12-15; 11:13-15, 26-28; 28:1-68; 30:15-20). But obedience in Deuteronomy is not merely following a list of laws. Rather, obedience is the proper *response* to God and his will (Deut 7:7-11; 11:1-15). Those who love God will obey him. Deuteronomy teaches that God's people are *already* chosen and *therefore* should be holy (Deut 7:7-8; 9:4-6).[12] Obedience is thus an ethical response to what God has already done; it is, in a sense, a response to gospel, good news. This is similar to that which we saw in Exodus 19 and at the beginning of the Ten Commandments.[13] This call to ethical response will be seen again at the end Joshua and is found much later in Paul.

A misunderstanding. Unfortunately, this understanding later became somewhat legalistic and overly simplistic for many. They

---

[11]The "high places" were the tops of hills where people went to worship and sacrifice. Since the people of Canaan were already worshiping there, this often led to syncretism. Deuteronomy does not mention these high places, since it comes to us as a sermon of Moses preached *before* the people enter Canaan. But the many references to "the place which the LORD your God shall choose" are probably warning against *other* places – i.e., the high places.

[12]Similar statements are found in Exodus, Leviticus, and Numbers, where God rescues Israel not because of Israel's holiness but because of God's love and faithfulness. *Therefore* Israel is to *respond* with lives of faithfulness and holiness (Exod 2:23-25; 19:3-6; Lev 11:45; 19:2; 20:7,26; Num 15:40-41).

[13]Exod 20:2-17; Deut 5:6-21. See the discussion on page 37.

reduced it simply to "if you are good God will bless you; if you are bad God will punish you." When Deuteronomistic theology is over-simplified in this way, it becomes a problem as we will see in Jeremiah, Job and Jonah. Although obedience is a major theme in Deuteronomy, it is presented as the proper response of loyal people. Obedience is to be the result of a right attitude and a proper love of God who has first loved his people, not merely a fear of punishment or the curse.

Sin and confession. There is a difference between Deuteronomy and, for instance, Leviticus. In Deuteronomy sin is removed by confession and prayer, not by sacrifice. Sacrifice in Deuteronomy is done not to remove sin; rather, it is understood as an offering to God. That which is sacrificed is then eaten and drunk by the one who offers it and shared with those who are poor (Deut 12:5-27; 16:10-15).

Concern for the weak. A concern for justice and equality (1:16-17; 16:18-20) and for the rights of the poor and weak (10:17-19; 14:28-15:11; 24:10-22) is also characteristic of Deuteronomy. Again and again, the people are told, "Remember that you were a slave in Egypt and the LORD your God redeemed you from there; therefore I command you to do this" (10:19; 15:15; 16:12; 24:18,22). And, following this theme, another thing is unique to Deuteronomy: runaway slaves are not to be returned to their masters, but are free to live among the people (23:15-16). Certainly the people of Israel, who had been slaves themselves, should now be sympathetic to the plight of a slave who escapes.

Some important texts: Ten Commandments (Deut 5:6-21; also Exod 20:1-17); the *Shema*[14] (Deut 6:4-9); an early creed (Deut 6:20-25); duties of the king (Deut 17:14-20); another early creed (Deut 26:1-11); the blessings and curses (Deuteronomy 27-28); the death of Moses (Deuteronomy 34).

Verses for memory: Deut 6:4-9; 7:7-8

---

[14]*Shema* (שְׁמַע) means "Hear." The imperative cry of these verses, "Hear, O Israel, Yahweh is your God; Yahweh is One," became Israel's greatest confession of monotheistic faith.

The Deuteronomistic History
(and Ruth)
An Overview

The theology of the books of Joshua, Judges, 1-2 Samuel and 1-2 Kings is influenced by the book of Deuteronomy. Thus, these books are called the Deuteronomistic History (DH). Ruth is not part of the DH, and in the Hebrew Scriptures Ruth is found in the third and last section known as the Writings (see p. 3). In the (Christian) Old Testament,[1] Ruth has been placed after Judges because the story takes place "in the days when the judges ruled" (Ruth 1:1). This present overview covers only the DH, but since we are following the order of the Old Testament, Ruth will also be discussed below (p. 77), just after Judges.

The Background of the DH. This was briefly mentioned in the overview of Deuteronomy, above. In 622 B.C., an early version of Deuteronomy was discovered in the temple during the reforms of Josiah (2 Kgs 22:8). This discovery had a powerful effect because the text contained not only laws but also blessings and curses. These seemed to explain the trouble which had come upon Israel and Judah (primarily the invasion of Assyria). Thus, this early version of Deuteronomy became the first text to be considered "scripture" in Israel. That is, its words were the first written words which were considered to be "word of God."

This "book of the law" inspired many people, including a historian who decided to write the history of Israel. Perhaps this historian felt that good days now lay ahead, that Judah would now be saved, and that the good king Josiah would be God's tool of salvation. This historian quite likely began with the recently discovered "book of the law" (the early version of Deuteronomy) and other old material which had already been written. This older material included stories from the time of David and

---

[1]For the difference between "Hebrew Scriptures" and "Old Testament," see p. 2 and especially footnote 3 on that page.

Solomon which we call the "Court History" or "Succession Narrative."[2] This material became the foundation of the DH. The historian then added the earlier stories of the conquest under Joshua and the period of the Judges. These were placed before the Court History. Then he started writing the stories of the kings from Solomon to Josiah.

The Theology of the DH. As mentioned above, the theology of Deuteronomy guided the writer of the DH. Therefore, the DH also teaches that Israel is to be loyal to the LORD, and that this loyalty should produce obedience. No other gods are to be worshiped. Failure in these areas was the reason for the Assyrian invasion and for the Babylonian exile. Each of the kings of Israel and Judah is evaluated according to the standards of Deuteronomy, and the writer notes especially whether they remove the high places.[3] Almost all kings are given a failing grade. Like Deuteronomy, the DH often brings us major speeches and sermons by important people. And, also like Deuteronomy, the DH especially emphasizes the importance of worshiping only the God of Israel, and that this should happen in Jerusalem ("the place that the LORD your God shall choose," Deut 12:5, etc.).

The two endings. The DH seems clearly to have two parts. The main part was written when the temple was still standing (note the words "to this day" in 1 Kgs 8:8). Perhaps this was at the time of Josiah. However, the very end of the DH describes the destruction of the temple (2 Kgs 25:9) and so must have been written later, perhaps in exile.

In other words, the original ending of the DH may have been 2 Kgs 23:25. There, the historian wrote of Josiah with great hope:

> Before him there was no king like him, who turned to the LORD with all his heart and with all his soul and with all his might, according to all the law of Moses; nor did any like him arise after him.

This sounds as if the historian was expecting good things to happen during and after the reign of Josiah. But good things did not happen; Josiah was killed in a foolhardy confrontation with Pharaoh Neco (2 Kgs

---

[2]"Succession" refers to one king following after (or "succeeding") another. Thus, the Succession Narrative is the story of the end of David's reign and the difficulties and problems of passing the kingship to Solomon. Solomon, after all, was not the oldest son, and thus there was a challenge from first-born Adonijah (1 Kings 1).

[3]For "high places," see p. 61, footnote 11.

23:29).[4] Babylon then destroyed Jerusalem and the temple, and the leadership of the people was taken into exile. What did this mean? When the exiles arrived in Babylon, they reflected upon this situation. It appears that a second ending was added to the DH at that time. Note the contrast between the original ending (2 Kgs 23:25) and the following verses (2 Kgs 23:26-25:30) which were probably added later.

Why was the DH written? The writer(s) of the DH seems to have several reasons for his work. One reason may simply have been the optimism at the time of Josiah which I mentioned above. But those who later edited the DH (while in exile in Babylon) also seemed to be trying to answer some difficult questions.

- **The first question** was: Why did the unfaithful northern kingdom of Israel last for two hundred years? The DH suggests that it was because even the evil kings of Israel did have moments of repentance (for instance 1 Kgs 21:27-29; 2 Kgs 13:4). In the end, however, the curses of Deuteronomy fell upon Israel (2 Kgs 17:5-20); Samaria was destroyed and the people were removed from the land.
- **The second question** was: Why was Judah destroyed just when they had a good king (Josiah)? The DH answers that the sins of King Manasseh, Josiah's grandfather, had been so great that even Josiah's faithfulness could not save them (2 Kgs 23:26-27; 24:3-4). Manasseh receives a great deal of blame in the DH.
- **The third question** was the most crucial one for the editors in Babylon: Is there now any hope? And as they watched events develop, the editors of the DH eventually said yes. The very last verses of 2 Kings tell us that, in the thirty-seventh year of exile,

---

[4]It was a classic example of geo-political realities. Assyria ruled Mesopotamia (see map on p. xiii) but was losing its grip. Thus, in 605 BC, Babylon decided to move against Assyria. Egypt, however, the third super power of the day, wanted to preserve the status quo of power ("The devil you know is better than the devil you don't know," after all) and thus headed north to help Assyria hold off Babylon. Josiah, on the other hand, had suffered under the rule of Assyria and wanted to help Babylon. Thus, he tried to stop the advance of Egypt, foolishly placing himself in front of Pharaoh Neco and one of the world's largest armies. The result was tragic for Judah: Neco easily rolled over Judah's army and killed Josiah in the process. Neco then went on to meet defeat at the hands of the Babylonian army at the climactic Battle of Carchemish.

King Jehoiachin was freed from prison and was honored by the king of Babylon (2 Kgs 25:27-30). This was seen as a sign of hope and an indication that good things lay ahead.

Outline

- **I. "Charismatic"[5] leadership** (Joshua through 1 Samuel 12)
  - A. Conquest of the land under Joshua (Joshua)
  - B. Temporary leadership under the Judges (Judges)
  - C. Transition to kingship under judge/prophet Samuel (1 Samuel 1-12)
- **II. The Kings** (1 Samuel 13-2 Kings 23)
  - A. Saul (1 Samuel 13-31)
  - B. David (2 Samuel)
    1. King of Judah at Hebron (2 Samuel 1-4)
    2. King of (united) Israel at Jerusalem (2 Samuel 5-24)
  - C. Solomon (1 Kings 1-11)
  - D. Kings after Solomon (1 Kings 12-2 Kings 23)
    1. The Divided Monarchy (Israel and Judah) (1 Kings 12-2 Kings 17)
    2. Judah alone (after fall of northern kingdom of Israel) (2 Kings 18-23)
- **III. The fall of Jerusalem to Babylon** (2 Kings 24-25)

Message

As mentioned above, the writer of the DH was influenced by the book of Deuteronomy, and his theology comes from there. Thus, in the DH, loyalty to the God of Israel is of the greatest importance and this loyalty should show itself in obedience and monotheistic worship. Therefore, the DH emphasizes the removal of the high places (where other gods were worshiped) and insists upon centralizing worship in the Jerusalem temple. The DH tells us that the Assyrian and Babylonian exiles happened because the people failed to be loyal to God and they

---

[5]In the study of the Old Testament, *charismatic* leadership means leadership which was temporary (the son did not rule after the father). It depended upon the dynamic personality of the leader rather than a structure or institution. The judges were charismatic leaders. Samuel was a charismatic leader. Saul was a successful charismatic leader but was not able to make the transition to institutional kingship. David was successful in both kinds of leadership.

worshiped other gods. Behind all this lies the Mosaic covenant of Deuteronomy.

But there is another theme at work in the DH. In addition to the call for loyalty and obedience from the book of Deuteronomy, there is the promise to king David and there is the covenant which God made with him (2 Samuel 7). The Mosaic covenant in Deuteronomy was conditional; the covenant with David was without conditions. A tension[6] develops between these two promises. As we shall see, one result is that the unconditional promise of 2 Samuel 7 later gains some conditions (1 Kgs 2:4; 6:11-13; 9:1-9). However, another result of this tension is even more important: when disloyalty and disobedience bring down the curses of the Mosaic covenant (i.e., the Babylonian exile), hope is maintained because of the unconditional promise of the Davidic covenant. At the very end of the DH, King Jehoiachin, a descendant of David, was freed from prison in Babylon and given a position of honor (2 Kgs 25:27-30) (Note again the "third question" regarding hope, above.)

---

[6]A "tension" can be thought of as two truths which challenge and conflict with each other, and yet both are necessary and both are true.

JOSHUA

❧

Overview

The book of Joshua is the first book of the Deuteronomistic History. It has a simple structure (see the outline below): preparation, conquering the land, dividing the land, final sermons by Joshua. The first chapters are chapters of preparation. In these chapters, God encourages Joshua, the people cross the Jordan River, and then they are circumcised and celebrate the Passover (Joshua 1-5). These last events are important since neither Passover nor circumcision had been observed while the people were traveling through the wilderness with Moses. The heart of the book is Joshua 6-21 in which the land is conquered and then divided among the tribes. Throughout the book, the message is clear: the land is a gift from God; it is not something the people have gained for themselves.

At the end of the book, after the division of the land, we find a series of sermons or speeches by Joshua (Joshua 23-24). These speeches again emphasize that the land is a gift of God and is not something that the people have gotten for themselves. Finally, at Shechem, Joshua makes a covenant with the people after reminding them of all that God has done for them in the past.

Outline

I. **Preparation for Conquest** (Joshua 1-5)
   A. Words of promise to Joshua from God and the people (Joshua 1)
   B. Spies sent to Jericho (Joshua 2)
   C. Crossing the Jordan (Joshua 3-4)
   D. Circumcision and Passover, and a vision (Joshua 5)

II. **The conquest of the land** (Joshua 6-12)

III. **The division of the land among the tribes** (Joshua 13-21)

IV. **Concluding sermons and covenant by Joshua** (22-24)

Message

As already mentioned, the book of Joshua is the first book of the Deuteronomistic History.[1] Perhaps the editor wanted the life of Joshua to inspire and encourage King Josiah in his brave stand against the King of Assyria.[2]

The book of Joshua brings us several historical and moral challenges. The historical questions[3] will not concern us here, but the moral ones will. The largest moral question is that of genocide. Would God really tell Joshua and Israel to kill entire cities of people – men, women, children and even animals – in order to give the land to Israel? This question is troubling and certainly deeply theological.

As we seek to answer this question, we need to note several points. The first point is that, although there is fighting in Joshua, it is not the fighting which seems to be important to the writer. Only six chapters (Joshua 6-11) involve the battles of conquest. Something else lies at the heart of Joshua, and that "something else" is the message that the land is a gracious gift from God. Yes, the people fight; but they are neither strong enough, nor do they have the ability, to take the land on their own. Indeed, unless God is with them, they suffer embarrassing defeats (for instance, at Ai, Josh 7:1-5).

Thus, the *point* of the battle stories is not the killing of innocent people (though that certainly catches *our* attention!). Rather, the point of the stories is to show, again and again, that the source of all they have is God's faithfulness to his promises, not the worthiness or ability of the people.

This is seen from the very beginning of Joshua, even before the conquest begins. The first chapter begins with a change of leadership. In Josh 1:5-9, God encourages Joshua:

---

[1]It is possible that Deuteronomy itself was originally used as the first book of the Deuteronomistic History. See the discussions on pp. 20 and 58, above.

[2]See the overview of the Deuteronomistic History, p. 63, which includes a discussion of the motives that may have been behind the writing of the first edition of this work.

[3]Those most often noted are the differences between what Joshua says and what archeology has discovered, and the contrast between the amount of land conquered and described in chapters 6-12 and the land divided in chapters 13-22. Another issue – the difference between the descriptions of the conquest in Joshua and those at the beginning of Judges – will be noted briefly below.

> As I was with Moses, so I will be with you; I will not fail you or forsake you. Be strong and of good courage; for you shall cause this people to inherit the land which I swore to their fathers to give them. ... Be strong and of good courage; be not frightened, neither be dismayed; for the LORD your God is with you wherever you go.

This point is made again in Joshua's three sermons at the end of the book. There he reminds the people that "not one thing has failed of all the good things which the LORD your God promised concerning you; all have come to pass for you, not one of them has failed" (Josh 23:14). Note also the "therefore" in Joshua's famous "choose this day whom you will serve" sermon of Joshua 24. Like Paul, and even like the Ten Commandments (see p.37), Joshua first begins with good news, gospel, reminding the people of all that God has done for them (Josh 24:2-13). Only after this tremendous review of God's gracious provision does Joshua then tell the people to choose (Josh 24:14-15). At that point the choice is easy! Those who preach this text would do well to follow Joshua's example, beginning with a reminder of all God has done for us. Only *then* comes the call to "chose this day whom you will serve." For people who have been made children of God because of the cross, the choice will again be clear and easy.

So the battles and killing are not themselves the primary point in Joshua. In addition, there is another point to consider concerning the killing of innocent people. In Joshua, we read of a single large army which conquers the land.[4] The book of Judges, however, tells a milder story. In Judges 1, we read that the people entered the land to conquer it *after Joshua had died*, and that they entered in smaller groups. And they are not completely successful. What can we say about this? The two stories are quite different.

Again, we need to recognize what the *point* is in each case. Indeed, there are differences between Joshua and Judges. But the most basic point of both books is the same: the land was a gift given by God, and Israel did not conquer Canaan using its own strength. "Thus the LORD gave to Israel all the land which he swore to give to their fathers ... not one of all their enemies had withstood them" (Josh 21:43-44). This is said in spite of the defeat at Ai, mentioned above, because the story is told by an Israelite writer for Israelite readers in order to emphasize God's grace toward them.

---

[4]See, for instance, Josh 4:13; 8:3; 9:1-2; 10:40-42; and the many mentions of "all Israel" in Joshua 10.

We, however, are gentiles not Israelites or Jews. We must always remember this when reading the Old Testament in general and especially when reading a book like Joshua. If we read Joshua as gentiles – as if we were Canaanites or modern Palestinians! – the story will have a very different sound. We will hear genocide, and the cries of the innocent. If, on the other hand, we imagine ourselves to be Israelites as we read Joshua, we will hear the writer saying, "Do not think this land is yours because you deserve it or because you yourself conquered it. This land is yours because God gave it to you." Those two voices are very different. The same is true when we read Exodus. Do we read Exodus as Israelites or as ("fellow gentile") Egyptians? The way we read a text often determines the message we hear in the text.

Reading is not a Game

In the section above, we have moved beyond mere overview to a discussion of the intent of the author. We have also made a comparison to another book. This kind of investigation is known as *hermeneutics* (see p. 16, where we briefly discussed this word). In general, we do not do hermeneutics in this book, but in the case of Joshua we need to understand at least one important hermeneutical principle – a principle important in reading *any* literature, not just the Bible. The point is this: In order to understand a writer, you must (at least temporarily) accept the viewpoint of the writer.

Although reading is not a game, there is one important way in which we can compare it to a game. If you play basketball, you must accept its rules and boundaries. You may not run with the ball under your arm. You may not kick the ball or carry it outside the boundaries of the court. When the game is over, you may do these things. When the game is over, you may put the ball under your arm, walk off the court, and go home. But you may not do this while the game is being played. *If you cannot accept these rules, you may not play the game. If you can accept them, you may play.*

Reading is at times similar. *While you are reading* an author's words, there are certain "rules," certain viewpoints and perspectives, which you must *at least temporarily* accept if you want to understand the writer. When you have understood the writer and finished reading, you then may or may not decide to continue accepting his perspective. But while you are reading, if you want to understand the writer, you must "play the game" of accepting the writer's rules, the writer's perspective, the writer's view of the world.

This is what we must do as we read Joshua. If you can temporarily imagine yourself to be an Israelite while you read Joshua, then you may be able to understand what Joshua is all about. You may be able to hear the voice which is saying, "All that you have is a gift from God; you have not earned what you have." If, however, you are unable to place yourself "in the game" of the writer like this, even temporarily, then you may indeed miss this message. You may only hear the voice crying "Genocide!" and it is possible that you may not be able to understand Joshua.

Truly, reading is not a game. It is a serious business. But there is this one point where understanding games and their rules may indeed help us in our reading and understanding.

Genocide is a serious matter, and we may not minimize this fact as we read Joshua. But Joshua is not *about* genocide. This is not what *the writer* is concerned about, and to understand what the book of Joshua is saying we will temporarily (though not permanently!) have to set aside the question of genocide. We will *temporarily* have to become Israelites in our minds as we read.

And there is also this: as already mentioned, the book of Judges (which is discussed next) suggests that we may not really know entirely what happened historically when Israel came into Canaan. Thus, the first chapters of Judges need to be read alongside the book of Joshua, and both need to be read with an awareness of God's message to Israel in these books:

> It was not by your sword or by your bow. I gave you a land on which you had not labored, and cities which you had not built, and you dwell therein; you eat the fruit of vineyards and oliveyards which you did not plant.
>
> Josh 24:12b-13

Some important texts: Promises to Joshua (Josh 1:1-10); crossing the Jordan (Josh 3:14-17); the twelve stones of testimony (Josh 4:19-24); Joshua's final sermon (Josh 24:1-15).

Verses for memory: Josh 1:9; 24:15

Judges

❧

Overview

The book of Judges continues the story of the conquest, which began in the book of Joshua, but the story is somewhat different. At the beginning of Judges, we read that Joshua has died (Judg 1:1, cf. 2:6-10). And it is at this point, *after* Joshua's death, that the people make plans to go up and fight against the Canaanites. In Judges, they go not as a single large group, but as one or two tribes at a time. Sometimes they succeed and sometimes they fail (Judges 1). So we do not see the same overwhelming picture of genocide that we saw in Joshua.

This mixture of success and failure is the result of a great forgetting of what God had done for Israel. The struggle which follows is described in two ways in Judges: as a **test** and as a **cycle**.

- In Judg 2:20-3:6, we are told that God left some of the Canaanites to live in the land as a **test** for Israel – to see if they would "walk in the way of the LORD as their fathers did" (Judg 2:22).
- Elsewhere, the experience of the people is described in terms of a repeating pattern or **cycle**, an example of which can be seen in Judg 3:7-12a:

> And the people of Israel did what was evil in the sight of the LORD, ... Therefore the anger of the LORD was kindled against Israel, and he sold them into the hand of Cushanrishathaim king of Mesopotamia .... But when the people of Israel cried to the LORD, the LORD raised up a deliverer ..., Othniel the son of Kenaz,... The Spirit of the LORD came upon him, and he judged Israel; ... and the LORD gave Cushanrishathaim king of Mesopotamia into his hand; .... So the land had rest forty years. Then Othniel the son of Kenaz died. And the people of Israel again did what was evil in the sight of the LORD ....

This cycle repeats throughout the book, showing clearly that the people do not learn. They turn to God only as long as the judge is alive; when the judge dies, they return to their old ways.

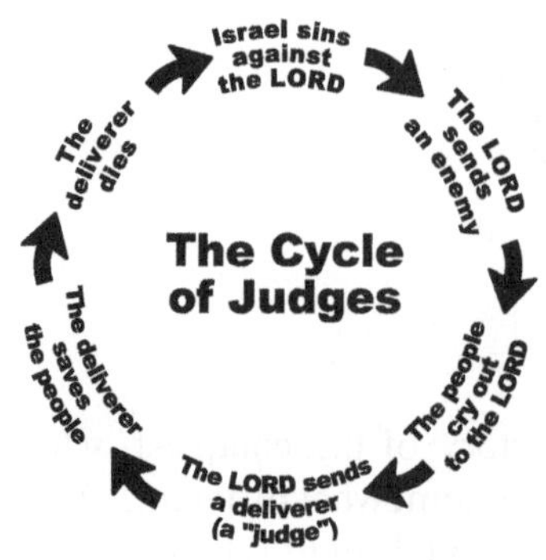

- Israel sins against the LORD
- The LORD sends an enemy to oppress them
- The people cry out to the LORD
- The LORD sends a deliverer (a "judge")
- The deliverer saves the people
- The deliverer dies
- Israel again sins against the LORD

Note that the "judges" actually did not do much judging. They spent more time ruling the people and leading them in battles. They were "charismatic"[1] leaders who were raised up by God for a period of time, and then died without making their sons leaders. They did not provide permanent, stable leadership. They were not kings, and this is important. Israel was at this time a theocracy.[2] Later, in 1 Samuel, the matter of charismatic leadership and theocracy becomes a hot issue.

The judges were a mixed blessing; the book tells us of both good and bad judges. One of the good ones was a woman, Deborah, a prophetess (Judg 4:4) who encouraged a timid military commander named Barak. Some of the most well-known judges were not very good. Gideon is known for laying out his fleece (Judg 6:36-40), an act which seemed to show not faith but lack of faith and mistrust of God. Although he did defeat the Midianites, later he became an idol worshiper (Judg 8:27). And, although Gideon himself refused when the people tried to make him king (Judg 8:22-23), his son, Abimelech,[3] later tried to become king (Judges 9). Samson, perhaps the most well-known judge, caused a great deal of trouble for his people and was not very wise.

The last chapters of Judges (Judges 17-21) contain some very strange stories involving Levites. In Judges 17, a man named Micah has stolen money from his mother. When he returns it, they "consecrate the

---

[1]See p. 66, footnote 5.

[2]Theocracy is government in which God rules. In Israel, this later raised serious issues and challenges with regard to kingship. Many believed that *God*, not a human being, should be king.

[3]The name Abimelech means "my father is king"!!

silver to the LORD ... to make a graven image and a molten image ... and an ephod and a teraphim" (Judg 17:3-5).[4] We are then told, "In those days there was no king in Israel; every man did what was right in his own eyes" (Judg 17:6), and this becomes a refrain in Judges. Micah hires a Levite to become a priest for his idol, and the Levite agrees to do so! Then men from the tribe of Dan come and steal both the idol and the Levite from Micah, after we again read that "In those days there was no king in Israel" (Judg 18:1). The third and worst story also begins with "In those days when there was no king in Israel" (Judg 19:1). In this story, a Levite takes his concubine[5] and goes to Gibeah in the tribal area of Benjamin. The men of the city act much like those in the story of Sodom and Gomorrah, and they rape and kill the concubine. The Levite then cuts up her body and sends the parts, along with a message about what happened, throughout the other tribes of Israel. The rest of Israel is enraged and almost destroys the tribe of Benjamin. The last verse of the book of Judges once again repeats the refrain, "In those days there was no king in Israel; every man did what was right in his own eyes" (Judg 21:25).

Outline

I. **Introduction:** Israel's failures and Joshua's death (Judg 1:1-3:6)
II. **The Judges** (Judg 3:7-16:31)
III. **Final stories of Levites, etc.** (Judges 17-21)

Message

The stories of Judges are interesting and contain many lessons. Three lessons in particular stand out. **First**, we learn that the harsh genocidal picture of Joshua may not be entirely accurate. As noted above in the section on Joshua, the point of that book is not the killing, but rather that the land was a gift from God. It had not been earned or deserved by the people. The **second** lesson found in Judges is that God

---

[4]An "ephod" usually refers to a garment worn by a priest (see Exodus 28 and 39). When mentioned along with the word "teraphim," however, both words seems to refer to cultic objects like idols. See also p. 50, footnote 9.

[5]A concubine is a woman who lives with a man and has sexual relations with him but is not married to him. Sometimes she is a slave, sometimes a contract is involved. Thus she is not a wife and certainly not a prostitute, but her legal status and rights are not always clear.

sometimes allows testing of his people (see discussion of Judg 2:20-3:6, p. 73, above). The **third** lesson: without good leadership, people again and again wander away from God. This seems to be a major concern in Judges and, as noted above, it is shown in three ways:

1. *The great forgetting*: After Joshua's death, the new generation "did not know the LORD or the work which he had done for Israel" (Judg 2:10).
2. *The cycle*: Every time a judge died the people returned to their sin (many times).
3. *The refrain*: "In those days there was no king in Israel; every man did what was right in his own eyes" (Judg 17:6; 18:1; 19:1; 21:25)

Thus, there is an emphasis upon the need for good leadership – a lesson which applies just as much today, too, when people need good leaders both spiritually and politically. At the end, Judges seems to be saying that the people really need a king – though we will see that there are mixed feelings about this in the next book of the Deuteronomistic History, 1 Samuel.

Some important texts: Entry into Canaan (Judges 1); the cycle (Judg 2:11-19; 3:7-12a); the test (Judg 2:20-3:6); the need for a king (Judg 17:6; 18:1; 19:1; 21:25)

Verses for memory: Judg 21:25

RUTH

❧

Overview

Fortunately, not "*every* man did what was right in his own eyes" during the time of the judges (see the discussion of that phrase in Judges, above). Boaz, in the book of Ruth, is a refreshing exception. The book of Ruth is not part of the Deuteronomistic History, but it is discussed here because it is found after Judges and before 1 Samuel in the (Christian) Old Testament.[1]

The small book of Ruth is a marvelous short story, like the book of Jonah. Both books have four carefully written chapters which carry the reader from a very interesting beginning to an important point at the end. Ruth is one of the five "festival scrolls" of Judaism,[2] and is read publicly when Jews gather to celebrate the Feast of Weeks.[3] A good story is sometimes like a scorpion: the sting is in the tail! The book of Jonah does carry a sting at the end; the end of Ruth, on the other hand brings us a surprise rather than a sting (this is discussed in the "Message" section, below). The style of Ruth is also different from that of Jonah and is more like that of Genesis 22, 24, 38 and the Joseph stories.

The story takes place during the time of the Judges. A Jewish couple, Elimelech (his name means "My God is King") and his wife Naomi ("pleasant"), go to live in Moab where Elimelech dies. Naomi's two sons (whose names mean "sickness" and "spent") also die. By the end of the fifth verse of the book, Naomi is alone in a foreign land with her two Moabite daughters-in-law, Ruth and Orpah. Naomi heads back

---

[1]For the difference between the "Hebrew Scriptures" and the "Old Testament," review p. 2 and especially footnote 3 on that page.

[2]Festival scrolls are books which are read when people gather at special Jewish festivals. The other books which are used as "festival scrolls" are Ecclesiastes, read at the Feast of Booths; Song of Solomon, read at Passover; Lamentations, read at Ninth of Ab (see p. 185); and Esther, read at Purim.

[3]Weeks is renamed "Pentecost" in the LXX, see p. 38 footnote 17.

to Israel and tells Ruth and Orpah to return to their families in Moab. Orpah (whose name means "back of the neck") turns and shows her back to Naomi as she returns to her people, but Ruth clings to Naomi and says she will not leave her.

Ruth (whose name means perhaps "friend" or "companion") leaves her own people of Moab and goes back to Israel with Naomi. The rest of the story is a delightful telling of how Ruth meets and marries Boaz ("in him is strength"), a fine and honorable man of Israel. At the end, a son is born to them and is named Obed ("serving, servant").

Outline

I. Naomi travels with her husband from Israel to Moab and returns to Israel with Ruth (Ruth 1)
II. Ruth meets Boaz the first time (Ruth 2)
III. Naomi arranges Ruth's second meeting with Boaz (Ruth 3)
IV. Ruth marries Boaz, and their son Obed is born (Ruth 4)

Message

God does not speak in the book of Ruth, but is certainly present throughout the story. The name "the LORD" appears 17 times in just four chapters. It appears five times in the phrase "May the LORD" bless you or do this or do that. The LORD provides food for his people (1:6) and is at first accused of afflicting Naomi (1:21); but finally he brings joy to Naomi and Ruth and Boaz by giving Ruth a son (4:13)

Two themes are very strong in the book: the first is **loyalty, faithfulness**. The important Hebrew word is *chesed*, חֶסֶד. This word is often used in the Old Testament to refer to God's covenant faithfulness and is sometimes translated "steadfast love" or "lovingkindness." The second theme is **blessing** (*berakah*, בְּרָכָה). God is faithful and blesses, but people also display faithfulness in this story. Ruth is faithful to Naomi in staying with her and going back to Israel with her. Naomi is faithful to Ruth in seeking a husband for her when they get to Israel. Boaz acts with great integrity and faithfulness toward Ruth, both at the threshing floor and before the community. And Ruth shows faithfulness toward Boaz[4] by taking him as husband rather than seeking a younger man. At the end, we read in Ruth 4:13-14:

---

[4]See Ruth 3:10, the only verse in Ruth that uses the word *chesed* (חֶסֶד) of a human being. RSV translates "kindness," NRSV translates "loyalty."

> So Boaz took Ruth and she became his wife; and he went in to her, and the LORD gave her conception, and she bore a son. Then the women said to Naomi, "Blessed be the LORD, who has not left you this day without next of kin; and may his name be renowned in Israel!"

And indeed his name was renowned in Israel. The last verse of Ruth tells us that Obed's grandson was King David. This is **the surprise at the end** of the story which was mentioned above: David's grandmother was a woman of Moab, not a Jew. There were traditions in Israel which were quite negative toward Gentiles and especially toward Moab.[5] But there are several places in which the Old Testament makes strong statements that God loves the whole world. The book of Ruth is one of those places; for in Ruth we read that even King David had a faithful Gentile ancestor!

Some important texts: Ruth's faithfulness toward Naomi (Ruth 1:15-18); David's family line (Ruth 4:18-22).

Verses for memory: Ruth 1:16-17

---

[5]In Numbers 22-24, Balak, king of Moab, hires the prophet Balaam to curse Israel. He fails, but this is remembered in Deut 23:3-6 where it is said that, because of this, "No Ammonite or Moabite shall enter the assembly of the LORD; even to the tenth generation none belonging to them shall enter the assembly of the LORD for ever." Later, this verse becomes important in the reforms (some would say "purges"!) of Nehemiah. See p. 118 for the very different response of Neh 13:1 to this proscription again Ammonites and Moabites.

1-2 Samuel

❧

Overview

The books. The books of 1-2 Samuel describe the beginning of kingship for Israel. This beginning involves the lives of Samuel (judge and prophet), Saul (Israel's first king), and David (Israel's greatest king). David becomes the model against which all other kings are measured; later he becomes the foundation of messianic hope.

Kingship in the Ancient Near East and Israel

The king was a very important religious figure throughout the ANE; he was thought to have a special relationship with the gods. Economic prosperity and the fertility of wives and of the land depended upon this relationship. In Egypt, they believed that the king (Pharaoh) was *actually* a god, his birth being the result of a sexual union of the queen mother and the god Amon. In Mesopotamia (for instance, Assyria and Babylon), the people did not think the king was an actual god; but they thought he was *adopted* by their god. And kingship itself was considered divine and a gift of the gods. The opening lines of the Sumerian King List reads:

> When kingship was lowered from heaven, kingship was (first) in Eridu. (In) Eridu, Alulim (became) king and ruled 28,800 years. Alalgar ruled 36,000 years. Two kings (thus) ruled it for 64,800 years.[1]

The years are mythological, but the point is clear. The people believed (and certainly the kings taught!) that kingship was from the gods and thus should not be challenged or questioned.[2]

---

[1]"The Sumerian King List," *ANET*, 265.

[2]See p. 271, and especially footnote 4 on that page, for a discussion of this "common theology" of the Ancient Near East.

In Israel, too, we find that the king had a special relationship with God, and that the fate of the nation was affected by this relationship. This is one reason why the prophets are so concerned about the activities of the king. Indeed there are several places where the relationship between God and the king of Israel (or Judah) seems particularly close. In five places[3] the king is called God's "son," and in the last of these (Ps 2:7) God even says of the king "today I have begotten you."

But in Israel the king was never considered to be actually divine. Indeed, there are many places in the Old Testament where the writers deliberately show the weaknesses and sins of the kings. And the king's power was not to be unlimited. In 1 Sam 10:25 the "rights and duties of the kingship" are spelled out. And Deut 17:14-20[4] describes what the ideal king would be like: he should study *torah* rather than make war! This, at least, was the ideal. What actually happened was usually rather different.

It may seem odd that we have a book called 2 Samuel which does not mention Samuel. Originally, 1-2 Samuel was a single book. When it was translated into the Greek Septuagint (LXX), however, it was put on two scrolls because it was too large for one. Thus, we now have 1 and 2 Samuel.[5]

Tensions. 1-2 Samuel is filled with tensions. As mentioned earlier,

---

[3]2 Sam 7:14; 1 Chr 17:13; 22:10; 28:6; Ps 2:7.

[4]This passage may contain unpleasant memories of the people's experience with Solomon.

[5]The origins of 1-2 Samuel is actually much more complicated, and is one of the more difficult challenges for scholars. Three issues are widely discussed. **First**, those who wrote and edited 1-2 Samuel used several early sources for their information. In particular, they used the stories of the Ark of the Covenant (1 Sam 4:1b-7:2), the rise of Saul, the rise of David, and Absalom's revolt (2 Samuel 13-20). (The large section 2 Samuel 9-20, plus 1 Kings 1-2, is often called the "Succession Narrative" or "Court History.") **Second**, the Hebrew text has many places where it has been badly copied from older texts and so is difficult or impossible to understand. In such cases, scholars use the LXX to try to reconstruct what the original Hebrew said. **Third**, however, the LXX is itself sometimes quite different from the Hebrew, and may have been translated from a Hebrew text that we no longer have. For all these reasons, technical study of 1-2 Samuel can at times be quite complex.

a "tension" can be thought of as two truths which challenge and conflict with each other, and yet both are necessary and both are true. Two times in 1-2 Samuel there is a tension between God's unconditional "forever" promises on the one hand, and later conditions which are added to them on the other. The first of these tensions sets the pattern for the second: in 1 Sam 2:27-36 God withdraws an unconditional promise previously given to Eli. The second tension has huge implications for the future of Israel: the unconditional promise to David in 2 Samuel 7 becomes conditional in 1 Kgs 2:4; 6:11-13; 9:1-9.[6]

Another great tension is seen in the choosing of Saul as king. Did the *people* ask for a king and thus reject God (a bad idea)? Or was the

1 Samuel 8	1 Sam 9:1-10:16	1 Sam 10:17-27	1 Samuel 11	1 Samuel 12
Negative	Positive	Negative	Positive	Negative
People chose the king and rejected God	God told Samuel to anoint Saul	People chose the king and rejected God	Spirit of the LORD was upon Saul	People chose the king and rejected God

king *God's* idea (and thus a good idea)? 1 Samuel 8 says that the people are rejecting God when they ask for a king. However, in the very next chapters (1 Sam 9:1-10:16) we read that it was God who told Samuel to anoint Saul as king. But then the words after that (1 Sam 10:17-27) are negative again. This pattern continues through 1 Samuel 12 (negative-positive-negative-positive-negative; see the diagram above). This is not simply a contradiction, and we will say more about these various tensions in the "Message" section, below.

Relationships. Difficult relationships are found throughout 1-2 Samuel. Samuel wanted to make his sons judges after him, but the people recognized that they were corrupt and rejected this idea (1 Sam 8:3-5). Saul, the first king, was a gifted leader, but he disobeyed Samuel (and thus God) on several occasions,[7] and so was found to be unfaithful.

---

[6]This raises the question of the freedom of God and whether anything can bind him – even his own word. The question is too big to discuss in depth here, and really belongs in the area of Systematic Theology. But it will return when we consider Jeremiah (especially chapters 7 and 18). The people said, "God cannot punish us for our sin; we are his people and we have his promises and his temple." Jeremiah said they were wrong in this belief and that it would lead to the destruction of Jerusalem. In the end, Jeremiah was right.

[7]1 Sam 13:6-14; 15:7-23; 15:34-16:1.

In addition, after Samuel's death, Saul attempted to contact Samuel for advice by using a medium.[8] It has also been suggested that Saul was unable to move from charismatic leadership to the more structured kind of kingship which was necessary for an expanding Israel.

David also had relationship problems. Certainly he is remembered as being more faithful than Saul. And he was very successful, first as a charismatic leader, then as a military and political leader, and finally in establishing a formal monarchy.

David conquered the Philistines. The Philistines had learned how to work with iron before the Israelites did. Thus, for a time, they were able to develop better weapons than Israel. David was also successful in the area of religion. He maintained a positive relationship with the prophets and even originated the idea of the temple. But David was unsuccessful within his own family; there we read of adultery (Bathsheba, 2 Samuel 11), rape (Tamar by her brother Amnon, 2 Samuel 13), and fighting between David's sons.[9] At one point, David's son Absalom tries to overthrow his father and become king. The section 2 Samuel 9-20 + 1 Kings 1-2 is sometimes called the "Succession Narrative" because it describes the very troubled succession (change of kingship) in moving from David to Solomon.

Prophets. Prophets are important in 1-2 Samuel. These "pre-classical" or "former" prophets[10] do not have books in the Bible which carry their name (as Isaiah and Jeremiah do, for example); but they sought to advise the king as kingship developed in Israel. Samuel began as a judge but ended up being a prophet who tried to advise Saul. And at two points, the prophet Nathan had important encounters with David: (1) he brought God's promise to David in 2 Samuel 7, and (2) he confronted David in 2 Samuel 12 after his sin with Bathsheba.

---

[8]1 Sam 28:3-28. A medium (sometimes called a necromancer and sometimes a "witch") is one who claims to be able to communicate with the dead. The Bible forbids such activity in many places. See Lev 19:31; 20:6,27; Deut 18:10-11; 2 Ki 21:6; 23:24; 1 Chr 10:13; 2 Chr 33:6; Isa 8:19; 19:3.

[9]See for instance Absalom's arrangement of the murder of Amnon in 2 Sam 13:22-29, the struggles for kingship between Adonijah and Solomon in 1 Kings 1, and Solomon's command to kill Adonijah in 1 Kings 2.

[10]The "former prophets" are Samuel, Nathan, Elijah and Elisha, etc., who are found in 1-2 Samuel and 1-2 Kings. The terms "pre-classical" and"former" are popular phrases rather than technical terms. See p. 3.

Outline

I. Samuel (1 Samuel 1-7)
- A. Samuel the boy (1 Samuel 1-3)
- B. Loss and return of the ark (1 Samuel 4-6)
- C. Samuel the judge (1 Samuel 7)

II. Samuel and Saul (1 Samuel 8-15)
- A. Saul chosen as king (1 Sam 8:1-10:27)
  1. The people demand a king (part 1) (1 Samuel 8)
  2. God chooses Saul as king (1 Sam 9:1-10:16)
  3. The people demand a king (part 2) (1 Sam 10:17-27)
- B. Saul's early activities as king (1 Sam 10:28-15:9)
- C. God rejects Saul (1 Sam 15:10-35)

III. Samuel anoints David (1 Sam 16:1-13)

IV. Saul and David (1 Sam 16:14-30:31)
- A. David in Saul's court[11] (1 Sam 16:14-19:24)
- B. David as a fugitive from Saul (1 Samuel 20-30)

V. The death of Saul (1 Samuel 31)

VI. David (2 Samuel)
- A. King of Judah at Hebron (2 Samuel 1-4)
- B. King of (united) Israel at Jerusalem (2 Samuel 5-24)
  1. Establishing David at Jerusalem (including God's covenant) (2 Samuel 5-8)
  2. "Succession Narrative" (2 Samuel 9-20 [+ 1 Kings 1-2])
  3. Concluding texts (2 Samuel 21-24)

Message

Two views of kingship. The books of 1-2 Samuel tell us about the beginning of kingship for Israel. As noted above (p. 80), the king was an extremely important figure in Israel. He was a religious figure, and not merely a political or military one. The king stood between the people and God, and thus the future of Israel depended upon whether or not the king had a good relationship with God.

But who was *really* king in Israel? Many in Israel remembered the "old days" in which Israel was led by charismatic figures such as Moses, Joshua or the judges. *God* was Israel's king,[12] and many felt that to

---

[11]A king's "court" is his family, servants, advisors and ministers. It has nothing to do with judges or lawyers.

[12]The word for this kind of government is *theocracy*. See also p. 74.

speak of having a *human* king (a monarchy) was to reject God. This is the tension we mentioned above (p. 81) – the tension which exists in 1 Samuel 8-12.

1 Samuel 8-12 is an extremely important passage, and it puts together two opposing viewpoints:

- Seeking a human king is necessary for stable leadership and military success.[13]
- Seeking a human king is to reject God who is the *real* king.

This passage keeps these two opinions in tension, and the tension is a fruitful one. Today we might also ask, is political leadership good or bad? A person with a broad understanding of human nature and politics would say "leadership is often *both* good and bad." We need political leaders to keep peace and to provide justice. But political leaders are also human and often corrupt. They must always be watched, often challenged, and sometimes removed. All of this is being said in the tension of 1 Samuel 8-12 regarding the kings. But it does not say this abstractly, as I have just done. Rather, it uses two stories which have opposing viewpoints, and it lets the opposition of these stories create a tension for the reader. This tension allows the two stories *together* to say more than either story could say *alone*. And it says it in the full awareness that Israel's *true* king really is God.

Are there Contradictions in the Bible?

Readers are sometimes troubled when they find contradictions in the Bible. For instance, 1 Samuel 8-12 has five parts which seem to contradict each other.[14] What can we say about this?

The first thing we must recognize is that the Bible is both human and divine. We know this is true of Jesus – Jesus is both God and Man. But sometimes, while confessing Jesus' divinity, we have a hard time pointing to examples of how he is human. We talk easily about his miracles, but we become uncomfortable when even Jesus himself says that he did not know everything (Matt 24:36; Mark 13:32). And sometimes we experience a

[13]It has also been suggested that a king was needed to organize the massive stonework terracing of the hillsides necessary to make the land farmable.

[14]See the diagram on p. 82, above.

similar discomfort when we talk about the human side of the Bible. Indeed, there are contradictions in the Bible. 1 Kgs 4:26 says Solomon had forty thousand stalls for horses and 2 Chr 9:25 says there were just four thousand. One of those texts is probably right and the other is wrong; and it does not really matter which. It is simply not important. Someone probably made a very human mistake and copied a number wrongly. And sometimes there are misunderstandings, such as in Lev 11:19 where a bat is called a bird. The Bible, like Jesus, is both human and divine.

But contradictions are not always a matter of human error. There are times when a Biblical writer or editor seems deliberately to allow a contradiction to arise. At this point, the reader will be puzzled and will need to decide what to do. And what the reader does will depend a great deal upon what the reader expects. A reader who expects incoherence[15] will simply say "The text is incoherent; it is contradictory." But a reader who generally expects the Bible to be coherent will pause and ask some questions. The writers and editors were not foolish people. Is the writer or editor trying to say something by deliberately creating or allowing a tension? A more theological question would be, Is *God* using this writer and this tension in order to say something to us?

The writers of the Old Testament do not speak abstractly or theoretically. They are not philosophical like the Greeks. Thus, when they consider an abstract or many-sided question, they will not give us an essay which says "on the one hand this, on the other hand that." Rather, they will sometimes take Story A which says "this" and Story B which says "that," and then they will combine the two stories. This will create a new story, a combination-story, a "final form"[16] story. And this new "final form" story will have a tension, as we see in 1 Samuel 8-12. This tension

---

[15]To *cohere* is to stick together. If a story is coherent, its parts fit together with each other and with other parts of the book. Incoherence is like confusion. An incoherent story is one which does not make sense. It has parts which do not fit with each other or which do not fit with other parts of the book. An incoherent story will lack order or reason or structure.

[16]The "final form" is the text as we have it today. Perhaps an editor combined several sources. It is possible to attempt to separate those sources and study them individually, and this is what source criticism does. But modern literary criticism is usually more interested in the *result* of the editor's work, not the sources of it. Modern literary criticism will thus usually discuss the text as we have it today – its "final form."

may make us uncomfortable. But the new combination-story is then able to say things that neither Story A nor Story B were able to say by themselves.

Here are **three examples**: The **first** is found in the story of Joseph and his brothers. In Genesis 37, Joseph is sold to traders who are going down to Egypt. But is he sold to Ishmaelites or to Midianites?[17] The story goes back and forth; it says both (see Gen 37:25-28,36; 39:1).[18] Are these contradictions? It would appear so. Did the editor see them? Most likely yes. Then why did he leave them? He does not tell us and so we do not know for certain. But perhaps this literary incoherence is supposed to reflect the incoherence of the family of Jacob.[19] Certainly there is a good deal of strife not only in Jacob's family but throughout Genesis (see the discussion on p. 26, above). And perhaps we are expected to remember that even the Ishmaelites and the Midianites were also part of this family of strife, for both are descendants of Abraham (Gen 16:15-16; 25:1-2).

The **second** example is more theological. At the beginning of Exodus (Exod 1:7) we read that the number of Israelites in Egypt increased so much that "the land was filled with them." Yet this is not really true, and the writer knows this. In Exod 8:22 and 9:26, he tells us that they were only in "land of Goshen," not in all of Egypt. But in Exod 1:7, the writer is showing us that God's command in Gen 1:28 has been fulfilled. A close comparison of the two verses makes this clear (compare the words in boldface): Gen 1:28 "Be **fruitful** and **multiply**, and **fill** the **earth** (*'erets*, אֶרֶץ)." Exod 1:7: "the descendants of Israel

---

[17]Furthermore, the story (deliberately?) leaves unclear even the question of who actually pulled Joseph up from the pit and sold him. Gen 37:28 says only "they" pulled him up (not "his brothers" as in the NIV). Does "they" refer to the brothers or to the Midianites mentioned at the beginning of the verse?

[18]The only way to make the story consistent is to translate the preposition אֶל (*'el*) in Gen 37:36 as "toward." That is, "The Midianites sold him *toward* Egypt [through the hands of the Ishmaelites]." In that case, The Midianites pull Joseph up from the pit and sell him to the Ishmaelites (Gen 37:28) and the Ishmaelites then sell him to the Egyptians (Gen 39:1). Between those two events, we read of the brothers' report to their father, Jacob, after which Gen 37:36 then becomes merely a summary of this whole series of events. Opinions will vary as to whether this is to stretch the preposition too far.

[19]This was first suggested in a conversation with Terence E. Fretheim, Luther Seminary, St. Paul, Minnesota.

were **fruitful** and increased greatly; they **multiplied** and grew exceedingly strong; so that the **land** (*'erets* again) was **filled** with them." The words "land" and "earth" are different in English, but in Hebrew it is the same word (*'erets*). Israelite readers and hearers would certainly recognize this as a fulfilment of the command of Genesis.

The **third** example is the most important theologically. It has to do with the tensions between the major covenants and theologies of the Old Testament. The theology of Deuteronomy says many things including "If you are good, God will bless you; if you sin, God will punish you." Yet people like Job looked around and said, "Sometimes good people suffer, and sometimes evil people succeed in the world." And so the book of Job argues against those who would take too simple a view of Deuteronomistic theology. The editors of the Bible decided to keep both Deuteronomy and Job in the Bible. The presence of both these books creates a tension in the Bible, and this tension is a healthy, good and fruitful one. More is said about this in the section on Job, below.

Thus, when you find contradiction, the first thing you should do is seek coherence. Ask "Is this a deliberate tension? If so, why is it here? What does it say to us?" We should do this because the Old Testament does not generally give us essays or philosophical or ethical discussions. Rather, it does its best teaching by using stories, and sometimes, it uses tensions between contradictory stories to teach complex truths.

The failures of Saul. 1 Samuel opens with God's rejection of the corrupt priesthood at Shiloh (Eli and his sons). Later, Saul was rejected because he was disobedient twice (making the sacrifice in 1 Sam 13:8-14, and not destroying Amalek in 1 Samuel 15). After the death of Samuel, Saul's reign ends extremely badly when he goes to see the medium[20] at Endor in 1 Sam 28:3-28. He asks her to bring Samuel back from the dead to get advice from him. But any attempt to communicate with the dead is sin (see 1 Chr 10:13) and the Bible rejects such activity. Whether or not the woman actually brought Samuel back from the dead

[20]See p. 83, footnote 8.

is not the point of the story.[21] Rather, the point is that Saul had been completely rejected, and any attempt to communicate with the dead is wrong.

David as the ideal king. David is the ideal king; other kings are compared to him. David is described as being a "servant of the LORD;" only Moses and Joshua are also described this way. Saul was unsuccessful in moving from charismatic leadership to more structured kingship, but David brings the ark of the covenant to Jerusalem and unites the religious and political centers of Israel.[22] By so doing, he prepares the way for the temple (which was both a blessing and, eventually, a source of misunderstanding[23]). The last act of David is recorded in 2 Samuel 24. Here, he buys the threshing floor of Araunah the Jebusite in order to build an altar. This later becomes the site of the temple itself.

David is the ideal king in 1-2 Samuel, but he is not perfect.[24] After reaching the high point of his success as king (2 Sam 10:16-19), he fails badly. First, he takes Uriah's wife, Bathsheba, and murders Uriah (2 Samuel 11). Second, he fails to deal successfully with various relationship issues among his sons (p. 83, above). Finally he takes a census in the last chapter of the book (2 Samuel 24). In general, there is nothing

---

[21]What actually happened? The text does not tell us. Some would say that the medium knew how to deceive people into *thinking* they were seeing someone return from the dead. This is not unusual, although in this case the woman herself seems frightened, as if God showed her something she did not expect to see. Others suggest that the event was psychological, and that Saul convinced *himself* that he was seeing Samuel, but that he really was not; it was all in his mind. Others say that when people think they are talking with the dead, they are really talking with demons. One thing is clear, however: the Bible says we should neither try to speak with the dead nor make offerings to them (Deut 26:14; Ps 106:28; Isa 8:19; see also Lev 19:28; 21:1; Deut 14:1).

[22]Though note the preview of north-south animosity in 2 Sam 19:41-43, where the "men of Israel" complain about favoritism toward the "men of Judah."

[23]The people eventually began to believe that the presence of the temple was a guarantee that God would protect them even if they oppressed the poor and worshiped false gods. See the discussion of the temple beginning on p. 46, and see p. 181 for Jeremiah's reaction to the people's attitude.

[24]This is one difference between 1-2 Samuel and 1 Chronicles. 1 Chronicles never mentions any sin or shortcoming in David.

wrong with taking a census.[25] However, the purpose of this census was probably to determine the size of the army – a sign that David was beginning to depend upon human resources rather than upon God. Yet, in both these cases David repents. Thus, David remains in close relationship with God; God's covenant with him remains in place and David and his descendants become the basis for later messianic hope.

Two great covenants in tension. Throughout the Deuteronomistic History, the tension remains between Israel's two greatest covenants. In the overview above, we saw that the unconditional promise to David in 2 Samuel 7 appears to become conditional in 1 Kgs 2:4; 6:11-13 and especially in 1 Kgs 9:4-7. This inconsistency creates a necessary theological tension between the unconditional nature of the Davidic covenant and the very conditional Mosaic covenant. This is the *Deuteronomistic* History, after all, and its theology is based upon Deuteronomy. In 2 Kings, the curses of Deuteronomy[26] take effect when Assyria and Babylon destroy Israel and Judah. At this point, it may seem that the tension breaks. The conditional Mosaic covenant appears to overwhelm the unconditional promises of the Davidic covenant. Yet it is the Davidic covenant which will finally bring hope in exile. During and after the exile, the religious leaders of Israel waited for God to fulfill his promises to David in new and unexpected ways. This hope is seen at the end of 2 Kings when King Jehoiachin is released (see p. 102 below). We shall also see this hope in the Psalms and in Isaiah.

Some important texts: Hannah's prayer (1 Sam 2:1-10); the tension of choosing Saul as king (1 Samuel 8-12); Samuel anoints David as king (1 Sam 16:1-13); the Davidic covenant (2 Sam 7:8-16); David and Bathsheba (2 Samuel 11-12); the census (2 Samuel 24).

Verses for memory: 1 Sam 16:7; 2 Sam 7:12-13

---

[25]See, for instance, Exod 30:11-16; Num 1:2; 4:2,22; 26:2,4.

[26]Deuteronomy 27-28. See p. 59.

1-2 Kings

❧

Overview

The books of 1-2 Kings continue the story of the kings of Israel and Judah which began in 1-2 Samuel. Just like 1-2 Samuel, the two books of 1-2 Kings were originally a single book which was put on two scrolls when it was translated into Greek (see p. 81).

The editors of 1-2 Kings used several sources, and they often mention them (for instance, "the book of the acts of Solomon" in 1 Kgs 11:41). However, when they mention "the Book of the Chronicles of the Kings of Israel" (or of Judah) they do *not* mean the books of 1-2 Chronicles which are found in the Bible. Rather, they are referring to the archives of the kings of Israel and Judah, and those books no longer exist. (1-2 Chronicles were written later.)

At the beginning of 1 Kings, David dies and Solomon becomes king. The transfer of power is not an easy one. Solomon's older brother Adonijah at first tries to become king (1 Kgs 1:5-53) and eventually Solomon has him killed (1 Kgs 2:25). The priesthood is also greatly affected. David had two priests and one of them, Abiathar, supported Adonijah while the other, Zadok, supported Solomon. In the end, Abiathar is banished (1 Kgs 2:26) and descendants of Zadok (called the Zadokites) then control the priesthood for the next 800 years.

Solomon is remembered as a *wise* king, but he was not a particularly *good* king. He was also known for collecting horses and for having 700 wives and 300 concubines (1 Kgs 11:3, cf. the warning of Deut 17:14-20). The many wives and concubines may seem strange, but when a king made an international treaty in those days, he often took a wife from the other nation. It was hoped that this "family relationship" would then strengthen the national relationships. Unfortunately, such arrangements also involved recognizing the gods of other nations. Thus, the prophets often spoke not only against idol worship, but also against such international treaties. In his old age, Solomon was led astray by these foreign relationships and gods (1 Kgs 11:4-10).

The Divided Kingdom (Samaria was built later by King Omri)

Solomon was also a great builder and was remembered for laying heavy taxes on the people and for using forced labor (as Samuel had warned, 1 Sam 8:10-18). When Solomon died, the northern tribes sent a representative named Jeroboam to speak with Solomon's son Rehoboam and ask that he lighten the heavy load (1 Kings 12). Rehoboam refused, and so the ten northern tribes rebelled and withdrew and made Jeroboam their king at Shechem. This led to a civil war, and for the next 200 years the nation was split between the northern kingdom (which kept the name "Israel") and the southern kingdom (which took the name "Judah"). One of Jeroboam's first acts was to set up golden calves in Dan and Bethel, the extreme northern and southern ends of Israel, in order that his people might worship there and no longer go south to Judah to worship at the Jerusalem temple (1 Kgs 12:26-30).

Certainly one reason for northern discontent was tribal (see p. 89, footnote 22). The united kingdom (all twelve tribes) had so far been ruled only by southern kings (Saul, David, Solomon, Rehoboam). It was clear that this was going to continue because of the Davidic covenant. Thus, the north rebelled and withdrew under Jeroboam.

The northern kingdom of Israel had an unstable and chaotic series of kings who gained power several times by killing the previous king. It was more orderly in the south where Judah continued under the house (dynasty) of David. In addition, the kings of Judah are described as being somewhat more faithful to God than were the northern kings, though not by much. God sent prophets to warn both the north and the south, but they were usually ignored.

In the eighth century B.C., Assyria began to gain power in Mesopotamia (modern day Iraq) and to expand. In 732 B.C., Assyria conquered Syria and destroyed Damascus, and in 722 B.C. the northern kingdom of Israel and its capital city Samaria fell. Israel's king and other leadership were taken away and scattered throughout the Assyrian empire, and the northern kingdom disappeared from history. However, its archives (perhaps including the original version of Deuteronomy) were probably brought south to Jerusalem at that time. Assyria then brought refugees from other conquered nations to settle in the land of Israel (2 Kgs 17:24-34). This produced a mixture of traditions and religious practices as well as a mixed people whom we later meet as "the Samaritans" in the New Testament.

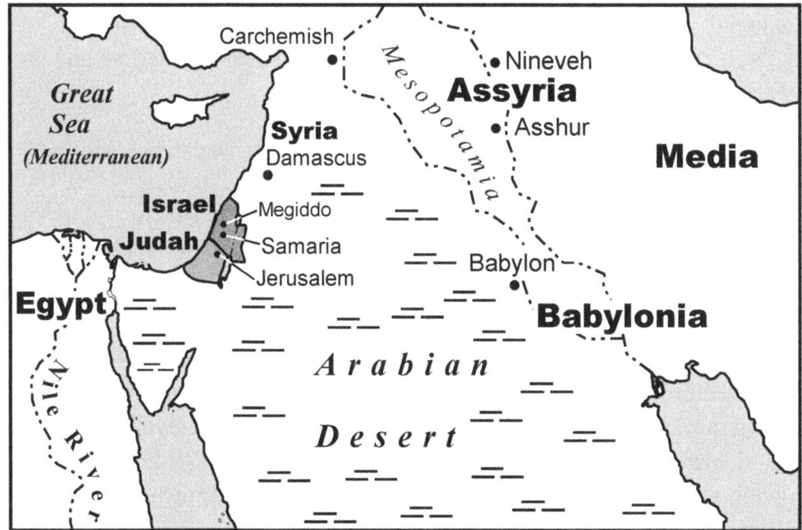

The Eighth and Seventh Centuries B.C.

The southern kingdom of Judah was also attacked by the Assyrians and suffered terribly at this time. Many villages were destroyed, although Jerusalem and the temple were spared as the prophet Isaiah said they would be (2 Kings 19). But this sparing would last for only another century. By 610 B.C., Babylon had arisen and challenged Assyria, and then began to move toward Egypt. The leaders of Judah thought that the promise of Isaiah a century earlier would save them or that Egypt could be of help. They were wrong in both cases: Jerusalem was destroyed in 586 B.C. and the temple was torn down.

Again, the king and other local leadership were removed, but in this case the Babylonians kept them together as a group. It is at this point that 1-2 Kings ends. But it ends on a word of hope: in 562 B.C., former king Jehoiachin was freed in Babylon and treated favorably by the king of Babylon. (Review the summary of the Deuteronomistic History on pp. 63-66.) This was seen as a sign that the people would eventually be able to return to Judah and rebuild Jerusalem.

Timeline

732 B.C.	Assyria destroys Syria and its capital city, Damascus
722 B.C.	Assyria destroys Israel and its capital city, Samaria
701 B.C.	Assyria invades Judah and attacks its capital, Jerusalem
627-610 B.C.	Weakening of Assyria; struggles with rising Babylon
609 B.C.	Pharaoh Neco of Egypt attempts to help Assyria against Babylon. King Josiah of Judah attempts to interfere and is killed at Megiddo.
	Babylon defeats Assyria
605 B.C.	Babylon defeats Egypt at Carchemish. Judah becomes a vassal of Babylon
600-586 B.C.	Judah's attempts to rebel against Babylon lead to deportations of Judah's leadership and finally to the destruction of Jerusalem and the temple.
562 B.C.	King Jehoiachin freed in Babylon

The Deuteronomistic Historian gives all the northern (Israel) kings failing marks. In the south (Judah), only three kings receive high marks: David, who is the model for all of the others, and kings Hezekiah and Josiah, who engaged in reforms. Six others receive approval except for failing to remove the high places.[1]

THE KINGS OF ISRAEL[2]

The United Monarchy (1025-922 B.C.)

Saul	(ca. 1025?-1000? B.C.)
David	(ca. 1000?-960? B.C.)
Solomon	(ca. 960?-922 B.C.)

The Divided Monarchy (922-722 B.C.)

Judah (south)		Israel (north)	
Rehoboam	(922-915 B.C.)	Jeroboam I	(922-901 B.C.)
Abijam	(915-913 B.C.)	Nadab	(901-900 B.C.)

[1]The six are listed on p. 98, footnote 5. For "high places" see p. 61, footnote 11.

[2]Dating of the kings of Israel is difficult, especially in the early years. The above list is based upon information found in *The Harper Collins Study Bible* ed. Wayne A. Meeks (London: Harper Collins, 1993), particularly the table found on p. 537. Other resources may give slightly different dates.

Asa	(913-873 B.C.)	Baasha	(900-877 B.C.)
		Elah	(877-876 B.C.)
		Zimri	(876 B.C.)
		Omri	(876-869 B.C.)
Jehoshaphat	(873-849 B.C.)	Ahab	(869-850 B.C.)
		Ahaziah	(850-849 B.C.)
Jehoram	(849-843 B.C.)	Jehoram/Joram	(849-843/2 B.C.)
Ahaziah	(843/842 B.C.)		
Athaliah	(843-837 B.C.)	Jehu	(843/2-815 B.C.)
Joash/Jehoash[3]	(837-800 B.C.)	Jehoahaz	(815-802 B.C.)
Amaziah	(800-783 B.C.)	Jehoash/Joash[3]	(802-786 B.C.)
Azariah/Uzziah	(783-742 B.C.)	Jeroboam II	(786-746 B.C.)
Jotham	(742-735 B.C.)	Zechariah	(746-745 B.C.)
		Shallum	(745 B.C.)
Ahaz	(735-715 B.C.)	Menahem	(745-737 B.C.)
		Pekahiah	(737-736 B.C.)
		Pekah	(735-732 B.C.)
		Hoshea	(732-724 B.C.)

Assyria destroys Israel (Samaria) and some of Judah (722/1 B.C.)

— The Remaining Monarchy (Judah) (722-586 B.C.) —

Hezekiah	(715-687/6 B.C.)
Manasseh	(687/6-642 B.C.)
Amon	(642-640 B.C.)
Josiah	(640-609 B.C.)
Jehoahaz	(609 B.C.)
Jehoiakim	(609-598 B.C.)
Jehoiachin	(598/7 B.C.)

Babylonian conquest of Judah (597 B.C.)

Zedekiah	(597-587/6 B.C.)

Babylon destroys Jerusalem and its temple (586 B.C.)

---

[3]Joash is probably a short form of the name Jehoash. (Note also Jehoram/Joram and Azariah/Uzziah.) The Bible uses both names, Jehoash and Joash, for the king of Judah who reigned 837-800 B.C. and for the king of Israel who reigned 802-786. The king of Judah is more often called Joash and the king of Israel is more often called Jehoash.

Outline

- **I. United Monarchy (960?-922 B.C.): the reign of Solomon (1 Kings 1-11)**
  - A. Solomon's early days as king (1 Kings 1-4)
  - B. Building and dedication of temple (1 Kings 5-8)
  - C. Renewal of Davidic promise (now conditional) (1 Kgs 9:1-9)
  - D. Solomon's remaining years, including his apostasy and death (1 Kgs 9:10-11:43)
- **II. Divided Monarchy (922-722 B.C.): Israel and Judah (1 Kings 12-2 Kings 17)**
  - A. Division of Israel into north and south: Jeroboam and Rehoboam; Israel's golden calves (1 Kings 12-14)
  - B. Kings of Israel and Judah (1 Kings 15-2 Kings 16)
  - C. Assyria destroys Israel and its capital Samaria (2 Kings 17)
- **III. Remaining Monarchy (Judah) (722-562 B.C.): (2 Kings 18-25)**
  - A. Hezekiah and his reforms (2 Kings 18-20)
  - B. Manasseh and Amon (2 Kings 21)
  - C. Josiah and his reforms; discovery of "book of the law" (2 Kgs 22:1-23:30)
  - D. Last kings of Judah; Babylonian destruction and exile (586 B.C.); release of Jehoiachin in Babylon (562 B.C.) (2 Kgs 23:31-25:30)

Message

The central issues. 1-2 Kings is the conclusion of the Deuteronomistic History, and its theology is very similar to that of the books we have just discussed (Joshua, Judges, 1-2 Samuel):

- Israel has only one God: the LORD
- Worship is to be at the place of God's choosing (the temple, once it is built by Solomon)
- Formal relationships with other nations are unhealthy
- The curses of Deuteronomy will fall upon Israel if the Mosaic covenant is not honored
- The covenant with David provides (unconditional) hope even after the curses fall

Two major goals of 1-2 Kings are to explain (1) why the unfaithful north (Israel) lasted so long, and (2) why the south (Judah) perished in spite of Josiah being so faithful. See the discussion of these issues in the introduction to the Deuteronomistic History (p. 65, above).

The nations. At times, it may seem that nothing good is said about the nations of the world, and that God loves only Israel, but this is not really the case. In 1-2 Kings, the LORD is indeed the God of all nations and works through them and sometimes even *for* them. For instance, in the story of Naaman, commander of the army of the king of Syria, we read that "by him the LORD had given victory to Syria" (2 Kgs 5:1). Likewise, in 2 Kgs 18:25, the Assyrian Rabshakeh claims that the LORD has sent him to destroy Jerusalem. And, although his words are political and manipulative, by the end of Israel's history it becomes clear that God is able to use both Assyria and Babylon to accomplish his will in the lives of his people. Furthermore, not only 1-2 Kings show God's interest in other nations; we have already seen this in Genesis and Ruth, and will see it again in other books – especially Isaiah and Jonah.

Evaluation of the kings. The heart of Israel's confession of faith was that the LORD alone is God (Deut 6:4-5). Thus, the kings of both Israel and Judah are evaluated in 1-2 Kings according to their faithfulness to this Mosaic covenant. David is the "gold standard;" next to him all other kings fall short. The northern kings (of Israel) are all judged unfaithful, and their reigns begin with formulas like the following:

> **Beginning of reign:** "In the thirty-ninth year of Azariah king of Judah Menahem the son of Gadi began to reign over Israel, and he reigned ten years in Samaria. And he did what was evil in the sight of the LORD; he did not depart all his days from all the sins of Jeroboam the son of Nebat, which he made Israel to sin" (2 Kgs 15:17-18).

Here, the year of reign of a king of *Judah* is used to date the beginning of reign of a king of *Israel.* Note the mention of Jeroboam, whose sin of setting up the two golden calves at Dan and Bethel (p. 92) was remembered as the root of Israel's apostasy. A second formula, such as the following, is used to note the end of each northern king's reign:

> **End of reign:** "Now the rest of the deeds of Menahem, and all that he did, are they not written in the Book of the Chronicles[4] of the Kings of Israel? And Menahem slept with his fathers, and Pekahiah his son reigned in his stead" (2 Kgs 15:21-22)

The southern kings of Judah are evaluated using a similar formula which also includes their age and their mother's name. Again, David is the standard. Only he and two of the other kings of Judah are found to

---

[4]This is not referring to 1-2 Chronicles of the Bible. See p. 91, above.

be completely faithful; they are the reforming kings Hezekiah and Josiah. Six others "did what was right in the eyes of the LORD"[5] except that they failed to remove the high places.[6] Finally, however, Josiah *did* remove the high places and "did what was right in the eyes of the LORD, and walked in all the way of David his father, and he did not turn aside to the right hand or to the left" (2 Kgs 22:2).

In the end, however, 1-2 Kings notes that both Israel and Judah sinned repeatedly against the covenant and were destroyed. In the case of northern Israel, blame is repeatedly laid at the feet of their first king, Jeroboam, who set up the golden calves (1 Kgs 12:26-30[7]). Note again how he is mentioned above in the "beginning of reign" formula. In the south, the fall of Judah was blamed on Manasseh who "made Judah ... to sin with his idols" (2 Kgs 21:10-16). Manasseh's sin was considered to be so great that even the faithfulness of his grandson Josiah was unable to save Judah (2 Kgs 23:26-27).[8] The descriptions of the fall of north (2 Kgs 17:5-23) and of the south (2 Kgs 24:1-4, 20; 25:1-12) emphasize the failure of both nations to live faithfully to the covenant.

The temple and proper worship. The temple is both a high point (Solomon builds and dedicates the temple, 1 Kings 6-8) and a low point (Manasseh defiles the temple, 2 Kgs 21:4-9).[9] In the 47 chapters of 1-2 Kings, it is both built and destroyed. During this period, the temple became the center of Israel's worship; Israelite males were to appear

[5]Those six are Asa, his son Jehoshaphat, and the four-generation series of Jehoash, Amaziah, Azariah (also called Uzziah) and Jotham. Of these six, Asa is given the greatest approval and "was wholly true to the LORD all his days" (1 Kgs 15:14).

[6]For "high places," see p. 61, footnote 11.

[7]As noted in our discussion of Exodus 32 (p. 39), this was prefigured in the words of the people who built the golden calf at Mt. Sinai. The words they spoke were the same as Jeroboam's later words, "Behold your gods, O Israel, who brought you up out of the land of Egypt" (1 Kgs 12:28).

[8]A different opinion of Manasseh is found in Chronicles (p. 110), where we read that he repented. Theology is interpretation of events (see the discussion on p. 108), and different theologians will at times give us different interpretations of what happened. This is true of John and the Synoptic Gospels, and is also true of the Deuteronomistic History and Chronicles.

[9]Later Jeremiah criticizes the people's taking it for granted (see p. 181).

there three times each year for the major feasts.[10] Note that the people themselves did not enter the temple for worship. The altar was outside, and the people gathered in the courtyard as priests performed sacrifices and led rituals. Only priests ever entered the temple itself.

But, as we saw in Exodus 32 with the golden calf incident, there is right worship and there is wrong worship. In 1-2 Kings, a major challenge comes from the Baal cult. The heart of 1-2 Kings is concerned with attempts by the house of Omri[11] to introduce Baal worship into Israel. This threat is challenged primarily by the prophets Elijah and Elisha. Elijah's conflict with, and destruction of, the priests of Baal at Mt. Carmel (1 Kings 18) is very much like the strong stand of Moses against the golden calf (Exodus 32).

A concentric pattern[12] and Elijah. Structure is very important in the Old Testament. Note the following concentric outline which covers all of 1-2 Kings. Centers of concentric patterns are often very important, and the center of the pattern below is the conflict with King Omri and

---

[10] Passover (and Unleavened Bread), Weeks (Pentecost), Ingathering (and Booths). See p. 37 for details.

[11] Omri was the most important king of the (northern) kingdom of Israel – at least politically. However, he was an unfaithful king and, perhaps because of this, his reign is given only six verses in the Bible (1 Kgs 16:23-28). But he was the king who built the city of Samaria. He was also the father of a short but infamous dynasty: his son was Ahab, and both of Ahab's sons Ahaziah and Jehoram ruled after Ahab. But Omri's family is most noted for its attempts to introduce the worship of Baal to Israel.

[12] A concentric pattern is often used in Hebrew literature. The author begins and ends a story or a section with similar things. Then he puts another set of similar things after the first one and before the last one. Consider the following "concentric" story: "John left his house. He got on a bus and rode. He walked from the bus stand to the market. He bought food. He walked from the market to the bus stand. He got on the bus and rode. He returned to his house." The story begins and ends with similar things: "John left his house" and "John returned to his house." We could call those two things A and A'. Then, after A, we read "He got on a bus and rode." We read that again just before A' near the end of the story. We can call those two sentences B and B'. Then C and C' describe his walking from the bus stand to the market and then back again later. The middle of the story is often the most important part. In our concentric story, the middle is "He bought food." We will call that D. Thus, the story goes A B C **D** C' B' A'. The relationship of 1-2 Kings and Elijah can also be diagramed this way, as it is in this chapter.

his descendants, who tried to bring the Baal cult into Israel. This was a critical moment in Israel's history. The pattern shows the crucial importance of Elijah, who stood against this royal attempt to replace worship of the LORD with worship of Baal.[13]

- A Single kingdom (united Israel and Judah) (1 Kgs 1:1-11:25)
  - B Northern tragedy (withdrawal of northern kingdom) (1 Kgs 11:26-14:31)
    - C Kings of Israel and Judah (strife between them) (1 Kgs 15:1-16:22)
      - **D Elijah & Elisha versus Omri dynasty (rise and fall of Baal cult) (1 Kgs 16:23-2 Kgs 9)**
    - C' Kings of Israel and Judah (strife between them) (2 Kings 10-16)
  - B' Northern tragedy (destruction of northern kingdom) (2 Kings 17)
- A' Single kingdom (Judah alone) (2 Kings 18-25)

Note in particular the following:

A and A' represent the rise and fall of house of David (and the kingdom of Judah)

B and B' represent the rise and fall of northern kingdom of Israel. B is the withdrawal of the northern 10 tribes under Jeroboam, and B' is the destruction of Israel and Samaria by Assyria

C and C' describe bad relationships, and at times war, between Israel and Judah

D is at the heart of the structure and is the heart of the problem. Here we read about 40 years of the house of Omri sponsoring the Baal cult, and the struggles of (primarily) Elijah and Elisha against it. At the heart of this section is the "prophetic succession"[14] from Elijah to Elisha (2 Kgs 2), something which occurs nowhere else in the OT.

---

[13]The pattern (which I have modified slightly) was suggested by G. Savran, "1 and 2 Kings" in *Literary Guide to the Bible* ed. R. Alter and F. Kermode (Cambridge, MA, 1987) 148-49.

[14]See p. 64 footnote 2 for "succession."

Elijah and Elisha are extremely important in this struggle which runs through a large part of the center of 1-2 Kings. They have been compared to Moses and Joshua, as may be seen in the following chart.

Moses	Elijah
Provided manna in the wilderness (Exodus 16)	Provided meal and oil for the widow of Zarephath (1 Kings 17)
Confronted the people about the golden calf (Exodus 32)	Confronted the people about Baal (1 Kings 18)
Called the people to renew their vows to the covenant (Exodus 33-34)	Called the people to renew their vows to the covenant (1 Kgs 18:19-40)
Went to Mt Horeb (Sinai) (Exodus 3)	Went to Mt Horeb (1 Kings 19)
Passed his leadership to Joshua (Num 27:18-23; Deut 31:14,23; 34:9)	Passed his leadership to Elisha (2 Kings 2)
Joshua then parted the Jordan and crossed to Jericho (Joshua 3)	Elisha then parted the Jordan and crossed to Jericho (2 Kings 2)

Finally, the deaths of both Moses and Elijah are hidden events, never seen by Israel.[15]

Two covenants in tension. As we come to the end of 1-2 Kings, and thus the end of the Deuteronomistic History, the two major covenants (Mosaic and Davidic) are still in tension. The Mosaic covenant was conditional, and promised blessing if Israel was faithful and the curse if Israel was not. But the Davidic covenant was unconditional and simply promised blessing.[16] Both were necessary. The Mosaic covenant allowed Israel to understand why both Israel and Judah were destroyed and why their king and other leaders were taken to Babylon.

[15] In the New Testament, Jesus is compared to Moses in similar ways in several places (especially in Matthew, and in Hebrews where he is shown to be superior to Moses, the priesthood, the law, etc.).

[16] At the same time, we must remember that there are places where the Davidic covenant gains Deuteronomistic conditions. See the earlier discussion of *Two great covenants in tension* which begins on p. 90.

In the midst of this darkness, however, the Davidic covenant provided hope for the future. And it is the Davidic covenant that had the last word. The very end of the Deuteronomistic History (2 Kgs 25:27-30) tells us that in the thirty-seventh year of the Babylonian exile, King Jehoiachin was freed from prison and was honored by the king of Babylon. The exiles saw this as a sign of hope and an indication that national restoration might lie ahead.

Some important texts: Solomon's prayer for wisdom (1 Kgs 3:5-15); dedication of temple (1 Kings 8); Solomon's decline (1 Kings 11); Rehoboam and Jeroboam (1 Kgs 12:1-19); Jeroboam's sin (1 Kgs 12:26-32); Elijah and priests of Baal (1 Kgs 18:17-40); destruction of Samaria (2 Kgs 17:1-23); Manasseh's sin (2 Kgs 21:11-15); discovery of book of the law (2 Kgs 22:3-23:3); death of Josiah (2 Kgs 23:28-30; destruction of Jerusalem (2 Kgs 23:26-27; 24:1-3,10-16 ; 25:1-12); release and elevation of Jehoiachin (2 Kgs 25:27-30)

Verses for memory: 1 Kgs 18:21; 19:11-12; 2 Kgs 22:8,10

Later History
-An Overview-

The period after the return from the Babylonian exile is called the **post-exilic period**. It began in 538 B.C. when Cyrus the Great of Persia conquered Babylon and wrote a decree that the Jews could return to rebuild Jerusalem and the temple.[1] This was recognized as a fulfillment of Jeremiah's 70-year prophecies (Jer 25:11-12; 29:10). Both the end of Chronicles (2 Chr 36:22-23) and the beginning of Ezra (Ezra 1:1-4) mention the prophecy of Jeremiah and give Cyrus' decree.

1-2 Chronicles, Ezra and Nehemiah were written during this post-exilic period. 1-2 Chronicles was originally a single book which was later divided, just as were 1-2 Samuel and 1-2 Kings. Ezra and Nehemiah were also originally a single book, Ezra-Nehemiah. Some even think that all of Chronicles and Ezra-Nehemiah was originally a single work by a single editor, though there are some problems with that idea. For instance, the Chronicler encourages people from the former northern kingdom of Israel to worship in the new temple, whereas Ezra and Nehemiah oppose the idea of any foreign involvement.

These books show great interest in the temple and worship. David and Solomon are very important in Chronicles, because they were instrumental in planning and building the first temple. David is also seen as founder and organizer of worship practices. For instance, he established the Levites as leaders of worship, singers of praise, and many other things (see p. 107).

In Ezra and Nehemiah, David and Solomon are mentioned as sources of instructions for worship. These books are most interested in the reconstruction of the temple, the rebuilding of the wall around

[1]2 Chr 36:22-23; Ezra 1:1-4. See also the chronological list of Post-Exile Events on p. 112.

Jerusalem, and Ezra's public reading of "the book of the law of Moses."[2]

In this section on "Later History" we will also consider the book of Esther. Esther is not at all related to Chronicles, Ezra or Nehemiah. It is, however, a story about the Persian period and it is found after Nehemiah in the Christian Bible, and so it is discussed here. (In the Hebrew Scriptures, Esther is found in the third section called the Writings,[3] near the end, between Lamentations and Daniel.)

---

[2]This event is possibly the first public reading of the Pentateuch. We will say more about this later.

[3]See p. 3 for a discussion of the Writings and the organization of the Hebrew Scriptures.

1-2 Chronicles

❧

Overview

1-2 Chronicles was written around the year 400 B.C., about 150 years after the Deuteronomistic History[1] (DH) was finished. As noted on the previous pages, 1-2 Chronicles was originally a single book which was later divided by the translators of the Septuagint because of its length. The editor of 1-2 Chronicles is known as "the Chronicler," and his concerns were different from those of the DH. He wrote at a time when some of the Babylonian exiles had already returned to Judah and had rebuilt Jerusalem and the temple. One goal of the Chronicler was to encourage not only people from Judah, but also people from the former northern kingdom of Israel, to come to Jerusalem and worship at the temple.

Chronicles is thus not part of the DH, and in the Hebrew Scriptures Chronicles is placed not after Kings but rather at the very end of the Writings. This means that the last two books of the Hebrew Scriptures are 1-2 Chronicles, not Malachi, as in the Christian Old Testament. Remember the discussion on p. 5 concerning how ending with Chronicles gives the reader a different feeling than ending with Malachi.

Chronicles does not merely repeat the story which is found in the DH (although it borrows and copies much from Samuel and Kings[2]). Rather, it offers an alternative to the "Primary History" of Israel.[3] The DH started with Joshua, but Chronicles, like Genesis, begins with Adam. Unlike Genesis, however, Chronicles does not tell the stories of Creation and Fall. Rather, it begins with a very long genealogy from Adam to

---

[1]Joshua, Judges, 1-2 Samuel and 1-2 Kings. See p. 63 for an overview of the Deuteronomistic History.

[2]The Chronicler also used material from Genesis, Exodus and Numbers, as well as some of the prophets.

[3]The Primary History is the continuous story which begins in Genesis and continues through the end of 2 Kings.

Saul in 1 Chronicles 1-8. Then, before Chronicles discusses the time of Saul and David in chapter 10, it gives a genealogy in chapter 9 of those who returned from the Babylonian exile. Thus the beginning of Chronicles is quite different from the beginning of the DH or the beginning of Samuel-Kings.

And there are other differences between Chronicles and Samuel-Kings. Sometimes important material in Samuel and Kings is missing in Chronicles.[4] Other times, there is information in Chronicles which is not found in Samuel or Kings.[5] Furthermore, Chronicles primarily tells the story of the kings of Judah. There is little mention of the kings of Israel, and there is no linking of years of reign of southern kings to dates in the northern kingdom.[6] Elijah, who is so central to the story in Kings,[7] appears just once in Chronicles (2 Chr 21:12). Finally, the impact of the Babylonian exile upon the land is more severe in Chronicles than in the DH. In Chronicles, the land is left completely empty after the Babylonian invasion and destruction of Jerusalem. As we shall see on p. 111, this allows the land to get its sabbath rest![8]

Saul gets very little attention in Chronicles. We read only of his death (1 Chronicles 10), and there is no mention of his years of conflict with David. This is because Chronicles is primarily interested in those kings who established the temple (David and Solomon) or who supported religious reforms (especially Hezekiah, Manasseh[9] and

---

[4]For instance, most of the stories of David found in 2 Samuel 9-20 are missing in Chronicles. Likewise, the story of the medium ("witch") at Endor (1 Sam 28:3-28) is not told, though 1 Chr 10:13 assumes the reader knows the story from Samuel and condemns Saul's "seeking guidance" from the dead.

[5]For instance, David's preparations for the building of the temple in 1 Chronicles 28-29 is not mentioned in 2 Samuel.

[6]It was different in the book of Kings, where the year in which a king came to the throne was connected to the year of reign of the king in the other kingdom. See p. 97.

[7]Remember the concentric pattern which was described on p. 99.

[8]See also p. 38 regarding the Sabbatical Years described in Exodus and Deuteronomy and the Years of Jubilee described in Leviticus. Remember that the curses of Leviticus 26 came, in part, because the people had failed to give the land its sabbath rests (p. 45).

[9]Manasseh's name here should surprise you, since the Deuteronomistic History describes him as one of Judah's worst kings and blames the Babylonian exile on him (2 Kgs 23:26-27). More will be said below.

Josiah). As a result, Chronicles skips most of the negative material found in the DH. Thus, Saul gets little mention.

David's first act is to capture Jerusalem (the future location of the temple) and to bring the ark there. Chronicles tells only positive things about David, and we do not read, for instance, of his sin with Bathsheba or his murder of Uriah. Rather, David is described as the real force behind the construction of the temple. He himself does not build it, because he has been a man of war and has shed blood (1 Chr 28:3). But it is David who draws up the plans and gives them to Solomon (1 Chr 28:11-12). It is David who gathers all the necessary supplies (1 Chr 22:2-5; 29:1-9). And it is David who organizes all aspects of worship, and presents the finished plan to young Solomon (1 Chr 28:13-21).

Solomon also receives complete approval. There are no stories of conflict within the family of David at the beginning of his reign, as there were in 1 Kings. Solomon is chosen by God (1 Chr 28:5-6,10; 29:1). This is significant. Only the Chronicler describes any king other than David as "chosen." Finally, Chronicles does not mention Solomon's apostasy at the end of his life. Again, this is because the Chronicler wants to tell his story in a way that brings no negative view of anything associated with the temple or its worship.

The **Levites** are also very important in Chronicles. David brings them to Jerusalem and gives them new tasks (1 Chr 23:25-32).[10] They become even more important than they were before, and become teachers, singers, leaders of praise, gatekeepers, and bakers of the Bread of the Presence for the temple. They are placed in charge of the holy things of the temple, and even serve as judges.

Outline

I. Genealogies and a list of returned exiles (1 Chronicles 1-9)

- A. Genealogy of Abraham through Jacob/Israel (1 Chronicles 1)
- B. Genealogies of Israel (1 Chronicles 2-8)
- C. List of those who returned from exile (1 Chr 9:1-34)
- D. Genealogy of Saul (1 Chr 9:35-44)

---

[10]The Levites are traditionally understood to be the descendants of Jacob's son Levi. Moses and Aaron were of the tribe of Levi. The descendants of Aaron became the priesthood of Israel, and the rest of the tribe became the "Levites" who carried the ark and tabernacle. The actual origins of the Levites as a priestly group may actually be more complex. For instance, Judg 17:7 mentions "a young man ... of the family of Judah, who was a Levite."

II. Death of Saul (1 Chronicles 10)

III. Reign of David (1 Chronicles 11-29)

A. General events in the life of David (1 Chronicles 11-20)
B. Preparations for building the temple (1 Chronicles 21-28)
C. Transition from David to Solomon (1 Chr 29:1-25)
D. David's death (1 Chr 29:26-30)

IV. Reign of Solomon (2 Chronicles 1-9)

A. Solomon receives the gift of wisdom (2 Chronicles 1)
B. Building and dedication of the temple (2 Chronicles 2-7)
C. Later events; death of Solomon (2 Chronicles 8-9)

V. Reigns of kings of Judah: Rehoboam to exile (2 Chronicles 10-36)

Message

The Chronicler looked at Israel's history 150 to 200 years after the Deuteronomistic Historian did. He thus "preached" to different people and a different situation. They had gone into exile in Babylon, and now they were back in Jerusalem again; God had taught them new things through their contacts with the Babylonians, the Medes and the Persians. Furthermore, there were now separated brothers and sisters living to the north of them in the former northern kingdom of Israel. The Chronicler thus looked back over Israel's history and asked, "What does this mean for *us today*?"

The Nature of Theology

Theology is an interpretation of events. One might consider Pharaoh and Moses standing on opposite sides of the Reed Sea looking at Egypt's destroyed army. They both see the same event, the same data. Pharaoh mutters, "Bad luck! The wind changed and the water came back;" but Moses says, "It was the hand of God." The event is the same for both of them, but their interpretations are very different.

Theology is also an interpretation of texts.[11] Theologians look at texts and situations and ask, "What does this mean?" and "What does this mean *for us*?" Situations change, and this

[11]Technically, we should also be talking about *hermeneutics* here. See the brief comment which begins on p. 15 regarding exegesis, hermeneutics and theology. See also the discussion block, "Reading is not a Game," p. 71.

changes what we teach and preach. 50 years ago, there were preachers who looked at the same texts from the Bible that we look at today, but the sermons they preached to our grandparents were somewhat different from sermons preached today. They tried to be faithful interpreters of God's word as they preached; so do preachers today. But different situations produce different answers to the question "What does this mean *for us*?" And this produces different theologies.

Therefore, the Chronicler answered the question "What does this mean *for us*?" in a different way than did the Deuteronomistic Historian. He looked at the same history but he lived at a later time, and thus he emphasized different things.

The temple and worship. The primary interest in Chronicles is the temple and worship. The Chronicler wants to glorify the temple and emphasize worship so that people come to Jerusalem to worship the LORD. David and his descendants had been chosen by God to rule his people forever.[12] David and Solomon were involved in building the first temple. But people in the northern kingdom had resented both the Jerusalem temple and the house of David.[13] The Chronicler hoped for a reunited Israel in which even former northerners recognized and worshiped in the temple. Thus he described the lives of David and Solomon in very positive terms.

The north (Israel). For the Chronicler, the true Israel is found among those who remain faithful to the house of David; thus, Judah and Benjamin receive special approval. Yet there are several places where Chronicles is positive toward northerners who live in the former kingdom of Israel (for instance 2 Chr 28:8-15; 2 Chronicles 30-31). Note in particular the invitation by King Hezekiah (Judah's king when Samaria was destroyed) in 2 Chr 30:1-9. Here, he invites the northern tribes of Ephraim and Manasseh to come south and join the Passover celebration. This invitation is generally mocked and rejected (2 Chr

---

[12]Note, however, that this unconditional promise has also gained a condition in Chronicles (1 Chr 28:7).

[13]Remember (northerner) Jeroboam's confrontation with (southerner) Rehoboam (1 Kgs 12:1-16), and then his building of the golden calves so that people would not go to Jerusalem to worship (1 Kgs 12:26-30). See p. 92.

30:10), but later we read that many people came not only from Ephraim and Manasseh but also from Issachar and Zebulun (2 Chr 30:18-19). There was "great joy in Jerusalem" because this had not happened "since the time of Solomon" (2 Chr 30:26) – that is, since the days of the united kingdom. This positive tone continues throughout the rest of the next chapter.

Retribution and the individual. Deuteronomistic theology teaches, among other things, that faithfulness brings blessing and unfaithfulness brings retribution (punishment, the curses of Deuteronomy 27-28). This understanding is also found in Chronicles, but again there are some differences. In Kings, we saw that it often took several generations for sin to bring punishment. In Chronicles, the king who sins is punished within his own lifetime (for instance, Saul in 1 Chr 10:13-14). Perhaps the Chronicler was reacting against a misunderstanding by people who blamed all their suffering (especially the exile) on what their parents and grandparents had done and who did not admit their own sin or responsibility. Jeremiah and Ezekiel had already begun to emphasize individual responsibility,[14] and the Chronicler may be moving in the same direction. The point: when we sin, we are not to make excuses and try to blame those who went before us; in Chronicles, sin is punished within the lifetime of the one who sins. Yet this punishment is not unavoidable; some kings respond to the preaching of the prophets and repent.

Thus, Chronicles does not blame the destruction of Jerusalem and the temple upon King Manasseh who lived several generations earlier. (Compare to 2 Kgs 24:3-4 which *does* blame it on him.) Chronicles reports that Manasseh suffered and repented and then engaged in reforms as did Hezekiah before him and Josiah after him (2 Chr 33:10-17). In Chronicles, it is the people of the time of Zedekiah[15] who are blamed because they rejected God's word and his prophets (2 Chr 36:11-16). Furthermore, they had neglected the Jubilee years of Lev

---

[14]Both reject the popular proverb, "The fathers have eaten sour grapes, and the children's teeth are set on edge" (Jer 31:29; Ezek 18:2), which the people were using in order to say "All our suffering is because of our parents' sins; we ourselves are innocent." Ezekiel 18 is particularly strong on this issue: "It is only the person who sins that shall die" (Ezek 18:4,20 NRSV). We will say more about this in the sections on Jeremiah and Ezekiel.

[15]The "likewise/also" (*gam*, גַּם) of 2 Chr 36:14 links the priests and people with Israel's last king, Zedekiah, mentioned in verse 11.

25:8-55 (see p. 38), and so the punishment of Lev 26:34-35 had fallen upon them. Thus, in Chronicles, the land is left completely empty during the exile "until the land had made up for its sabbaths" (2 Chr 36:20-21).

Hope. In spite of its strong theology of retribution, Chronicles is yet a book of hope. The Chronicler refers to the return from Babylon even before starting to tell the story of Israel's origins and later failures. He does this by placing a list of all of those who returned from exile in 1 Chronicles 9, just after the opening genealogy and just before the death of Saul. This is, of course, long before the people actually went into exile or returned. And Chronicles (and thus the modern Jewish Bible, see p. 5) ends with words which encourage people to "go up" to help rebuild Jerusalem. Even today, Passover services around the world end with the hopeful cry, "Next year Jerusalem!"

Chronicles was written after the exile at a time when Israel no longer had a king. Is there a messianic hope for God to restore the monarchy of David? Perhaps. On the one hand, Israel's king is the LORD (note "kingdom/throne of the LORD" in 1 Chr 28:5; 29:23; 2 Chr 13:8). On the other hand, there is still God's unbreakable link with the house of David (1 Chr 17:11-15; 2 Chr 21:7). The very last words of Solomon's prayer of dedication of the temple plead for God not to turn away from his "anointed one" (messiah, *mashiach*, מָשִׁיחַ),[16] and to remember his *chesed* (חֶסֶד)[17] with David his servant (2 Chr 6:42).

Praise and Rejoicing. Finally, Chronicles is a book in which people rejoice in and praise God. Chronicles reports that when David brought the ark to Jerusalem, he gave the Levites new responsibilities and turned them into leaders of singing and praise (1 Chr 23:25-32). And it is the goal of Chronicles that all people, including those in the former northern kingdom, should come and worship the LORD.

Some important texts: David's preparations for the temple (1 Chr 28:1-12; 29:1-9); Solomon's dedication of the temple (2 Chr 6:1-7:11); the proclamation of Cyrus (2 Chr 36:22-23).

Verses for memory: 2 Chr 7:14-15

---

[16]For *mashiach*, see p. 9, footnote 10

[17]*Chesed* is a Hebrew word, often translated "steadfast love" or "lovingkindness." It means God's covenant faithfulness or loyalty to Israel's king and to the people of Israel. See also p, 78 for *chesed* in Ruth.

EZRA

❧

Overview

The book of Ezra is connected to what comes before it as well as to what comes after it. It continues the story from the end of 2 Chronicles, where King Cyrus of Persia gives a decree which lets the exiles in Babylon return to rebuild Jerusalem and the temple. In fact, the last words of 2 Chronicles (36:22-23) are identical with the first words of Ezra (1:1-3a). Ezra also connects with the book of Nehemiah which follows it. In the Hebrew Scriptures, Ezra and Nehemiah form a single book.

Ezra the priest does not appear in the first six chapters of Ezra the book. This is because Ezra 1-6 describes events which happened more than half a century before Ezra came from Babylon to Jerusalem. Study the following time line, which begins with the decree of Cyrus:

Post-exile events: 538-445 B.C.[1]

538 B.C.	Cyrus lets the exiles return	} Ezra 1-6
520 B.C.	Work on the temple is begun	
515 B.C.	The temple is completed	
458 B.C.	Ezra arrives	Ezra 7-10 (more than 50 years after Ezra 1-6)
445 B.C.	Nehemiah arrives	Nehemiah

Cyrus let the people return in 538 B.C., under the leadership of Sheshbazzar (Ezra 1:11) and Zerubbabel (Ezra 2:2). This was more than 50 years before Ezra arrived.[2] Reconstruction of the temple did not

---

[1]This table is found again on p. 245.

[2]It is difficult to know the date of Ezra. People generally agree that Nehemiah came to Jerusalem from Babylon in 445 B.C. during the reign of Artaxerxes I (465-424 B.C.). Ezra also came to Jerusalem during the reign of an Artaxerxes, but it is not entirely clear whether it was during the reign of Artaxerxes I or Artaxerxes II (405-359 B.C.). If it was the latter, then Ezra

begin until 520 B.C., 18 years later.[3] From 520 B.C. until 515 B.C., work continued under the encouragement of the prophets Haggai and Zechariah (Ezra 5:1; 6:14), although the work faced opposition. Two sets of enemies opposed the rebuilding of the temple. In Ezra 4:1-3 we read of "the adversaries of Judah" and this probably refers to people from the north (former Israel). Their request to help seems very kind and reasonable, but those who returned from Babylon suspect that they have bad motives and reject their offer. The second set of enemies is "the people of the land" (4:4-5), that is, peasants and others who had been left behind when Judah's leadership class was taken to Babylon. With the wealthy and powerful gone, these "people of the land" had no doubt experienced freedom, and did not appreciate it when, 50 years later, the former power people returned.

These opponents wrote letters to the kings of Persia (Ezra 4-5), trying to stop the work.[4] King Darius searched the Persian archives and found that Cyrus had given the returning Jews permission to rebuild (Ezra 6). Reconstruction of the temple resumed and soon was finished.

The second part of the book (Ezra 7-10) begins more than fifty years later, with Ezra's preparations and travel to Jerusalem in 458 B.C. Just as the activities in the first part of the book rest upon the authority of the decree of King Cyrus, so Ezra's activity rests upon a letter of authorization from King Artaxerxes. When he arrives, he discovers that the people, and even the priests and Levites, have intermarried with foreigners. In Ezra 9 and 10, they make a covenant to send away these foreign wives and children, and they offer a guilt offering.

As already mentioned, Ezra-Nehemiah is really a single book.[5] The climax is found in the reading of the Book of the Law of Moses in Nehemiah 8-9 which is discussed in the section on Nehemiah, below.

---

arrived around the year 398 B.C. In our present discussion, we assume Ezra came earlier, around 458 and before Nehemiah, and that Ezra and Nehemiah then worked together at one point.

[3]Possibly a small start had been made earlier. See Ezra 5:14-16.

[4]This section of the book of Ezra is written not in Hebrew, but in Aramaic, the language of Persia. Aramaic is a sister language to Hebrew, and uses the same alphabet. Many words are almost exactly the same.

[5]And, as also mentioned earlier, some think that all of Chronicles-Ezra-Nehemiah was originally one book by a single author or editor. However, the attitude of Ezra and Nehemiah toward northerners (former Israel) is rather negative, whereas it is generally positive in Chronicles.

Outline

I. Exiles return to Jerusalem and rebuild temple (Ezra 1-6)
   A. Decree of Cyrus (Ezra 1)
   B. List of those who returned (Ezra 2, also found in Nehemiah 7)
   C. Beginning the rebuilding of the temple (Ezra 3)
   D. Opposition to the rebuilding of the temple (Ezra 4:1-6:12)
   E. The temple completed and Passover celebrated (Ezra 6:13-22)

II. Ezra's ministry (Ezra 7-10) (See also p. 116 footnote 4)
   A. Ezra's plans to leave Babylon and go to Jerusalem (Ezra 7:1-10)
   B. Letter of authorization from King Artaxerxes (Ezra 7:11-28)
   C. Preparations for the journey (Ezra 8:1-30)
   D. The return to Jerusalem (Ezra 8:31-36)
   E. Ezra's opposition to mixed marriages (Ezra 9-10

Message: See this section in Nehemiah, p. 117, below.

Some important texts: Decree of Cyrus (Ezra 1:1-4, cf. 2 Chr 36:22-23); completion of the temple (Ezra 6:14-18); covenant to send away foreign wives and children (Ezra10:1-5).

Verses for memory: Ezra 7:27

Nehemiah

❧

Overview

Nehemiah and the books before it. Ezra-Nehemiah was originally a single book, and thus Nehemiah continues the story which was begun in Ezra. Some think that all four books, 1-2 Chronicles, Ezra and Nehemiah, were originally a single work which began with Adam, continued through the exile of Judah to Babylon, and then concluded with the people's return to rebuild Jerusalem and the temple after the decree of Cyrus. But, whereas Chronicles appeals to the former northern kingdom of Israel to join in worship at the temple in Jerusalem, Ezra and Nehemiah generally have a negative attitude toward foreigners.

Nehemiah the man. Nehemiah, a Jew, was cupbearer to the king of Persia in Susa, the capital city. In 445 B.C., he heard that the wall of Jerusalem still lay in ruins and that the people were discouraged (Neh 1:1-4). He thus requested and received permission to go to Jerusalem. The restoration of the temple had been completed seventy years earlier, and Ezra had already been in Jerusalem for 13 years.[1]

Rebuilding the wall. When Nehemiah arrived, he first inspected the condition of the fallen wall, and then went to the leaders of the people. When they heard why he had come, they eagerly said "Let us rise up and build!" (Neh 2:18). But again there was opposition.[2] This time, the enemies were "Sanballat the Horonite and Tobiah the Ammonite and Geshem the Arab" (Neh 2:19 and throughout the book). But the work began on August 11, 445 B.C.[3] in spite of the opposition. The people "labored on the work with one hand and with the other held a weapon" (Neh 4:17). Attempts were made to assassinate Nehemiah (Nehemiah 6), but even this did not prevent the completion of the wall on October

---

[1]This is traditional dating. See p. 112 for a general discussion of dating in the books of Ezra and Nehemiah, and p. 112 footnote 2 for a discussion of the dating of Ezra's arrival in Jerusalem.

[2]See the Overview of Ezra, p. 112, regarding those who opposed the rebuilding of the temple 75 years before.

[3]See Neh 6:15. Once we get to the period of Haggai and beyond, dating becomes quite accurate because of connections to the calendars of Persia. See the discussion of the dating of Haggai on p. 245, footnote 6.

2, 445 B.C. in less than two months of work.

The high point of Ezra-Nehemiah. Rebuilding the wall was important. But in Ezra-Nehemiah, there is something even more important than the rebuilding of the temple (Ezra) or the wall (Nehemiah). The high point of Ezra-Nehemiah is found in Nehemiah 8-10,[4] where Ezra is called before the people to read "the book of the law of Moses, which the LORD had given to Israel" (Neh 8:1). It is possible that this "book of the law" was the Pentateuch, which had been edited and completed in exile. Thus, this might have been the first time the people of Israel had heard it read. Imagine hearing for the first time the words "In the beginning, God created the heavens and the earth." No wonder the people "bowed their heads and worshiped"[5] (Neh 8:6) and even wept (Neh 8:9). The people then made a covenant in which they promised to obey this book of the law and support the temple (Nehemiah 9-10).

The rest of the book describes the populating of the city of Jerusalem,[6] the dedication of the wall, and Nehemiah's reforms. The reforms of Nehemiah are very strict and, like those of Ezra, involve the removal of all foreigners.

Outline

I. **Nehemiah's first governorship: rebuilding the Jerusalem wall (Nehemiah 1-7)**
   A. Nehemiah travels to Jerusalem and makes plans to restore wall (Nehemiah 1-2)
   B. Rebuilding begins and is opposed (Nehemiah 3-4)
   C. Nehemiah deals with the rich oppressing the poor (Nehemiah 5)
   D. The wall is completed; plans to repopulate the city (and a

---

[4]Some think that Nehemiah 8 was originally located between Ezra 8 and 9, and that Neh 9:1-5 was originally located between Ezra 10:15 and 10:16. If this is true, then they were moved in order to emphasize their importance by putting them near the end of Ezra-Nehemiah.

[5]This is an important phrase. The people "bow their heads and worship" four times in the Old Testament. The first is in Exod 4:31 when Moses first comes to the people to tell them that God would save them. The second is Exod 12:27, when Moses announces that the LORD is going to "pass over" the houses of Israel and strike the Egyptian first-born. The third is in 1 Chr 29:20 where kingship is passed from David to Solomon. The fourth is here, when the people hear the reading of the law by Ezra.

[6]People preferred living in outlying villages before the wall was rebuilt.

census[7]) (Nehemiah 6-7)

II. Ezra reads the law and the people make a covenant to obey it (Nehemiah 8-10)

A. Ezra reads the book of the law to the people (Neh 8:1-12)

B. The people celebrate the Feast of Booths (Neh 8:13-17)

C. Confession of sin and covenant to keep the law and support temple (Nehemiah 9-10)

III. Final steps in restoring the community of Jerusalem (Nehemiah 11-13)

A. Repopulation of the city and dedication of the wall (Nehemiah 11-12)

B. Nehemiah's second governorship and his reforms (Nehemiah 13)

Message

God controls history. One major purpose of Ezra-Nehemiah is to show that God fulfilled Jeremiah's 70-year prophecies,[8] and that God was able to move great kings and emperors (Cyrus, Darius, Artaxerxes) in order to do so. The very first words of Ezra 1 (and the last words of 2 Chronicles) are:

> In the first year of Cyrus king of Persia, **that the word of the LORD by the mouth of Jeremiah might be accomplished**, the LORD stirred up the spirit of Cyrus king of Persia so that he made a proclamation ...: "Thus says Cyrus king of Persia: The LORD, the God of heaven ... has charged me to build him a house at Jerusalem, which is in Judah.

Two major royal decrees were the foundation for the restoration of Jerusalem, the temple and worship: the decree of Cyrus (Ezra 1, above) and that of Artaxerxes (Ezra 7:11-28). This shows that God is the God of all nations, and that his power extends even over kings of other lands.

The high point of Ezra-Nehemiah. Above we mentioned the importance of Ezra reading of the law to the people in Nehemiah 8. This was followed by a national confession of sin and a covenant to obey the book of the law (Nehemiah 9-10). This may have been the first time Israel heard the Pentateuch read as a single unit.

Certainly, various parts of the Pentateuch had been around for a long time. Many years before Ezra and Nehemiah, the prophets were using ideas and phrases which we now hear in Genesis and Exodus. And the discovery of an early version of the book of Deuteronomy

---

[7]The census of Neh 7:6-73 is a list of the people who came out of Babylon many years before. It is the same list as we find in Ezra 2, and Nehemiah may have used this old list to determine who were true Jews.

[8]Jer 25:11-12; 29:10.

during the reign of Josiah had inspired a whole generation. But during the exile, all of this was collected into a single large unit – the Pentateuch – and it was recognized as God's word. Nehemiah 8 may be a record of the first public reading of this great work.

The written word. This reading of the law meant several things to the people and their leaders. First of all, God's word was more and more becoming the *written* word. In Ezra and Nehemiah, neither God nor prophets ever speak. Rather, actions are taken because of what is found in "the book of the law."

Second, the people and their leaders understood that the Assyrian and Babylonian exiles had happened because Israel had been unfaithful. So *now they would be a faithful people* – and they would do so by carefully following all the words of this written "book of the law of Moses" which Ezra had read. Earlier, Ezra had made the people expel foreign wives and children (Ezra 9-10). Now, in Nehemiah, we find out why. The last chapter of Nehemiah (13:1) begins

> On that day they read from the book of Moses in the hearing of the people; and in it was found written that no Ammonite or Moabite should ever enter the assembly of God; ... When the people heard the law, they separated from Israel all those of foreign descent.

Nehemiah's interpretation of this text (Deut 23:3-6[9]) is very rigid, as is his attitude toward foreigners. In Neh 13:25, we read of his rebuking men of Judah who had married foreign wives:

> And I contended with them and cursed them and beat some of them and pulled out their hair; and I made them take oath in the name of God, saying, "You shall not give your daughters to their sons, or take their daughters for your sons or for yourselves."

This is harsh, and perhaps it is too harsh. Was this attitude really commanded by God? Or was this perhaps a human excess? Was it a misinterpretation and a misapplication of the law? Nehemiah and the people wanted to be faithful and pure and true to the covenant. But they seem to have forgotten that the *purpose* of God's original call to Abraham was so that "all the families of the earth shall be blessed" (Gen 12:3). The *purpose* of God bringing them to Mt. Sinai was that they should become "a kingdom of priests and a holy nation" (Exod 19:5). All of this was for the sake of a world of "foreigners."

This, therefore, raises a third issue. As the written word of God now becomes the primary form of God's address to the people, life begins to depend upon human *interpretation* of this written law. This,

---

[9]For a different attitude toward Moabites, see the discussion of Ruth 4 on p. 79.

in turn, leads to the possibility of *mis*interpretation and to the need for careful work and humility on the part of interpreters.

For instance, note that they had read that "no Ammonite or Moabite should ever enter the assembly of God" (Neh 13:1, above). But then they rejected "all those of foreign descent." Why all? Did they perhaps go too far in their interpretation at this point?[10]

The books of Ezra and Nehemiah often receive little attention. Some may feel that these books have lost the sense of living graciously and grace-fully before God. Yet it is important to recognize two things. First, Ezra and Nehemiah were striving to keep the people faithful to their commitments to God in light of a history of their having failed to do so. But, second, it is important to note that Ezra and Nehemiah are not books which tell us what God *wants* people to do; rather Ezra and Nehemiah are a record of what God's people *did*. In that sense, Ezra-Nehemiah is neither law nor prophecy, but rather is history. It is the first record of a community's attempt to live by the written word of God. As such, Ezra-Nehemiah leads us to ask:

What does it mean:

- To be a people seeking to live faithfully before God?
- To have God's *written* word as his primary means of address?
- To have the heavy human responsibility of interpreting that word?
- To realize that there might be other interpretations than ours, and that they may be right?
- To be a leader who is both strong enough to lead and humble enough to listen to others?

Some important texts: Completion of the wall (Neh 6:15-16); reading of the law (Neh 8:1-12); dedication of the wall (Neh 12:27-43)

Verses for memory: Neh 6:15-16; 12:43

---

[10]Could they perhaps have handled things more moderately even in the case of Ammonites and Moabites? Today, for instance, when the church expands into polygamous areas it forbids *new* polygamous marriages among its members. But sometimes it allows previous polygamous marriages to remain intact so as not to throw out helpless women and children. Certainly other parts of the Old Testament show a great concern for widows, orphans and the marginalized. See Exod 22:22; Deut 10:18; 14:29; 16:11,14; 24:17-21; 26:12-13; 27:19; Ps 68:5; 146:9; Isa 1:17; Jer 7:6; 22:3; Zech 7:9-10.

Esther

❧

Overview

The story of Esther is meant to be read and enjoyed. It is one of the five "festival scrolls" of Judaism (see p. 77), and is read publicly when Jews gather to celebrate the festival of Purim. The major purpose of the book of Esther may simply be to explain Purim. A *pur* (plural *purim*) is a "lot" – that is, something which is thrown on a table or on the ground to make a decision or to predict the future. In Esth 3:7, Haman, the enemy of the Jews, "cast Pur, that is the lot" in order to determine the best day to annihilate the Jews, whom he has come to hate. In Esth 9:24-28, Haman's actions are remembered, and thus the festival is named Purim.

The style of Esther is similar to that of other court[1] stories such as those involving Joseph (Genesis 39-41) and Daniel (Daniel 1-6). Esther is also a book in which two women have strong central parts to play. First, there is Queen Vashti, who refused to be treated as a piece of property even by the king (Esth 1:10-12); second, there is Esther, herself (throughout the book).

The story begins in the court of Ahasuerus,[2] king of Persia. Queen Vashti, called by a tipsy Ahasuerus to display her beauty before his guests at a party, refuses such a degrading spectacle. This displeases the king and she is dismissed as queen. A new wife is sought for the king, and Hadasseh, a beautiful young Jewish girl, is chosen. She is given a new name, Esther, which is related to the Persian word "star." Her cousin Mordecai[3] had previously been caring for her, and the story describes several plots (against the king and against the Jews) which they discover and expose. At the end of the story, the Jews gain a great

---

[1]A king's "court" is his family, servants, advisors and ministers. It has nothing to do with judges or lawyers.

[2]Ahasuerus may be either Xerxes I (486-465 B.C.) or Artaxerxes II (405-359 B.C.).

[3]It has been noted that the name Mordecai is a form of the name Merodach (Marduk), the chief god of Babylon. This is all the more interesting when it is also noted that the name Esther is not only related to the Persian word for "star" but also to the name Ishtar, the Babylonian goddess.

victory over their enemies and establish the festival of Purim to celebrate this moment.[4]

Perhaps the most unusual feature of the book of Esther is that it never mentions God.[5] This has caused much discussion by both Jews and Christians over the centuries. Perhaps this is why the book of Esther has not been found among the Dead Sea Scrolls. Luther at one point rejected Esther. In his "Table Talks" we find, "I am so great an enemy to the second book of the Maccabees, and to Esther, that I wish they had not come to us at all, for they have too many heathen unnaturalities."[6] However, in the introduction to his translation of Esther, Luther said that Esther contains "much that is good." In spite of this very mixed opinion, Christians and Jews have agreed over the centuries to include Esther in the Bible.

The LXX version of Esther has "additions" which are not found in the Hebrew text. They are probably intended to add excitement or to show Esther and Mordecai in a more religious light. In these "additions":

- Mordecai has a dream at the beginning which lets him know what lies ahead,
- The king becomes enraged at Esther's first unrequested appearance before him, and
- Esther and Mordecai are more pious and Haman is more evil.

These additions appear in the Roman Catholic Bible but they are not found in the Protestant Bible since they are not in the Hebrew text.

Outline

It is better simply to read the book of Esther than to try to outline it. Esther is a marvelous story and should be enjoyed. There is much that is humorous, much that is ironic. The audience is expected to laugh and to jeer (though, as we will see in the "Message" section, below, there is a theological side to Esther in spite of the book never mentioning God).

Although Esther does not outline very well, the story may have a

---

[4] The book of Esther not only explains why there is a festival of Purim, but also why there are *two* days of Purim celebration (Esth 9:16-22,27).

[5] Song of Solomon is the only other book of the Bible which never mentions God.

[6] See "The Table Talk of Martin Luther," translated by William Hazlitt (Philadelphia: Lutheran Publication Society, nd.), XXIV.

concentric pattern.[7] Note how the whole story is built around feasts and banquets (the Hebrew word is *mishteh*, מִשְׁתֶּה).

A King Ahasuerus removes Queen Vashti from his presence (Esther 1)
  B A Feast (*mishteh*): after Esther is made the new queen (Esth 2:1-18)
    C The enemies of the king are destroyed (Esth 2:19-23)
      D Haman plots to destroy the Jews (Esther 3)
        E Esther agrees to help (Esther 4)
          F Esther's first banquet (*mishteh*) (Esth 5:1-8)
            G Haman's rise to glory (Esth 5:9-14)
              H The king honors Mordecai (Esth 6:1-11)
            G' Haman's fall to shame (Esth 6:12-13)
          F' Esther's second banquet (*mishteh*) (Esth 6:14-7:3)
        E' Esther helps (Esth 7:4-5)
      D' Haman is destroyed by his own plot (Esth 7:6-8:2)
    C' The enemies of the Jews are destroyed (Esth 8:3-9:19)
  B' A Feast (*mishteh*): Purim, after slaughter of enemies (Esth 9:20-32)
A' King Ahasuerus raises Mordecai in his presence (Esther 10)

In this case, the center of the story, as well as its end, becomes the honoring of Mordecai (and the great shaming of Haman in the process).

Message

As mentioned above, the book of Esther has troubled many Jews and Christians over the years. Not only is God not mentioned in the book, but Esther and Mordecai seem to be rather secular (especially to conservative Jewish eyes).

There are, however, two points at which God may be seen in the background. First, when Haman, the enemy of the Jews, makes a plan to kill all of them, there is a crucial moment in the story where Mordecai encourages Esther to speak to the king. She has been made queen, and Mordecai wants her to use her new position to tell the king about Haman's evil plot. She is afraid to do this, however, since no one may go before the king without first being invited. To enter without an invitation can mean death. However, Mordecai points out that, if she does not go, her exalted position will not save her. She will die along with the rest of the Jews. Then, in Esth 4:14, he adds the following admonition:

> For if you keep silence at such a time as this, relief and deliverance will rise for the Jews from another quarter, but you and your father's house will perish. And who knows whether you have not come to the kingdom for such a time as this?

---

[7]For "concentric patterns," see p. 99, footnote 12.

Many think that "another quarter" refers to God, and that Esther has "come to the kingdom" because of God's hidden activity. If Esther does not act to help her people, God will find another way.

The second place where God may be seen in the background comes immediately after that, in Esth 4:16. Esther says she will go to see the king, but that Mordecai should first have all the Jews "hold a fast on my behalf, and neither eat nor drink for three days, night or day." It would seem most logical to interpret this fast as an appeal to God.

And there is another interesting possibility. At least one theologian has noted similarities between the story of Esther and the Exodus:[8]

- Moses also was Jewish and kept his identity secret.
- There was danger to his people, and he was at first unwilling to act on their behalf.
- He appears in the court of the king (Pharaoh) several times.
- Finally, there is a great deliverance of the Israelites and a mighty destruction of the enemy.

Note also that women play central roles in both Exodus (see p. 33) and Esther.

Some important texts: Mordecai's advice to Esther (Esth 4:12-14); the honoring of Mordecai at Haman's expense (Esth 6:1-13); the beginning of the festival of Purim (Esth 9:20-23)

Verses for memory: Esth 4:14

---

[8]G. Gerleman, *Esther* in Biblischer Kommentar: Altes Testament (Neukirchen-Vluyn, 1973) 11-23.

Poetry and Wisdom

-An Overview-

The books of Job, Psalms, Proverbs, Song of Solomon and Ecclesiastes are books of poetry. In addition, the books of Job, Proverbs and Ecclesiastes are books of wisdom. Thus, it is important to understand the characteristics of Hebrew poetry and Hebrew wisdom.

Hebrew Poetry

Hebrew poetry is based upon structures and patterns rather than upon rhyme and meter. (It will sometimes make use of sound patterns but not in a way that could really be called rhyming.)

Parallelism. One of the most common structural features of Hebrew poetry is parallelism, in which a phrase is repeated with slightly different words. Psalm 24 is an excellent example of parallelism. Consider the four lines of verses 1 and 2:

First line:	[1]The earth is the Lord's and the fulness thereof,
Second line:	the world and those who dwell therein;
Third line:	[2]for he has founded it upon the seas,
Fourth line:	and established it upon the rivers.

Notice how the thought of the first line is repeated by the second line. Likewise, the thought of the third line is repeated by the fourth line. This is called *synonymous parallelism.* Two lines of poetry say the same thing (or very similar things).

Sometimes, however, the second line says the opposite of the first line, giving us *antithetic parallelism.* For instance, look at the last verse of Psalm 1 in which the way of the righteous and the way of the wicked have different ends:

First line:	for the LORD knows the way of the righteous,
Second line:	but the way of the wicked will perish.

A third kind of parallelism is called *synthetic parallelism.* In this case, the following line (or several lines) neither repeats nor says the opposite of the first line, but rather extends the thought. Psalm 1:3 has an example which is four lines long. Each line continues and extends the thought from the previous line:

First line: He is like a tree
Second line: planted by streams of water,
Third line: that yields its fruit in its season,
Fourth line: and its leaf does not wither.

So parallelism is a structure of two (or more) lines in which the second line presents a thought which is similar to or opposite from the thought in the first line – or else it expands and extends that thought. Much more could be said because recent scholarship has greatly expanded this discussion. However, this is enough to give a basic awareness of how this very common feature works in Hebrew literature.

Concentric patterns and chiasm. We have already seen several times how *concentric patterns* work (see p. 99). They give us patterns such as A B C D C' B' A', where A=A', B=B', and so on. A *chiasm* is just a concentric pattern with no center: A B B' A'. It is often found in parallel structures, where the first line is A B and the second line is then B' A'. Consider the first part of Gen 1:27:

First line A: So God created man B: in his own image,
Second line B': in the image of God A': he created him

Note how the arrangement of A and A', and then B and B', forms an X pattern (see the diagram to the right). This X looks like the Greek letter *chi* (X), and so the patterns is called *chiasm* (kī′-asm). More than four parts may be involved. For instance, see Isa 6:10 for a chiasm with six parts A B C C' B' A'.

Patterns such as this can carry theology. Gen 1:27 (above) actually has three lines, not two:

First line A: So God created man B: in his own image,
Second line B': in the image of God A': he created him;
Third line B": male and female A": he created them.

Here, the relationship of the first and second line is synonymous parallelism with chiasm (A B and then B' A'). But then the third line does something very interesting. It follows the synonymous parallelism of the second line, but adds a theological surprise. It places "male and female" (B") in parallel with "image of God" (B and B'). This shows that "image of God" is found in "male *and* female," not just male. Women are also in the image of God, just as much as men are. Important theology can be carried in poetic structures.

Acrostics. An acrostic is a poem in which the first letter of each line forms a pattern. In the Old Testament, the letters of the alphabet are often used in this way. In English, I could write:

Abraham and Sarah had a son,
But Hagar bore a son before.
Can these five people live as one?
Does God love Hagar any more?

Well, yes, God loved Hagar, too. But the point of this poem is to demonstrate an *acrostic*. Note the first letter of each line. The first line begins with an A, the second line with a B. There is a C at the beginning of the third line and the first letter of the fourth line is a D. ABCD. I could continue the poem ABCDEFGHI... until I had gone through the entire alphabet. That is called an *acrostic*.[1]

This is what the Hebrew poets often do. There are 22 letters in the original Hebrew alphabet, א ב ג ד (*aleph, beth, gimmel, daleth*) and so on.[2] Hebrew poets often wrote poems in which the first word of the first line began with א, the first word of the second line began with ב, the first word of the third line with ג, and so on. The poem thus had 22 lines or verses. You can see this in the book of Lamentations, for instance, where chapters 1, 2 and 4 each have 22 verses. Each of these chapters is an alphabetic acrostic.[3] Lamentations 3 is also an acrostic poem but it has 66 verses. The first 3 verses begin with א, the next three (verses 4-6) begin with ב, and so on. The largest acrostic in the Bible is also the largest chapter in the Bible: Psalm 119. The first *eight* verses begin with א; verses 9-16 all begin with ב, verses 17-24 with ג and so on. Twenty-two sections with eight verses each. 8x22=176, and so Psalm 119 has 176 verses. Other acrostic psalms are: Pss 9-10 (broken acrostic, originally one psalm), 25, 34, 111, 112, and 145. Prov 31:10-31 (the ideal wife) is also an acrostic poem.

Sound Patterns. All people enjoy sound patterns. Songs use words which rhyme. Jokes are often funny because they use words which have similar sound but different meaning. Thus, many jokes cannot be translated from one language to another, since the words do not have the same sound in the other language.

This also happens in Hebrew. Hebrew writers and poets loved to play with the sound of their language. But when we translate, we lose the sound patterns. In English, for instance, we cannot hear the subtle joke at the end of Genesis 2 and the beginning of Genesis 3: "And the man and his wife were both naked (*arummim*, עֲרוּמִּים), and were not

---

[1]Acrostics are not restricted to letters of the alphabet. They may also spell words or even sentences, though this does not happen in the Bible.

[2]These 22 primary letters are all consonants. See p. 267 for a listing and discussion of the Hebrew alphabet.

[3]Lamentations 5 also has 22 verses, but it does not have an alphabetic acrostic pattern.

ashamed. Now the serpent was more subtle (*arum*, עָרוּם) than any other wild creature." The words "naked" and "subtle" (clever) sound very similar in Hebrew. Did Hebrew listeners smile when they thought to themselves, "Yes, the snake is both more clever *and more naked* than any other wild creature"? Perhaps they did, although the story carries a theological seriousness which they would have recognized, too.

The prophets also often used word plays not for fun but seriously. In Amos 8:2, God shows Amos a basket of "summer fruit" (*qayits*, קַיִץ) in order to tell him that the "end" (*qets*, קֵץ) has come upon Israel. And in Isa 5:7, there is synonymous parallelism and chiasm in the first part of the verse (A B B' A') and sound patterns after that:

For the vineyard of the LORD of hosts — A
  is the house of Israel, — B
  and the men of Judah — B'
are his pleasant planting; — A'

and he looked for justice [*mishpat*, מִשְׁפָּט],
  but behold, bloodshed [*mispach*, מִשְׂפָּח] } sound pattern
for righteousness [*tsedaqah*, צְדָקָה],
  but behold, a cry [*tse'aqah*, צְעָקָה] } sound pattern

Thus, we should realize that the writers of books such as the Psalms and Lamentations did not merely sit down and effortlessly write scripture simply by the inspiration of the Holy Spirit. Yes, they were inspired by the Holy Spirit; however, in addition to that, they also worked very hard to put what God gave them into a form which would speak and appeal to people. And of course, this applies also to preachers and teachers today. For it is not only *what* is said which is important, but also *how* it is said.

Wisdom

The Biblical books of Wisdom are Job, Proverbs and Ecclesiastes. Books such as those in the Pentateuch and the Deuteronomistic History are concerned with telling us what God has done in the world. Wisdom is somewhat different. Wisdom is often less concerned with what *God has done* in the world than with what *people can discover* about the world. Wisdom books seek understanding.

Every society has "wisdom" teachings. There are simple proverbs such as "Haste makes waste" or "Penny wise and pound foolish." There are stories which the elders tell the young people in order to teach them about life and proper behavior. In Old Testament times, however, wisdom also included what we would call science today. Like the physical sciences, wisdom sought to understand the stars and planets, the life of animals, plants, etc. And, like the social sciences, wisdom sought to understand and teach how people can live properly and successfully. The latter included relationships between men and women, and proper behavior before leaders and other important and powerful people.

Characteristics of Biblical Wisdom. The books of wisdom sought to understand the world through human observation rather than through divine revelation. The wise men of Israel were fairly optimistic that they could do so. They knew there were limits to what people could understand, of course. One of the greatest limits was death which seems to strike us just as we are becoming truly wise. In general, however, the wise men of Israel felt that, using their human abilities, they could learn much about the world and then teach it to others in order to improve their lives. Other parts of the Bible say things like, "God has blessed you; therefore live in this way. God has saved you and had mercy on you; therefore, have mercy on others." But the teachers of Wisdom often appealed to self-interest, instead. They said, "Things will go better for you – you will have a successful life – if you live in this way." One of the things they emphasized was moderation in all things. Eating, drinking, speaking – all should be done moderately. Too much or too little brings trouble.

At the same time, wisdom tended to be socially conservative. The ANE had schools of wisdom which trained the wealthy young men of the king's court[4] to behave properly in their advantaged situations of life. The Wise were less concerned about speaking to the poor. The prophets continually spoke out strongly against injustice, but the wise men noted that it could be dangerous to do so; after all, "a living dog is better than a dead lion" (Eccl 9:4). The Wise tried to *understand* society, not to *change* it. If society was not fair or just, then Wisdom tried to teach people how to *live* in a society that was not fair. Thus, the prophets sometimes harshly criticized the wise men of Israel for being too close to the power people.[5] Again we have a tension in the Old Testament; perhaps Mikhail Sergeyevich Gorbachev would have understood it well in his careful rise to power in the Soviet Union prior to 1985. Sometimes it is wise to remain silent until we are in a better

---

[4]See p. 84, footnote 11, for the meaning of "king's court."

[5]For instance, Isa 19:11-12; 29:13-16; Jer 8:9. Walter Brueggeman makes the same point in *Old Testament Theology: Essays on Structure, Theme and Text* (Minneapolis: Fortress Press, 1992) 296-307.

position to speak; on the other hand, sometimes we *must* speak and not remain silent. There is a proper time for everything (Ecclesiastes 3), but it may be difficult to know which "time" we are in.

Three kinds of Biblical Wisdom. There are three types of Wisdom in the Bible, and each has its function.

- *Conservative Wisdom.* This type of Wisdom was very traditional. It did not seek change, but rather tried to understand the world. Its understanding of God was very orthodox and conservative. Often, this type of Wisdom used short proverbial sayings with parallel structures (synonymous, antithetic, or synthetic parallelism). The book of **Proverbs** is a typical example of conservative Wisdom. The point of view is similar to parts of Deuteronomistic theology, and says, "If you act wisely, you will have a good life (or God will bless you); but if you act foolishly you will suffer loss."
- *Challenging, Skeptical Wisdom.* Sometimes those who are good suffer, and those who are wicked succeed in life. There were times when conservative wisdom (and Deuteronomistic theology) did not seem to have all of the answers. At this point, "challenging" or "skeptical" wisdom began to ask serious questions. The books of **Job** and **Ecclesiastes** are examples of this kind of Wisdom. They do not use short proverbial sayings; rather, they present their thoughts as dialogues (discussions) or monologues. They look at traditional wisdom and traditional religion and ask difficult questions. *Why* do good people sometimes suffer? *Why* do the wicked seem to succeed in so many cases? Sometimes, traditional religion and traditional wisdom feel threatened by such questions; they may try to avoid them or deny them. But responsible religion and mature faith must respond and try to answer thoughtfully, carefully, and honestly. And when this happens – when challenging Wisdom confronts faith – the result will be that faith is strengthened in the encounter.
- *Mantic Wisdom* is the third type of wisdom found in the Bible. Mantic wisdom involves interpretation of dreams and is found in the **Joseph** stories and in **Daniel**. More is said about mantic wisdom in the section on Daniel.

Doubt and Questions. Those who collected the books of the Bible included the books of Wisdom along with the doubts and questions which those books raise. They did this because doubt and questions are neither bad nor sinful. They are part of a faith which is living and growing, as we shall see in Job. Faith without questions is faith which is not growing. Furthermore, the questions of "challenging wisdom" can become an entrance door to faith for a person who has doubts. Such questions may open a conversation. Someone may say, "I am not yet able to believe everything you tell me, but I *can* enter as far as the questions and debates which I see in the books of Wisdom." Later, as such people continue to talk with people of faith, their own faith and understanding are able to grow.

Some Themes of Biblical Wisdom.

- *We are to fear God.* Although we cannot understand everything about God and his ways, and although we may not be able to answer some of the most difficult questions, yet we are to fear (reverence, honor) God. Even in the midst of asking difficult questions about justice and meaning in life, the wise never doubt that God exists, and that he should be honored.
- *God reveals himself through Wisdom.* Biblical Wisdom writers talk about the revelation of God, but they find this revelation not through God's mighty acts in history, as other books of the Bible do. Rather, they look to the world of what we would call science – animals, plants, relationships between people – to discover the wisdom of God. In addition, Wisdom is sometimes personified[6] as a good woman who calls young men to come to her and learn. This is especially true in Proverbs 7-9. Her opposite is a woman who is described both as foolish and as a prostitute – a double warning to young men.
- *Wisdom asks about:*
    - **Justice.** Why do people so often get what they do not seem to deserve? Why, for instance, do good people sometimes suffer? Why do the wicked sometimes succeed?
    - **Meaning.** What is the meaning of life? Why are people placed in the world?
    - **God.** Is God just or unjust? How can he be just if there is injustice in his world? "Theodicy" is an attempt to explain God's actions, and to count him just, even when it may seem

[6] "Personification" means representing an object or an idea as a living person so that it can speak and act, display personality, etc.

that there is no justice in the world which he created. The book of Job is theodicy; it asks why good people suffer, and it seeks an answer to the question, "Why doesn't God do something about injustice?"

- *Wisdom affirms that:*
    - **Human wisdom has its limits.** People can investigate and discover many things about the world, even without the help of God, but we cannot discover and understand *everything*.
    - **We cannot avoid death.** One of life's great ironies[7] is that, when people finally gain a great deal wisdom, they are unable to use it because they have become very old and soon will die. This does not seem to make sense. The book of Ecclesiastes, in particular, pursues this question.
    - **There are good and proper ways to live.** Although there are limits to what we can understand, and although we all eventually die, yet we *can* learn useful ways of living which will be of benefit to us. Wisdom tries to teach these ways.

---

[7]See p. 33 footnote 6 for the meaning of irony.

Job

❧

Overview

A Summary of the book. The book of Job tells us about a good and rich man named Job, who lived in the land of Uz (which means, *counsel, advice*). A challenge takes place in heaven between the *satan* (see below) and God concerning Job and his faith. The *satan* suggests that Job is faithful only because God has blessed him. God disagrees and allows the *satan* to test Job. The *satan* does this and Job is reduced to poverty and suffering. Job's three friends Eliphaz, Bildad and Zophar come to comfort him – but instead of comforting him they argue with him about whether he has sinned or whether God is unjust. Later, near the end of the book, a young man named Elihu joins the discussion. He is frustrated with the inability of the three friends to answer Job effectively, although he himself does not add a great deal to our understanding in his six(!) chapters of monologue. The book finally concludes with two appearances of God, who commends Job and criticizes the friends.

The Subject of the book. The book explores the relationship of suffering and justice. If God is just, then why do good people suffer? This kind of question, and the arguments which follow, is called "theodicy."[1] Who would write such a book? It probably comes from a period in Israel's history in which there was great suffering, such as the time of the Assyrian destruction of Samaria and the northern kingdom of Israel (and much of the southern kingdom of Judah). Or it could have been written when Babylon destroyed Jerusalem and the temple and took the leadership of Judah into exile. In both cases, Israel asked, "Why did God let such wicked people conquer us, his people?"[2]

---

[1]See p. 131 for "theodicy."

[2]Since the *satan* figure appears in the story, it is possible that Job is connected with their post-exile experience of Persia (see OT Chronology, page xv). The Persians were dualists, believing in a balance of power between good and evil. The Jews didn't accept that world view, but their recognition of the *satan* figure as an adversary to God's people may have matured at that time.

Was Job an actual historical person? Perhaps, since the beginning and end of the story may be older than the middle. On the other hand, the only Old Testament reference to Job outside of the book of Job itself is in Ezek 14:14,20. And consider the following observation, from rabbinic Judaism, which speaks of the experience of suffering as a "study house":

> The Talmudic discussion on Job is very poignant. Resh Lakish and Rabbi Yochanan, who lived in the 200s in Tiberias, were discussing it. Resh Lakish says that "Job never actually existed; he is only the imaginary hero of the poem, the invention of the poet." Rabbi Yochanan, who had lost his parents in childhood and had lost his children too, told him, "Job did exist, and he had a study house in Tiberias."
>
> Rabbi Yochanan was referring to himself. In other words, even if you say these things never happened to a person named Job, tragedies just as terrible happened to other people over the ages and still happen in our time. So the book is as true as can be.[3]

Rabbi Yochanan of Tiberias had himself suffered greatly. He recognized in his suffering a "study house in Tiberias" in which he had struggled with the same questions raised by Job. And at times, Job has "study houses" in New York or London or small villages in Tanzania.

The "sons of God" and "the satan." Before we continue, we need to consider "the sons of God" and "the *satan*" (both found in Job 1:6), since many readers are troubled by the presence of both in heaven.

The Sons of God and the Satan

The sons of God. The Old Testament is indeed very old. Especially in the poetic sections, but also in some of its older prose sections, it uses *popular* language from the ANE which is not really *theological* language. That is to say, the writers of the Old Testament will at times mention other gods,[4] or mythological creatures,[5] which were part of their ancient cultural heritage but no longer part of their theology. Even the ancient "council of the

[3]From an e-mail conversation with Ephraim Brilliant, an orthodox Jew living in Raanana, Israel, 19 February 2006.

[4]See, for instance, Exod 15:11; Ps 82:1; Ps 95:3; Ps 135:5; 136:2; 138:1; etc. See also the discussion of ANE gods on pp. 271-275.

[5]Leviathan in Job 3:8; 41:1; Ps 74:14; 104:26; Isa 27:1; Rahab in Job 9:13; 26:12; Ps 89:10; Isa 51:9.

gods," which is sometimes called the "sons of God,"[6] occasionally appears. The Jews did not believe in other gods,[7] and they did not believe that there was a council of the gods or that God had sons. But this ancient imagery is found in well-known texts such as Genesis 6 (where the "sons of God" mate with the daughters of men) and here in Job. Some translators will try to hide this fact by calling them angels. They are not angels. Rather, the writers are simply using very old traditional imagery in order to tell their story.

The *satan* in the Old Testament. The Old Testament does not have the full understanding of Satan which we find in the New Testament. Even Genesis 3 never claims that the snake is Satan. That interpretation is a later Christian understanding. Actually, *satan* is simply a Hebrew word which means "adversary," and it is found with that simple meaning in many places throughout the Old Testament.[8] There are three places, however, in which the word *satan* begins to gain the sense of "enemy of God." Job is perhaps the first. Here in Job, we do not actually read of Satan (*satan*, שָׂטָן), but rather "the *satan*" (*hassatan*, הַשָּׂטָן). The Hebrew text has a definite article (the ה in הַשָּׂטָן), and this shows us that "the *satan*" is an office (job, position): the adversary. In Job, "the *satan*" appears to be working for God. He is in heaven with "the sons of God" (see above), and this means he is part of the divine council. His work in Job is to be God's "prosecuting attorney." That is, he roams the earth looking for sinners and then reports back to God. In this sense, "the *satan*" (again, note the definite article) is working *for* God in Job – though in a way that still makes him an adversary to Job.

In two other places, "the *satan*" is even less friendly. In Zech 3:1, he is found accusing Joshua the high priest,[9] and

---

[6]Gen 6:2,4; Deut 32:8; Job 1:6; 2:1; 38:7; Ps 82:1.

[7]This is probably somewhat of an overstatement. Most likely the patriarchs and early Israel did think there were other gods, but were (or became) convinced that the God of Israel (Yahweh, the LORD) was more powerful. It was later in Israel's history that they became absolute and confident monotheists, and could say things such as we find in Isa 44:6-20.

[8]See, for instance, Num 22:22,32; 1 Sam 29:4; 2 Sam 19:22; 1 Kgs 5:4, 11:14,23,25; Ps 109:6.

[9]This is not the Joshua who helped Moses. The Joshua mentioned in Zechariah was the high priest after the people returned from exile in 538 B.C. He ruled with a governor named Zerubbabel, and is mentioned in Haggai and

again it is "the *satan*" not "Satan." In 1 Chr 21:1 he causes David to sin. 1 Chron 21:1 is particularly interesting because

- It is the parallel text to 2 Sam 24:1 which says *God* caused David to sin, and
- In 1 Chr 21:1, the Hebrew text does not use the definite article: this one time it simply says "*satan*" (or "Satan"[10]). This time, as in the New Testament, we find Satan being treated as an individual, not just an office.

What is happening here? Why does the Old Testament mention Satan (or "the *satan*") only in these texts? Many think Israel came to an understanding of "the *satan*" while in Babylon through contact with the Persians. God taught his people through many different experiences, and it is not unreasonable to think that God used the Persians in this way, as well.[11] Both Zechariah and 1 Chronicles come from this period. (Review "Later History: an overview" on p. 103.) Perhaps Job came from this period, too.

Finally, what about the very popular story of Satan being a proud angel who tried to take over heaven and was cast to earth by God? This story is known by most Christians but is not found in the Bible. At least it is not found in just that way. The story may be a combination of Isa 14:12-15 and Ezek 28:12-17. Both sound very much like the story of "Satan's fall from heaven" – especially when we add Luke 10:18 and Rev 12:7-17 to the discussion. But note that Isaiah's words are really a "taunt against the king of Babylon" (Isa 14:4), and Ezekiel is raising "a lamentation over the king of Tyre" (Ezek 28:12). Now, certainly some of the language in these texts seems to speak of more than earthly kings (Isa 14:14 and much of the Ezekiel text). Are we supposed to see reference to a fall of Satan here? The text

---

Zechariah and was encouraged by them. See the discussion of this "dyarchy" on p. 245.

[10]However, Hebrew does not have upper case (capital) and lower case (small) letters. Thus, Hebrew cannot distinguish between *satan* and *Satan*.

[11]The Persians, however, were dualists, and Israel was not. **Dualism** believes that there are two opposite forces, one good and one evil. For the dualist, this explains why there is evil: the evil force does it. In the Bible, however, Satan or "the *satan*" is not equal and opposite to God. For instance, the Bible never suggests that Satan is omnipotent, omnipresent or omniscient. There is no question as to who will finally win out in the end. Satan is a creature, and, like all creatures, must finally obey God.

does not say this, and the answer to the question will vary from interpreter to interpreter.

The poetic debate. Although Job begins with a story (prose), the story is only two chapters long. The largest part of the book is the forty chapters of poetry which follow. In this long poetic section, we find

- The debate between Job and his three friends,
- Elihu's contribution, and
- The two appearances of God (plus Job's repentance).

The longest part of this poetic section is the debate between Job and his three friends in chapters 3-31. The argument moves around in a circle three times. Three times, each friend speaks and Job responds. The three friends represent traditional wisdom. In many and various ways they say, "Job, *everyone knows* that if you are good God will bless you, and *everyone knows* that if you are evil God will punish you. You are suffering; this shows clearly that you have sinned." But Job has not sinned. We have been told this from the beginning (Job 1:1). Thus, what "*everyone knows*" is not true. More to the point, this "truth" is no longer sufficient for Job. This is likely the whole reason for the book of Job. The writer seeks to answer the question of why good people suffer, and to argue against the too-simple answers of conservative wisdom. Truly, when we study the Old Testament, we are studying the *theologies* of the Old Testament, and not merely *the theology* of the Old Testament. Again, we have tension; and again it is a fruitful tension.[12]

The Center. In addition to the debate, there is a center to the book of Job. We have already discussed concentric patterns (see p. 99), and noted that important material is often found at their center. Entire books of the Old Testament sometimes have important things at their centers, too. As already mentioned, the poetry of Job has three sets of arguments, and in each set Job argues with each of the three friends. In the middle argument of the middle *set* of arguments, Job suddenly makes a tremendous statement of faith:

A	B	C	A	★	C	A	B	C
First set of arguments			Second set of arguments			Third set of arguments		

[12]Recall what was said about "tensions" on pp. 81 and 90.

The statement is found at Job 19:23-27 (marked with the ★ above). In the midst of the dark struggle, Job makes a surprising confession of trust in God. More will be said about this below.

God speaks. Finally comes the voice both Job and the reader have waited for. Twice, God answers Job "out of the whirlwind," and both answers appear to be the same. God uses powerful creation language and asks, "Job, where were you when I created the world? Can you do the great things that I have done?"

Job is left speechless, of course. At the very end, he repents in dust and ashes for having spoken of things which he did not understand. God criticizes Job's three friends (Elihu is now forgotten) and tells them to ask Job to pray for them. Then God gives back to Job double of everything he lost in the first chapter.[13] The *satan* is completely absent at the end.

What we see, therefore, is the following structure with prose at the beginning and end and a large section of poetry in the middle:

Chapter	**1:1-2:13**	**3:1-42:6**	**42:7-17**
Type of Literature	Prose (story)	Poetry	Prose (story)
People	Job, his family, God, the *satan*	Job and his three "friends," Elihu, God	All except the *satan*
Place	Earth and Heaven	Earth	Earth

[13]Everything except sons and daughters. Job started with ten, lost ten, and is given ten again at the end. One student of Job has suggested that this may be a hint of life after death (see also the discussion of *A Future Hope?* on page 142, below). That is, perhaps the first ten were not really lost, but "after [their] skin has been thus destroyed, then from [their] flesh [they] shall see God," too. This may be somewhat too imaginative, though Job would indeed then end up with double what he had at the beginning.

Outline

I. **Prose:** Job goes from health and wealth to sickness and poverty (Job 1-2)
II. **Poetry:** The debate and its conclusion (Job 3:1-42:6)
   A. Job debates with his three friends (Job 3-31)
   B. Elihu (Job 32-37)
   C. God answers out of the whirlwind – twice (38-41)
   D. Job repents in dust and ashes (Job 42:1-6)
III. **Prose:** The conclusion of the story (Job 42:7-17)

Message

Why was Job written? No one knows who wrote the book of Job. Job did not write the book, since it is all written in the third person (Job is "he" not "I"). But whoever wrote it had undoubtedly either suffered unjustly or *watched* good people suffering unjustly. And clearly, for the writer of Job, the traditional answers offered by conservative wisdom – and by scriptures such as Psalm 1 – were no longer satisfying.

In Job, those traditional answers are represented by Job's three friends who continue to throw them at Job; but Job continues to reject them. Statements like "God always blesses the wise and righteous, and always punishes the foolish and wicked" seem to make good sense when you are healthy and wealthy and powerful. But when you are sick, or poor, or oppressed, then these statements of conservative wisdom no longer seem quite as convincing. Or, as Santayana has said, "A lion must feel more secure that God is on his side than does a gazelle." Job insists that he is innocent and that his suffering is undeserved, and he demands to stand before God to ask him why all this has happened.

The conclusion of the matter. The arguments in the poetry section of Job are long and, in the end, not satisfying. Finally God appears, and his answer simply seems to be, "Job, I am God, you are man; I am bigger than you, and you are not able to understand." And Job seems to agree, since he repents. Then at the end everything is returned to him.

But we are left with some questions. First, where is the *satan*? He appears at the beginning to place his challenge before God, but he is not found at the end. We would expect God to turn to the *satan* at this point and say, "See, what did I tell you? Job is faithful." But he does not. So apparently the *satan* is not important to the writer or the story. We must remember, after all, that Job has problems with God, not with the *satan*.

Second, what has happened to the writer's argument? For thirty-five chapters (Job 3-37), Job argues that he is innocent and that conservative wisdom is wrong. Job says, "It is not *always* true that if you are good you will experience God's blessing." Job has even demanded to stand before God to ask him questions.[14] Then suddenly God appears and simply says "I am bigger than you," Job repents, and he gets back double of everything. Conservative wisdom can smile and say, "See, I was right." But then why was the book written?

Several suggestions have been made. Some have thought that the very end of the story (where the *satan* is missing) was added later by an uncomfortable conservative writer in order give a "good ending" to a troubling story. Others suggest that the writer started with a very old story and used it as a prose frame around his poetry. Since the story was old and well-known, however, he was then unable to skip the well-known "happy ending." Either of these suggestions could be true.

But perhaps we should leave the ending as it is and instead look carefully at Job 42:7. Job 42:7 says: "After the LORD had spoken these words to Job...." But "these words" (verses 1-6) have been spoken by *Job* not by God. So it appears that either

- Some words of God, originally located between verses 6 and 7, have become lost, or else
- Verses 1-6 were added by someone else and Job 42:7 originally came immediately after Job 41:34.

I will return to these two possibilities in the third paragraph below.

The Message of the Book of Job. Several possibilities have been suggested. Some, following James 5:11, suggest that the theme of the book is "the patience of Job." But Job does not seem very patient, and his repentance is found only at the very end. Others have suggested that the question is "the problem of evil;" that is, "Where did evil come from?" But, whereas that may be one of the questions of Genesis 3, this question of the *origins* of evil never comes up in Job.

A third suggestion is probably the best, and that is that Job is asking serious questions about "the nature of God." Is God just? If good people suffer – and sometimes they do – is God fair?[15] Job finally seems

---

[14]Job 9:34-35; 13:3,15-23; 31:35-37.

[15]The book of Jonah asks the other side of the question: If *wicked* people receive *mercy*, is God just and fair?

to arrive at two answers: yes, God is just, but no, we cannot find the complete answer to the large question of why he allows good people to suffer. This answer may not be completely satisfying; but it is honest, and is the best that can be offered in an age that had no clear picture of life after death.[16]

However, the book of Job may be saying something else about the nature of God as well. Above, I noted the problem of "these words" in Job 42:7. On the one hand, perhaps the words of the LORD, which should appear between 42:6 and 42:7, have gotten lost. Perhaps at one point someone forgot to copy them. This leaves us with a broken or incoherent[17] text, a text which just does not make sense. In some ways, that may be appropriate: the brokenness or incoherence of the text reflects the lack of resolution to Job's questions.

But what if, on the other hand, Job 42:1-6 (the repentance of Job) was added by a later pious writer? What if originally Job 42:7 came immediately after Job 41:34? What do we have if we leave out Job 42:1-6? Without Job 42:1-6, God finishes his second speech in Job 41:34 (where he speaks of Leviathan) and we then continue at 42:7. In this case, the text would read as follows:

> 41:33: [God speaking] Upon earth there is not his [Leviathan's] like, a creature without fear.
>
> 41:34: He beholds everything that is high; he is king over all the sons of pride."
>
> 42:7 After the LORD had spoken these words to Job, the LORD said to Eliphaz the Temanite: "My wrath is kindled against you and against your two friends; for you have not spoken to [see below] me what is right, as my servant Job has.

In this case, there is no repentance of Job. Instead, God finishes his description of Leviathan and then turns immediately to Eliphaz and says "My wrath is kindled against you and against your two friends; for you have not spoken to[18] me what is right, as my servant Job has." In other

---

[16]We will see below, however, that there may be a hint of life after death in Job 19:25-27. More is said about this on p. 200 in the chapter on Daniel.

[17]For coherence and incoherence, see p. 86 footnote 15.

[18]The English translations say "you have not spoken *of* me what is right," but the Hebrew is אֵלַי (*'elay*) and that may be better translated "to me." The translations seem to think that the issue is what has been said *about* God. I am going to suggest that the real issue is, instead, how Job spoke *to* God. That is, the book may be suggesting that his bold challenging was the right thing to do.

words, in all the arguments of Job 3-37, *Job has spoken rightly and properly and his 3 friends have been wrong.* This would mean that, although Job never finally got the answer to his question, he was right to ask his questions and make his argument. He was right to speak "what is right" to God, even if that meant arguing with God. Of course, such arguing is still to be done in an attitude of reverence and respect for God. At times, Job may indeed have crossed the line and gone too far (for instance, in Job 31:35-32:1), and God's speeches from the whirlwind may include some reprimand because of this. But overall, God says that Job was right to argue.

As was the case with Moses in Exodus 3, God encourages and even honors honest discussion and relationship with him. This is true even when it leads to strong words from us. This says much to us in terms of prayer and conversation with God. God takes us seriously and wants us to take seriously our relationship and conversations with him. And, even if we leave the repentance of Job in the text above and assume that some words of God got lost between 42:6 and 42:7, the same point is still made in God's strong words to Eliphaz. God wants honest, open relationships with his people. Asking questions – even challenging questions – is good and healthy and necessary for faith.

A Future Hope? Above, we noted that the book of Job has a center (marked with the star in the chart on p. 137). In the midst of Job's questioning and struggle, suddenly we find a statement of faith in which some would see the hope of life after death. There are only a few places in the Old Testament where such hope is possibly being expressed.[19] Here, in the very center of Job (Job 19:25-27), Job suddenly cries out:

> For I know that my Redeemer[20] lives, and at last he will stand upon the earth; and after my skin has been thus destroyed, then from my flesh I shall see God, whom I shall see on my side, and my eyes shall behold, and not another.

This hope is not found in the rest of the book. Indeed, we will not find anything similar until we get to Daniel. But in the midst of Job's dark

---

[19]Some possibilities are Isa 26:19; Daniel 12:1-3 and Psalms 71.20b and 73:23-26.

[20]The word is *go'el* (גֹּאֵל). It refers to a family member who buys back property for a poor relative who has had to sell it, or even redeems the relative if he has sold himself into slavery (see Lev 25:25-50). The word is also often used to describe God as Israel's Redeemer (e.g., Pss 19:14; 74:2; 78:35; 107:2).

night of struggle, we do not want to miss this very brief glimpse of the hope which, for Christians, finds its completion many years later in Jesus Christ.

A Final Note. The purpose of this book is to study the Old Testament, and so not a great deal is said about the theology of the New Testament which developed later. But it is worthwhile to note that the New Testament presents us with two pieces of information which might have helped Job in his struggle. The first is life after death. Although Job 19:25-27 hints at this possibility, the writer of Job generally does not know of it. Like those around him, he felt that death was the end, that both the good and wicked went to *Sheol*,[21] and that in *Sheol* there was no relationship or conversation with God. Thus, they believed, if a person is going to experience justice, this must happen *in this life*. If this does not happen, then something is wrong; perhaps God is unjust. At this point, an understanding of life after death would have allowed Job to work with some alternatives.

The second piece of information found in New Testament theology – but missing in the Old Testament – is that of the widespread nature of sin. Sin is not merely evil actions; rather, sin is a power (see Romans 7, for instance). It affects all people, quite apart from whether they themselves have committed a particular sin. People who work in offices filled with cigarette smoke will smell like smoke when they leave, even if they do not smoke. They may even get cancer. Likewise, people living in a world which has been invaded by the power of sin will suffer because of this pervasive presence of sin, even if they themselves have not committed particular sins. This understanding, too, could have helped Job.

But Job's struggle was not in vain. Although he did not finally arrive at a complete answer to his question, he did point to the problem. He did raise the question of suffering and justice in such a way that conservative wisdom could no longer simply say "if you are good, God

---

[21]*Sheol* (שְׁאוֹל) is the Old Testament "place of the dead." It is not the same as hell. Rather, it was thought to be the place where all people go when they die – both the good and the wicked, the wealthy and the poor. It was thought not to be a place of suffering, but rather a very drab, uninteresting place. No one ever came back from the dead, and the dead had no conversation with the living or with God. One might think of *Sheol* as a world in which television has lost its color and food has lost its taste – not a place of suffering but rather a very dull and tiresome place. See Job 7:21; Pss 88:4-5, 10-12; 115:17; Eccl 9:5-6.

will bless you." It may generally be true that those who are good are blessed, but it is not *always* true. Today, too, God's people cannot be theologically lazy and simply say that people are poor and oppressed because they have sinned. Rather, we are forced to think seriously about a world in which there are systems and structures which sometimes cause great suffering. Job does not yet have an understanding of "corporate evil," but he pushes his later readers to consider the possibility that our group actions – what we do as institutions or nations – can cause individual suffering for those who are innocent.

Some important texts: The wager (Job 1:9-12); Job curses the day he was born (Job 3:1-26); I know that my redeemer lives (Job 19:25-27); Job's boldness (Job 31:35-37); God answers (Job 38-40); Job repents (Job 42:1-6); God tells Job's 3 friends to ask Job to pray for them (Job 42:7-9).

Verses for memory: Job 19:25-26

Psalms

❧

Overview

The Psalms are not wisdom material. Rather, they are poems and hymns written for individuals as well as for communities of faith. But, like wisdom, they do something different from the other books of the Old Testament.[1] Other books tell *what God has done* in the world, the Psalms tell us *how God's people have responded* to what God has done.

The Hebrew name for the book of Psalms is "Praises" (*tehillim*, תְּהִלִּים). The word comes from the verb *halal* (הלל), which is the root of *Hallelujah!* or "Praise the LORD," and indeed the Psalms contain much praise of God.

However, the Psalms are not all praise, and we shall see that they also contain much lament. Indeed, we shall see that the whole book of Psalms, from beginning to end, is built like a large lament psalm. In general, Psalms 1-80 contain many psalms of lament (though they are not all lament), and then the end of the collection (Psalms 145-150) are Psalms of praise.

Almost every psalm has a short title or header, such as "Psalm of David when he fled from Absalom his son," or "To the choirmaster: with stringed instruments." Many of these headers mention David's name.[2] But other people are mentioned, too: Asaph (Pss 50, 73-83), the Sons of Korah (Pss 42, 44-49, 84, 85, 87, 88), Ethan bin Ezra (Ps 89) and even Moses (Ps 90). Indeed, the book of Psalms may be considered

---

[1]See p. 128 regarding how Wisdom is different.

[2]Most of Pss 3-41, 51-72, 108-10, and 138-45 have the words *mizmor ledavid* (מִזְמוֹר לְדָוִד) at the top. *Mizmor* means "a psalm," but *ledavid* is more difficult. *le* (לְ)is a Hebrew preposition which means many things including *to, for, of, about, by, according to*, etc. So it is not clear that all these psalms were written *by* David. Some may have been written *for* David or even *according to (the style of)* David. This is especially true of Psalms that mention the temple (see Pss 5:7; 11:4; 18:6; 27:4; 29:9; 65:4; 68:29; 138:2), since it was built not by David but by his son Solomon after David died.

the hymn book of Israel and contains contributions from many people.[3]

Outline

The book of Psalms is a collection, and so it cannot be outlined. But there are some features which should be noted. First of all, the first two Psalms act as an introduction to the rest of the collection. This is clear because of the following four points.

First, neither Psalm 1 nor Psalm 2 have a header, which is unusual.

Second, near the beginning of each psalm (in Ps 1:2 and Ps 2:1), we find the Hebrew word *hagah* (הָגָה) which means "to think hard, to plan." Thus, "Blessed is the man who ... meditates (*hagah*) on his law day and night" (Ps 1:2), and "Why do the nations conspire, and the peoples plot (*hagah*) in vain?" (Ps 2:1).

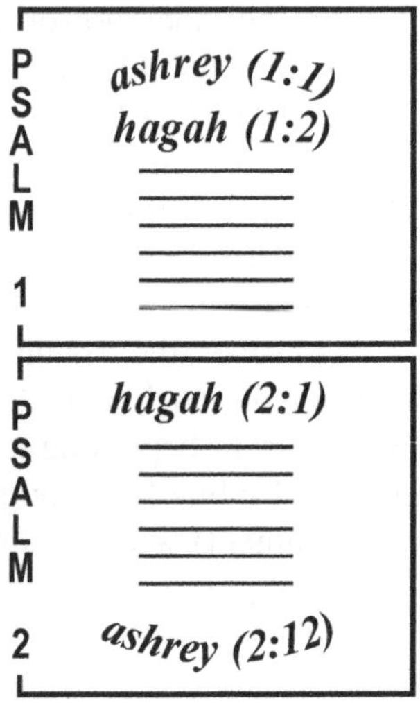

Third, a "frame of blessing" surrounds Psalm 1 and Psalm 2. The Hebrew word "blessed" (*ashrey*, אַשְׁרֵי) is found at the beginning of Psalm 1 ("Blessed (*ashrey*) is the man who ...") and at the end of Psalm 2 ("Blessed (*ashrey*) are all who take refuge in him").

Fourth, Psalm 1 is a psalm of an individual whereas Psalm 2 is a community or national psalm.

PSALM 1
ashrey (1:1)
hagah (1:2)

PSALM 2
hagah (2:1)
ashrey (2:12)

Thus, Psalms 1 and 2 function as an introduction to the rest of the psalms – an introduction which says that the *individual* person is invited to contemplate (*hagah*) the psalms, but that the psalms are also meant for the *community*. And there is *blessing* (*ashrey*) for all who study the psalms. There is also a reference to the Messiah[4] in Psalm 2. This may be significant, since the psalms were collected during the Babylonian exile, at a time during which messianic hope was beginning to grow.

---

[3]Another indication of the community use of the psalms may be the word *selah* (סֶלָה) which appears 71 times in the psalms (and 3 times in the psalm in Habakkuk 3). Its actual meaning is unknown, but it may be a musical notation or directions for the choir singing the psalm.

[4]The Hebrew word is *mashiach* (מָשִׁיחַ), and most English *Bibles* translate this word as "anointed." See p. 9, footnote 10.

There is another structure in the Psalms, as well. The entire collection is divided into five "books." This structure is not extremely important, but several things may be noted. First, Books I and II may

Book	I	II	III	IV	V
Chapters	1-2, 3-41	42-72	73-89	90-106	107-150

originally have been two separate collections of Psalms of David. Several psalms in Book I are found again in Book II, and Book II has a number of "Elohistic Psalms" in which the name *Yahweh* ("the LORD") has been changed to *Elohim* ("God").[5] For instance, compare Psalms 14 and 53. Book II ends with the words "The Prayers of David, the son of Jesse, are ended," which may mean that this was the end of the original collection of Davidic psalms. Second, while Books I and II have many lament psalms, Book V ends with psalms of praise. More is said about this feature on page 151.

Types of Psalms.

More important than any outline or structure of the whole book are the various *types* of psalms. The following types of psalms are found throughout the entire collection:

Lament psalms

Individual: 3-7, 9-10, 13, 17, 22, 25, 26 and many others

Community: 12, 44, 60, 74, 79, 80, 83, 85, 90, 94, 108, 123, 129, 137

There are two kinds of psalms of lament:
(1) individual and
(2) national or community.

Lament psalms often have a pattern, and this pattern can be seen clearly in Psalm 13:

Call upon God (13:1a)
Complaint (13:1b-2)
This involves "me," "you" (that is, God), and "them" (the enemy)
Prayer for Help (13:3-4)
Confession of Faith (13:5)
Vow to Praise God (13:6).

[5]The rabbis eventually began to consider the divine name *Yahweh* to be too holy to pronounce. This led to several things including sometimes replacing the name *Yahweh* with the word *Elohim*. See the discussion of *Yahweh* on p. 34.

Sometimes, instead of the final vow, there is simply praise of God. This may show that the lamenter received an answer from a priest or from God after presenting the first parts of the lament. Ps 7:11-16 may be an example of such an answer. The most famous individual lament psalm is Psalm 22: "My God, my God, why have you forsaken me?" Most lament psalms end with praise or some kind of resolution. But Psalm 88 does not, and neither does the book of Lamentations. Both end with the issue still unresolved and the question "Where is God in this?"

Historical psalms

78, 105, 106

In general, other books of the Bible tell about what *God has done*, while the Psalms tell us how God's *people have responded* to what he has (or has not) done. Thus, the psalms do not usually mention historical events. But there are a few psalms which do. Psalm 78 tells the history of Israel from the Exodus until the ten northern tribes are taken captive in the eighth century BC. Psalm 105 tells of events from the time of Abraham until the Exodus. Psalm 106 recalls God's faithfulness during the Exodus in spite of the unfaithfulness of the people – and it prays that God would act again to save his people, who have been taken into exile.

Royal psalms

2, 18, 20, 21, 45, 72, 89, 101, 110, 132, 144:1-11

These psalms were written about and for events in the life of the king. Psalm 2 was probably read at the crowning of a new king and warned Israel's neighbors not to attack at this sensitive time. Psalm 45 was for a king's wedding. The king was known as God's "anointed" (*mashiach*, מָשִׁיחַ, see footnotes on pp. 9 and 146). Thus, some of these psalms have become known as "Messianic Psalms" and are seen by Christians to be pointing ahead to Christ.

Wisdom psalms

37, 49, 73, 112, 127, 128, 133.

In these psalms we find neither lament nor praise. Rather, there is contemplation of the nature of life and of one's responsibilities in living before God (see the discussion of Wisdom on pp. 128-133, above). Psalms 37 and 112 are acrostic psalms (see p. 126 for acrostics). Psalms 37 and 73 consider the problem of the prosperity of the wicked, and Psalm 73 even begins to ask difficult questions similar to those of Job – though at the end it retreats to the safety and comfort of conservative wisdom.

Torah psalms

1; 19:7-14; 119

One of the major themes of wisdom is the *seeking* of wisdom. "Happy is the man who finds wisdom, and the man who gets understanding" (Prov 3:13). In the Torah Psalms, the theme is seeking the *law* (*torah*, תּוֹרָה) *of the* LORD instead of wisdom. "Blessed is the man who walks not in the counsel of the wicked ....but his delight is in the law of the LORD, and on his law he meditates day and night" (Ps 1:1-2). The greatest Torah psalm is Psalm 119 with its 176 acrostic verses. But be sure also to read Ps 19:7-14. Such love for the law may sound strange to Christians, but *torah* really means "instruction" or "guidance," not just "law" (see the discussion on p. 3). Israel believed that God's gift of the *torah* showed how much he loved them.

Imprecatory psalms

5, 6?, 11?, 12, 35, 37?, 40, 52, 54?, 56, 58, 69, 79, 83, 109, 137, 139, 143

Sometimes the psalmist asks God to destroy or punish enemies. Many readers find these psalms to be difficult. Four points may be considered:

(1) As mentioned, the psalms are *people's response.* They are not doctrine, but are rather a record of people's responses to what God has done. Perhaps sometimes people spoke too strongly.
(2) Vengeance itself is left in the hands of God; the individual does not plan personal vengeance, but calls upon God to make things right.
(3) Injustice is not a small thing. It is not to be minimized or ignored. At times, these psalms may be a proper response to injustice – prayers that injustice and unjust people might be stopped.
(4) Some have suggested that, especially in times of temptation or struggle, the imprecatory psalms may be used against the enemy within us: the "Old Adam."

Liturgical psalms

15, 24, 50, 81, 95, 115, 118, 132

These psalms were used during Israel's worship. "Liturgy" means "the work of the people," and some of these psalms may have been chanted back and forth between the priest and the people. Some think that Psalm 50 was used in a "covenant renewal" ceremony.

Pilgrimage psalms

Ascent: 120-134
Zion:46, 48, 76, 84, 87, 122, 132:13-18

Pilgrimage psalms were sung as people approached Jerusalem on their way to visit the temple. Jerusalem is set on a hill, and so people sang Psalms of Ascent as they went up the hill. The hill on which the temple sat was called Mt. Zion, and so there are also Psalms of Zion which glorify the temple or the city of Jerusalem. One of these psalms, Psalm 46, was the foundation and inspiration for Luther's great hymn, "A Mighty Fortress is our God."

Psalms of Praise and Thanksgiving

many, but especially 145-150

As mentioned above, the book of Psalms is called the book of "Praises" in Hebrew. It calls people to praise God, and even the lament psalms move in that direction, beginning with a cry of pain but ending with a cry of praise. The Bible has many psalms of praise and thanksgiving(not just in the Psalms; see, for instance, Exodus 15, 1 Samuel 2, 2 Samuel 22, Jonah 2). But they are found especially at the end of the book of Psalms (145-150). And these psalms usually begin with a *call* to praise, followed by a *reason* for praise. The Hebrew word *kiy* (כִּי) is used for this: "Sing to the LORD, *for* (כִּי) he has triumphed gloriously" (Exod 15:21). "O give thanks to the LORD *for* (כִּי) he is good" (Ps 118:1). This כִּי is missing in Psalm 150 (the "for" of v. 2 is -בְּ not כִּי), and perhaps this means that what has been said in all the previous 149 psalms is the *reason* for praise in this final psalm.

Message

Luther said that when we turn to the Psalms, "we look into the heart of all the saints," because the experiences we find in the Psalms are common to people throughout all ages. It is for this reason that the psalms are so popular and that they are used so frequently in worship. Some of the most neglected psalms are also some of the most important, however. These are the lament psalms. Those who deal with people in grief should be familiar with the lament psalms because they give a voice to thoughts and feelings that people sometimes find hard to express. Can we cry out to God in words of complaint? Can we ask God, "Where are you?" The psalmists did, and so can we. Several times they boldly call to God to wake up and help them! "Awake, O Lord! Why do you sleep? Rouse yourself!" (Ps 44:23, NIV; see also Ps 7:6; 10:1; 35:23; 59:4-5) These are not words of disrespect; rather, they are words of people who are so convinced that God cares for them that they can only think his absence must mean he is asleep. God wants to hear not only our cries of praise but also our cries of pain and even complaint.

The Movement of the Psalms. Although the Psalms do include bold cries of complaint, it is finally praise that is the goal. We have seen how the lament psalms begin with a cry of complaint but end up with praise (or a vow to praise). This pattern has also been adopted for the whole book of Psalms. That is, we find the largest number of lament psalms at the beginning, but psalms of praise at the end. Thus, the entire book of Psalms is like a large lament psalm; it begins where we are (our situation) and seeks to move us toward our purpose (praise).

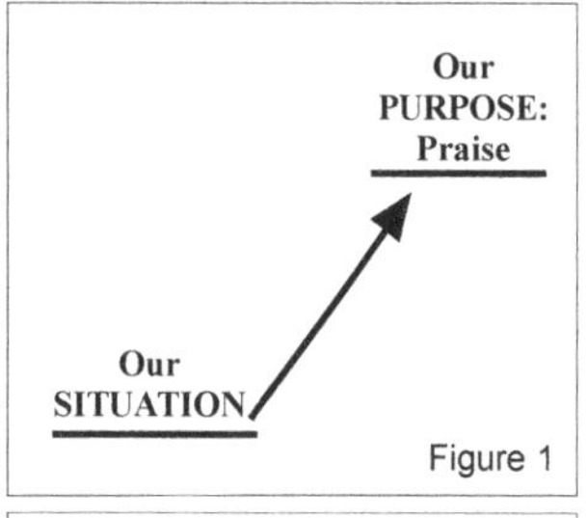

Figure 1

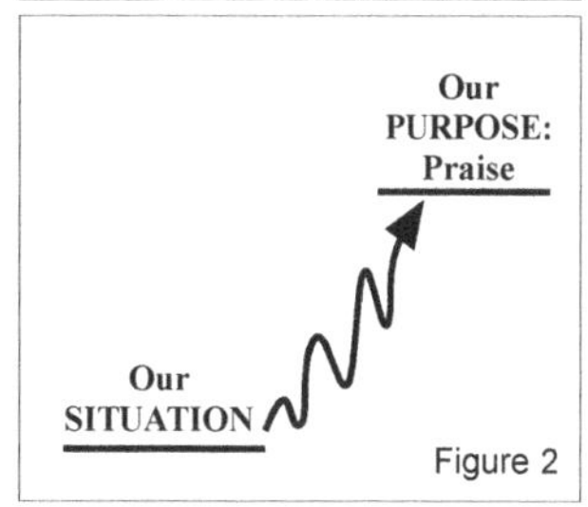

Figure 2

But this movement in the Psalms (and in life itself) is not a direct move as in Figure 1. Although the greatest number of lament psalms are found in the first half of the book of Psalms, there are laments in the latter part of the book, too. Likewise, there are praise psalms in the earlier part of the book, but they are most frequent toward the end. Thus, the movement of the book of Psalms, from beginning to end, like life itself, is more like Figure 2 – back and forth between lament and praise, but the final resting place is praise.

When we arrive at the end of the book of Psalms – as at the end of life – we arrive at praise of God. The last psalm invites the whole creation to praise God. The last verse of the book of psalms says:

> Let everything that breathes praise the LORD!
> Praise the LORD!
>
> (Psalm 150:6)

(There are too many "important texts" and "verses for memory" in the psalms to list them here. You might choose some of your own, beginning with Psalm 23, which all of God's people should know by heart.)

Proverbs

❧

Overview

Proverbs are short wisdom sayings, and are found in every culture. A proverb is meant for a specific situation. Thus, although a proverb may be *true*, it will not always be *appropriate*. For instance, at times it will be appropriate to say "haste makes waste" (that is, *do not act too quickly* or you will damage the results). At other times, however, it is more appropriate to say "a stitch in time saves nine" (i.e., *act quickly* before the problem becomes worse).

A proverb tends to "distill the wisdom of the ages." That is, it takes what has been known by many for a long time, and puts that knowledge into a short, memorable and often clever, group of words. For this reason, proverbs tend to be conservative and looking to the past, rather than new and creative and looking to the future.

Parallel structures. The book of Proverbs is, in general, a collection of conservative wisdom as described above. Much of Proverbs (though not all) uses parallel structures.[1] Proverbs 10-15 contain antithetic parallelism (A *but* B):

> A wise son makes a glad father
> *but* a foolish man despises his mother. (Prov 15:20)

Synonymous and synthetic parallelism are found throughout Proverbs 16-22. Another common parallel pattern involves comparison (A *is like* B; or *Like* A *is* B). This form is found especially in Proverbs 25-29:

> He who meddles in a quarrel not his own
> *is like* one who takes a passing dog by the ears. (Prov 26:17)
>
> *Like* clouds and wind without rain
> *is* a man who boasts of a gift he does not give. (Prov 25:14)

---

[1]See p. 125 for a description of parallelism and its various forms.

Poetry. Not all of Proverbs is short sayings in parallel structures. There are also several sections of extended poetry, especially at the beginning and at the very end. The first section, Proverbs 1-9, is the most structured part of the book. It begins with a collection of ten speeches aimed at the training of young men who were probably from the wealthy and privileged class of society. The goal is to teach them proper behavior, especially when they stood before those who ranked above them. The language of this section is that of a father to a son.[2]

After these opening speeches, there are two poems (Proverbs 8-9) in which Wisdom is personified[3] as a wise woman. In Proverbs 9 she builds a house[4] with seven pillars. She calls to the young men to come to her, and to avoid the "foolish woman" of Prov 9:13-18. In these texts, young men are being warned both to seek wisdom and avoid foolishness (folly), as well as to seek the good woman and avoid prostitutes. In general, in this section we find the following pairings:

wisdom = righteousness
folly = wickedness.

Some have suggested that Prov 8:22-31 points to Christ, but this is rather dangerous theology since Prov 8:22 can lead to Arianism.[5] (The verse is sometimes misused in this way by Jehovah's Witnesses.)

The last 22 verses of Proverbs (Prov 31:10-31) are an acrostic[6] poem about the ideal wife. Although most of what she does is for her husband's benefit, this poem does show that a wealthy woman in those days was able to do many things including buying and selling land and teaching wisdom.

The book of Proverbs is actually seven collections of material from several sources. The first verse of the book says "The Proverbs of

---

[2]The phrase "my son" occurs fifteen times in Hebrew between Prov 1:8 and Prov 7:1. Nine of these come at the beginning of a verse.

[3]See p. 131, footnote 6, for "personification."

[4]Cf. Prov 14:1, and note the footnote found there in RSV and NRSV.

[5]Arius (4th century A.D.) said that the Logos (the second person of the Trinity, the Christ, the Son) was not co-eternal with the Father. Rather, he said, the Son was the Father's first creation, and was thus of a different "substance" from the Father. This view, known as Arianism, was finally declared to be heresy by the Church.

[6]See p. 126 for acrostics.

Solomon," but those words only apply to the first, second and fourth collections (see outline below). Other collections are from "The Wise," Agur, and Lemuel. The final section is the poem about the "ideal wife."

Outline

I. **Proverbs of Solomon: poetry** (Proverbs 1-9)
II. **Proverbs of Solomon: sayings** (Prov 10:1-22:16)
III. **The words of The Wise** (Prov 22:17-24:34)
  A. Admonitions ("Hear the words of the wise") (Prov 22:17-24:22)[7]
  B. Sayings ("These also are saying of the wise") (Prov 24:23-34)
IV. **Proverbs of Solomon: sayings** ("These also are proverbs of Solomon") (Proverbs 25-29)
V. **The words of Agur** (Proverbs 30)
VI. **The words of Lemuel** (Prov 31:1-9)
VII. **The ideal wife** (acrostic poem) (Prov 31:10-31)

Message

The book of Proverbs is not a book of doctrine. It contains not "timeless truth" but rather "situation-specific" truths. That is, a given proverb will be appropriate in some situations and not appropriate in others. Thus, for instance, we do not use Proverbs in the same way we use Paul's letter to the Romans. Concepts such as *covenant, redemption* and *law* (*torah*) are not completely absent in Proverbs (*torah* occurs 13 times), but they are less central or important in Proverbs than they are in other books.

In general, Proverbs considers wisdom and righteousness to be closely connected to each other. Likewise, foolishness and wickedness are seen to be connected. There is a concern for justice in Proverbs, but the concern does not have the intensity that is found in the prophets. At times, the concern of Proverbs seems rather abstract and theoretical. When the concern is specific and practical, it often relates to bribery or unfair judgments.

The major goal of the book of Proverbs is to note how life works and to teach how to live properly. The emphasis is upon observation of life, obedience, self-control, and the fear of the LORD. The book may

---

[7]This section contains material which is quite similar to the earlier Egyptian "Instruction of Amenemopet."

seem rather secular at times, but the phrase "the fear of the LORD" occurs 14 times. And it is "the fear of the LORD" which is the beginning of knowledge (Prov 1:7) and the beginning of wisdom (Prov 9:10). Throughout the book, there are many other references to the LORD (a total of 85), and a wonderful cluster of them is found at the center[8] of the book (nine in Prov 15:33-16:9).

Some important texts: Advice to young men ("My son") (Proverbs 1-7); the virtuous and foolish women (Proverbs 8-9); wisdom as the first of God's creations (Prov 8:22-31); the ideal wife (Prov 31:10-31).

Verses for memory: Prov 3:11-12; 9:10

---

[8]The center of patterns and structures in Hebrew literature is often very important. See the discussion of concentric patterns on pages 99 and 126.

Ecclesiastes

❧

Overview

Ecclesiastes is a book of Wisdom, and is one of the most challenging books in the Bible. Scholars still do not agree about many things including where and when Ecclesiastes was written or what the message of the book is. In general, Ecclesiastes is a collection of personal thoughts and reflections. It was written by someone who had looked at the world carefully and decided that there is little purpose or justice or even hope in life. Everything we do in life becomes like smoke or vapor. The writer uses a Hebrew word[1] which means smoke or vapor or futility, and which is translated "vanity" in some English translations. Since life appears to be futile and meaningless, the writer suggests that we should simply do the best we can to enjoy the life we have been given, fear God, and keep his commandments.

Who wrote Ecclesiastes? Traditionally, people have said that Solomon wrote it, but his name appears nowhere in the book. The writer describes himself as having been "king over Israel" (Eccl 1:12), and refers to "all who were over Jerusalem before me" (1:16). But only David ruled over Jerusalem before Solomon,[2] and so it is unlikely that the writer was Solomon. Furthermore, the style of language in the book seems to come from the late Persian period (see OT Chronology on p. xv). Therefore, some think that the writer may have been a governor (thus a "king") over Jerusalem at that time.

The name which *does* appear in Ecclesiastes is *Qoheleth*, and this is another puzzle. The first words of the book are: "The words of *Qoheleth*, the son of David, king in Jerusalem. Vanity of vanities, says

[1]The Hebrew word is *hebel* (הֶ֫בֶל), and occurs 37 times in Ecclesiastes. In Genesis, this word is used as a name, Abel, the second son of Adam and Eve. Indeed, Abel's life was also like smoke and soon passed away.

[2]King Saul ruled at Gibeah (sometimes called "Gibeah of Saul"), not at Jerusalem. Jerusalem was later conquered by David.

Qoheleth, vanity of vanities! All is vanity" (Eccl 1:1-2). David had no son named Qoheleth, and none of his descendants bore that name. The name is found nowhere else in the Bible, but it seems to be related to the Hebrew word *qahal* (קָהָל, assembly), which is *ekklesiastes* (ἐκκλησιαστής) in Greek. That became the name of the book in the Septuagint, and the name has now come into English translations. Because of this connection to *qahal*, several suggestions have been made:

- Some think that *qahal* might refer to an "assembly" or gathering of the people, like a congregation. Thus, many English translations call Qoheleth "the Preacher." But that seems to be an unlikely suggestion; Qoheleth does not preach.
- Others have suggested that the name *Qoheleth* is related to the word *qehillah* (קְהִלָּה) found in Neh 5:7 ("I held a great *qehillah* against them"). Here, the word may mean "strong argument."[3] Thus, it has been suggested that Qoheleth means "arguer" – though he does not really argue; rather, he observes and reflects.
- Another suggestion notes that the verb *qahal* can mean not only to assemble things but to collect things. Perhaps Qoheleth was a collector of saying and proverbs.

Ecclesiastes does not mention Israel's scriptures or traditions except in two places: Eccl 5:4, where reference is made to Deut 23:21, and at the very end (Eccl 12:13) where God's commandments are mentioned. But Ecclesiastes is *used* in the traditions of Israel: it is one of the five festival scrolls and is read every year at the Feast of Booths.

Outline

The book of Ecclesiastes is a series of skeptical Wisdom reflections and does not outline well. The thoughts of Qoheleth tend to go through a cycle: something is mentioned and briefly discussed, then dropped for while as other ideas are considered. Then the first thought may return again. Thoughts are placed alongside other thoughts in patterns which change again and again. This gives the reader new perspectives and points of view to consider.

The only true structure of the book is found in a concentric "frame"

---

[3]However, English versions of Neh 5:7 usually simply translate this word "assembly."

at the very beginning and at the very end which encompasses the body of the book:

Title: "The words of the Preacher, the son of David" (Eccl 1:1)
***Inclusio*:** "Vanity of vanities, says the Preacher..." (Eccl 1:2)
Poem: "There is nothing new under the sun" (Eccl 1:3-11)
Body of the book (Eccl 1:12-11:8)
Poem: "Rejoice, O young man, in your youth" (Eccl 11:9-12:7)
***Inclusio*:** "Vanity of vanities, says the Preacher..." (Eccl 12:8)
Postscript: "Besides being wise, the Preacher also taught" (Eccl 12:9-14)

As can be seen above, there is a title at the beginning, then the first part of an *inclusio* and a poem. Then comes the body of the book, after which comes another poem, the other part of the *inclusio* and a postscript.

There also are a few distinct and very interesting units within the book of Ecclesiastes:

- *The "royal experiment*" (Eccl 1:12-2:26). Here, Qoheleth outlines his plan "to know wisdom and to know madness and folly."
- *"For everything there is a season*" (Eccl 3:1-8). Here, we are told that all things have their proper time – though we are not told how to know when that proper time has arrived.
- *"Two are better than one*" (4:9-12). This is a very short observation on how it is better to approach life as a pair of people, or a couple, rather than as an individual.
- *The decline of the "house*" (12:1-7). This is a clever poem (actually the latter part of the "Rejoice, O young man" poem), in which the aging body is compared to an old house which begins to weaken and fail.

Message

Ecclesiastes, like Job and Proverbs, is a book of Wisdom. It is a collection of thoughts and reflections which at first seem fairly secular. Ecclesiastes moves beyond Job in its questioning of life. Qoheleth often mentions God, but does not address God or seek an appointment with God as did Job. For Qoheleth, God exists but is rather distant and what God does is not completely clear. Qoheleth is, for the most part, either unaware of or not interested in Israel's scriptures or religious traditions (though we noted two exceptions above). There is enough injustice in the world to convince Qoheleth that God does not generally cause justice to rule. Yet there is a future judgment (Eccles. 11:9).

For Qoheleth, life seems to have no *ultimate* meaning, since the world is unjust and death finally reduces everything to emptiness and futility. Life is filled with limits, irony[4] and absurdity.[5] Death erases all gains. What you achieve in life eventually falls into hands of strangers or fools when you die.

So Qoheleth begins a search, a quest. He uses his wealth and position to finance a "royal experiment" in which he tries everything life has to offer – from wisdom to madness. He is asking, "What is good for people?" And, after trying everything, he finally concludes the following: although life seems to have no *ultimate* meaning, wisdom will still get you further than folly will. Furthermore, there are two things people can do to make their lot better:

1. Enjoy the life which God has given you – both the work that is placed before you as well as the leisure you find. Seek pleasure while you are able – though in moderation for, again, we will eventually face God's judgment.
2. "Fear God, and keep his commandments; for this is the whole duty of man" (Eccl 12:13).

The Old Testament sometimes asks questions it is unable to answer. Yet it knows that the questions are important, and so it asks them anyway. Ecclesiastes is one of the books which does this; to some extent, Job is, too. Qoheleth can see far but not quite far enough. He sees that one can work for a lifetime to earn money or build a house and then die; then someone else gets the money or the house. This seems to be such a waste of effort, and so Qoheleth describes life as futile and vain. And he is right – if that is all there is to our existence. What Qoheleth does not know, of course, is life after death. And he does not know of God in Christ who opens the door to that possibility. Ecclesiastes is thus a book of preparation. Qoheleth forces us to look at the emptiness of life if one lives just for earning wealth or even for gaining wisdom. He thus prepares us for, and creates a hunger for, the fullness of life eventually

---

[4]See p. 33, footnote 6, for the meaning of irony.

[5]That which is absurd is unreasonable, ridiculous and often strange. Absurdity does not make sense.

opened to us in the New Testament.

Some important texts: "Vanity of vanities..." (Eccl 1:2; 12:8); "For everything there is a season" (Eccl 3:1-8); the decline of the "house" (Eccl 12:1-7); "the end of the matter" (Eccl 12:13-14)

Verses for memory: Eccl 1:2; 3:1; 12:13

Song of Solomon

❧

Overview

"Song of Solomon" is a collection of love poems.[1] The book is sometimes called "Canticles," and title in Hebrew is "Song of Songs," which actually means "the greatest of all songs." Solomon's relationship to the book is somewhat of a puzzle. The first verse of the book says "The Song of Songs, which is Solomon's," but this may mean several things including "which is *to* Solomon" or "which is *for* Solomon."[2] The name Solomon appears six other places in the poem, but Solomon never speaks; so, again, his relationship to the book is somewhat uncertain.

Those who do speak in the poems are:

- A **woman** (who describes herself as "dark and lovely," Song 1:5)
- A **man** (described at times as a king and at times as a shepherd)
- The **"daughters of Jerusalem"** (once "daughters of Zion").

The "daughters of Jerusalem" are addressed seven times[3] by the woman, and they take part in her thinking about (and her searching for) her beloved.

The poems contain a fair amount of unusual vocabulary and *hapax legomena*,[4] and this at times makes translation difficult. But the general sense is never unclear or uncertain; the poems celebrate the (often quite sexual) love of a man and a woman. Song of Solomon is one of the

---

[1]Scholars disagree about how many poems there are, and have suggested anywhere from five to fifty.

[2]The Hebrew preposition is *le-* (-לְ), which can mean, to, for, according to, etc. See the discussion of the phrase "of David" in footnote 2 on p. 145.

[3]Eight times if you count the "daughters of Zion" reference.

[4]A *hapax legomenon* (*legomena* is the plural) is a word or phrase which appears only once in the Bible. This may make it difficult to translate, since there are no other places with which to compare the way the word is used.

festival scrolls of Israel and is read every year at Passover.

Outline

I. **Title and introduction** (the woman speaks) (Song 1:1-6)
II. **Dialogue** (the man and the woman) (Song 1:7-2:7)
III. **Monologues** (Song 2:8-5:1)
  A. Reflections by the woman (Song 2:8-3:5)
    1. About her beloved (Song 2:8-17)
    2. About losing and finding her beloved (Song 3:1-5)
  B. Description of Solomon's wedding procession (Song 3:6-11)
  C. The man describes his beloved (plus a short interchange in Song 4:16-5:1) (Song 4:1-5:1)
IV. **Dialogue** (woman and the daughters of Jerusalem) (Song 5:2-6:3)
V. **Monologue** (the man addresses the woman) (Song 6:4-12)
VI. **Dialogue** (the man and the woman) (Song 7:1-8:4)
VII. **Appendices** (additional material) (Song 8:5-14)

Message

In one sense, the Song of Solomon is not theological. Like the book of Esther, Song of Solomon never mentions God. On the other hand, the love poems celebrate God's gift of sexual love in a very healthy and unembarrassed fashion. This alone is reason enough for us to read the book, since all too often God's people seem to be uncomfortable discussing the subject of sexuality.

The book therefore does not need to be defended; it can stand upon its own merit. It fits well with the Old Testament's affirmation of the physical world as good (see Genesis 1) and of sexuality as a gift from God. (This is quite different from some ancient Greek points of view, of course, which considered the spirit good and the physical world something to be denied. The Old Testament does not hold such a point of view.)

Yet we must also recognize that for centuries both Jews and Christians *have* often interpreted Song of Solomon as a parable or allegory[5] of

---

[5]Parable and allegory are similar. But a parable often has just a single important point, whereas in an allegory we find several or many things representing other things. In Mark 4, we find examples of both. There is a parable in which Jesus compares the kingdom of God to a mustard seed which "grows up and becomes the greatest of all shrubs" (Mark 4:32). The point is

God's love for his people. Christian interpretation has often seen Christ and the Church in the poems. Until the seventeenth century A.D., this was the primary way this text was interpreted. And the book has been very popular. In the Middle Ages there were more commentaries written on Song of Solomon than on any other Old Testament book.

After the seventeenth century, it was generally recognized that the poems are indeed love poems, and that they do have sexual themes. Parabolic or allegorical interpretations were usually rejected as unfaithful to the text. In more recent years, however, many interpreters have begun to balance the parabolic or allegorical interpretation (God's love for his people) with the literal (poems of human love). While today almost everyone understands that Song of Solomon is a collection of love poems, it is also recognized that there are indeed places in the Old Testament where God's covenant relationship with Israel is described as a marriage,[6] and where God is described as "jealous" when Israel worships idols.[7]

Modern interpretation generally recognizes that texts can have more than one meaning for the reader. Thus, as long as one is aware that the original meaning of these poems is a celebration of love between and man and a woman, one may also see in these chapters an intensity and depth of love which illustrates God's love for his people – and which

---

merely the tremendous growth of the kingdom of God from very small beginnings. But just before that parable, he tells another one which is really an allegory: the sower and the seed (Mark 4:3-8). In this allegory, every detail has a special meaning: the seed means the word of God, and the birds and the rocky ground and the thorns and the good soil each have their meanings, as Jesus explains in vv. 13-20.

[6]For instance, Hosea 1-3; Isa 1:21; 54:4-8; Ezekiel 16 and 23.

[7]Jealousy is a very human emotion, and it seems strange to apply the word to God. But this term is used to describe God's reaction when his people turn to idols. At this point, the people's unfaithfulness is compared to unfaithfulness within a marriage. Unfaithful husbands or wives can create jealous feelings in their spouses. Likewise, when Israel went after idols, this unfaithfulness provoked God to anger, and this divine anger is thus called "jealousy." Again, this word is used only when discussing the problem of idolatry. See Exod 20:4-5; 34:14; Num 25:10-13; Deut 4:23-24; 5:8-10; 6:14-15; Josh 24:19-20. The Num 25:10-13 text at first does not seem to refer to idol worship, but this comes at the end of the infamous Baal of Peor incident, and one needs to read the first verses of Numbers 25 to see what was happening. In the New Testament, the theme is found once in 1 Cor 10:19-22.

can call God's people to respond in love to God.

Some important texts: The whole poem should be read; Song 2:8-17 is a good representative text.

Verses for memory: Song of Solomon 2:4; 8:6

Prophets (and Lamentations)

-An Overview-

Some terminology.

We noted on p. 3 that the book order in the Hebrew Scriptures differs from that of the Christian Bible. This includes the books of the prophets. The Christian Bible divides the prophets into two groups: Major Prophets (large books) and Minor Prophets (small books):

Major Prophets: Isaiah, Jeremiah, (Lamentations,) Ezekiel, Daniel
Minor Prophets: Hosea, Joel, Amos, Obadiah, Jonah, Micah, Nahum, Habakkuk, Zephaniah, Haggai, Zechariah, Malachi

The Hebrew Scriptures also divide the prophets into two groups, but in a different way:

Former Prophets: the Deuteronomistic History (Joshua, Judges, Samuel, Kings)
Latter Prophets: Isaiah, Jeremiah, Ezekiel, The Twelve (that is, the "Minor Prophets")

This division is also discussed on p. 3. The major difference between the Jewish and Christian prophetic canons[1] is that Jews do not include either Lamentations or Daniel among the prophets. Indeed, Lamentations is not a book of prophecy; rather, it is a collection of poems lamenting the destruction of Jerusalem. However, since it was thought that Jeremiah wrote Lamentations, the book was placed after Jeremiah in the Septuagint. Daniel is unique, and its placement among the Writings is discussed below, on page 193.

The "latter prophets" are sometimes called the "classical prophets." They are also sometimes called the "writing prophets" because "pre-

[1]See p. 3, footnote 6, for "canon."

classical" or "former" prophets such as Samuel, Nathan and Elijah did not leave any writings.[2]

The major *theological* difference between the Former and Latter Prophets is the difference of attitude. The books of the Former Prophets describe Israel's early days as a nation, and are optimistic about the future. The nation was young, and the theme of these books could be described as "Out of Egypt, into the land." The Latter Prophets were different. They lived during troubled times, when the nation was older and had sinned often against God. They are usually *not* optimistic, and warn that a good future is not guaranteed if the people continue to reject God. Their theme eventually becomes "Out of Egypt, into the land, *back to Egypt*" – where "Egypt" means exile in Assyria or Babylon.

The latter or classical prophets are generally found in three periods of Israel's history: in the **late eighth century**, before Assyria's destruction of Samaria; in the **late seventh century**, before and during the fall of Jerusalem to Babylon; and in the **late sixth century**, during and after the exile in Babylon:

Period	Location	Prophets
Late Eighth Century (750-700 B.C.)	**In Israel (north):** **In Judah (south):**	Amos and Hosea 1 Isaiah (of Jerusalem), Micah
Late Seventh Century (650-600 B.C.)	**In Judah:** **In Babylon:**	Jeremiah, Obadiah, Nahum, Habakkuk, Zephaniah Ezekiel
Late Sixth Century (550-500 B.C.)	**In Babylon (before 538 B.C.):** 2 Isaiah **In Jerusalem (after 538 B.C.):** 3 Isaiah, Joel, Haggai, Zechariah, Malachi	

The matter of 1, 2 and 3 Isaiah, as well as the absence of Jonah and Daniel in the table, are discussed below in the chapters on those books.

In the pages which follow, we will be considering the "major" and "minor" prophets (i.e., the "latter prophets" of the Hebrew Scriptures). Since we are following the order of books found in the Christian Bible, we will also include both Lamentations and Daniel in this section.

---

[2]The phrase "writing prophets" is not technically correct, because in most cases the words of these prophets were collected by others, and they themselves did not write anything.

Who were the prophets?

The prophets were men and women who received messages from God which they then delivered to the leaders or to the people of Israel and Judah. Most of the prophets are found at the time of the kings, though a few are found in the post-exilic period. They were not fortune-tellers, though at times they spoke of future events. They were not merely social critics, though they often spoke harshly and strongly against the wealthy and the nation's leaders when they abused the poor.

Sometimes earlier leaders such as Moses, Aaron, Miriam and even Abraham are called "prophets"[3] by later writers. This is because at times they also carried God's message to the people. However, they were not prophets in the sense we are considering here.

The prophets became one of the major institutions of Israel. Yet they are almost always found standing over and against the other institutions such as the kings, priests and wise men. Thus, the prophets were usually "outsiders," though we do find several of them standing alongside and advising kings (for instance, "pre-classical" prophets such as Samuel and Nathan and even "classical" Isaiah[4]). They warned the leadership classes because of their abuse of the poor and because they allowed the worship of false gods. They criticized the priests for putting false hope in sacrifice when God wanted changed hearts and justice. They condemned the wise men of Israel for being too closely connected with those who were wealthy and privileged.

At times they even had to speak against a class of "professional prophets" in Israel and Judah. Kings often employed these professional prophets who then spoke words which were pleasing to the king (1 Kgs 22:6; 2 Kgs 3:13). There are many strong words against those who falsely claimed to speak as prophets (Isa 9:15; 28:7; 29:10; Jer 2:8, 26-27; 5:13, 31 and many other places). At times, it must have been very difficult for the people to know which prophet was speaking for God (see, for instance, Jeremiah 28).

Because of the problem of false prophecy, we find that the prophets sometimes did not use the name "prophet" for themselves. Amos rejected the title completely (Amos 7:14), and often the first verse of a prophetic book does not mention the word "prophet." For instance, we

---

[3]See, for instance, Gen 20:7; Exod 7:1; 15:20; Deut 18:15,18; 34:10.

[4]Isaiah 7; see also 2 Kings 19-20. Even Jeremiah, who was usually rejected by the kings, was three times asked for advice by King Zedekiah in the final days of Jerusalem (Jer 21:1-7; 37:16-21; 38:14-28).

read "The vision of Isaiah the son of Amoz" (Isa 1:1) or "The words of Jeremiah, the son of Hilkiah, of the priests who were in Anathoth" (Jer 1:1). Finally, there came a day when people became suspicious of all who called themselves prophets and even threatened to put them to death (Zech 13:2-6; see p. 254). But that was late in Israel's history.

What did they believe?

The prophets believed that the people were responsible before God, that the word of the LORD was powerful, that God was powerful in history, and that they themselves were called to bring a message from this powerful God to his people.

Responsibility of God's people. The prophets believed that God's covenant people were to be responsible people, and this responsibility applied to two main areas:

- **Religious responsibility:** the people were to be faithful to the LORD who had saved them from Egypt and who had made them his people. Thus, the prophets spoke out strongly against **idolatry** or any involvement with the gods of other nations.
- **Social responsibility:** God had been merciful to his people; thus, they were to show mercy to others. The prophets spoke strongly against **injustice or any oppression** of those who were weak and poor (especially the widow, the orphan, and the sojourner).

In addition, the prophets often spoke against relationships with **foreign nations**, since treaty relationships involved acceptance of the other nation's gods. Thus, when the prophets oppose foreign relationships it is really part of their message about religious responsibility and their opposition to idols.[5]

The word of the LORD. The prophets believed that God's word was powerful, and that it accomplished his will in the world. Samuel said God rejected Saul because Saul had "rejected the word of the LORD" (1 Sam 15:26). When Nathan came before David to accuse him of sin, he did not merely say that David had sinned against Uriah. Rather, in taking Bathsheba, David had "despised the word of the LORD" (2 Sam 12:9). This was a very serious matter, and it led to the death of the child

---

[5]See, for instance, the concern expressed in Exod 23:31-33; 34:12-16.

in spite of David's fervent prayers (2 Sam 12:14-23[6]). Other pre-classical examples are found in the confrontations of Elijah and king Ahab in 1 Kings 17-19, 21 and the very interesting encounter of the prophet Micaiah with kings Ahab and Jehoshaphat in 1 Kings 22. Major classical texts are Jer 23:29 ("Is not my word like fire, says the LORD, and like a hammer that breaks a rock in pieces?") and Isa 55:10-11 ("my word ... shall not return to me empty, but it shall accomplish that which I purpose....").

God is active in history. The prophets believed that God was involved within history, and that he raised up nations and brought them down. He was able to use even nations such as Assyria and Babylon to punish his own people, as Jeremiah stated so clearly. The messages of the prophets therefore changed according to the period of history in which they lived. Three types of messages may be noted:

- **Words of warning** are found among earlier classical prophets as they tried to get the people to change their ways.
- **Words of judgment** came next, when the people refused to listen.
- **Words of hope** are found after God's judgment had fallen upon the people, especially when they were in exile in Babylon.

Called to bear a message. Finally, the prophets believed that God had called them to be his messengers. Thus, they used whatever methods they could to carry the "word of the LORD" to those to whom God sent them.

What methods did they use?

The prophets used several methods to get the people to listen.

- They spoke in places where they knew there would be many people, such as the market or the temple.
- They used visual examples (Isaiah walked barefoot and naked for three years; Jeremiah shattered a pot, and buried some underwear; Ezekiel built a model of Jerusalem and set a battle against it).

---

[6]This text is also important in discussions of death, the "living dead," and ancestors. When the child dies, David stops praying and fasting, and the people ask why. His answer is "Why should I fast? Can I bring him back again? I shall go to him, but he will not return to me." The dead do not return. We will one day go to them and will rejoice together in the Resurrection, but before that great event they do not return to us in this life.

- They used popular forms[7] such as love songs or courtroom scenes to carry their messages.

One of the most popular forms was the "messenger formula" used by messengers of the king: "Thus says the king; hear the word of the king" (see 2 Kgs 18:28-29). When those words were spoken by a representative of the king, people sat up and listened. Thus, the prophets made use of this form and would often begin their messages by crying out, "Thus says the LORD; hear the word of the LORD."

The following pages present overviews of the prophets in the order found in the (Christian) Old Testament. As mentioned above, both Lamentations and Daniel will also be included in this section.

---

[7]See p. 58, footnote 4, for "form."

Isaiah

❧

Overview

The book of Isaiah has 66 chapters, and much has been written concerning their structure. Many students of the Bible have noted three major sections in the book of Isaiah, and suggest that they were written by several different people at three different times.

One of the strongest pieces of evidence for this division is found at the beginning of Isaiah 40, where a surprising change takes place. Although Isaiah 1-39 comes from the eighth century B.C., the message of Isaiah 40 and following is an announcement to the sixth century exiles in Babylon that they are about to return home again. Thus, many would divide the book as follows:

I. **Isaiah 1-39 is usually called First Isaiah (1 Isaiah)**, and contains events and prophecies from Isaiah of Jerusalem during the approximate period 742-690 B.C.

II. **Isaiah 40-55 is often called Second Isaiah (2 Isaiah)**, and may come from a period approximately 150-200 years later (some time before 538 B.C.), when the people of Judah are in exile in Babylon. If this is indeed the case, then the actual name of this great prophet is unknown.

III. **Isaiah 56-66 is often called Third Isaiah (3 Isaiah)**. These chapters come from a time after the people have returned to Jerusalem from Babylon. It may be from the same person responsible for 2 Isaiah, and, if so, then it was written shortly after 538 B.C. On the other hand, it may have been written perhaps a century later, around the time of Ezra and Nehemiah.

Others, however, have noted that the book does not really divide quite this neatly. There is a certain amount of material in Isaiah 1-39 which seems to fit better in Second Isaiah. In addition, the "surprising change" which takes place at Isa 40:1 is perhaps a false surprise. It only appears to be something completely new because a block of historical material (Isaiah 36-39, found also in 2 Kgs 18:13; 18:17-20:19) has been inserted just before it. If that block of material had not been added, then the end of Isaiah 35 would flow very nicely into Isaiah 40, and we would not notice the change at Isa 40:1.

Many today seek to study Isaiah as a single literary unit. In doing so, they will often accept the idea that there were originally two or three "Isaiahs," but they will point out that the editor who put the three sections together did so with a purpose. The structure of the book is not an accident. Thus, they say, if we want to hear the book as the editor wanted it to be heard, we must finally read it as a single book.

Since the book of Isaiah does seem to contain material written over several centuries, the discussion below follows the assumptions found in the three-point outline above. This is because the historical arguments make sense, and because students of Isaiah should be familiar with the very common use of the terms 1 Isaiah, 2 Isaiah and 3 Isaiah. Students should also be aware, however, that there are today several "schools of thought" concerning how we should finally read the book of Isaiah.

First Isaiah (Isaiah 1-39)

In the last half of the eighth century B.C. (750-700 B.C.), the northern kingdom of Israel was at the peak of its economic development. It was also a time when the wealthy oppressed the poor in both Israel and Judah. Two prophets in the north (Amos and Hosea) and two in the south (Isaiah and Micah) spoke words of warning and judgment. Isaiah and Micah sometimes share the same words and so perhaps they knew each other.

Unlike most other prophets, Isaiah seems to have been politically and socially well-connected in Jerusalem. It is possible that he (like Jeremiah) came from a family of priests, since his call (Isaiah 6) came while he was in the temple[1] "in the year that king Uzziah died" (i.e., 742 B.C.). He had access to the kings (Isa 7:3; 37:1-2) and a good relationship with King Hezekiah (2 Kings 19-20).

---

[1]Only priests entered the temple. The rest of the people of Israel never did. See p. 46.

The Assyrian Invasions of the Eighth Century (745-701 B.C.)

(Review the maps on pp. 10, 13 and 93)

745 B.C. Tiglath-Pilesar III becomes king of Assyria, and starts expanding the Assyrian empire

732 B.C. Damascus (capital of Syria) is conquered by Assyria

727 B.C. Tiglath-Pilesar III dies and his son, Shalmaneser V, becomes king

722 B.C. Samaria (capital of Israel) is conquered by Assyria
Shalmaneser V dies, and his brother Sargon II becomes king
Those remaining in Samaria rebel against Assyria

720 B.C. Sargon II destroys Samaria and deports its people

705 B.C. Sargon II dies and his son Sennacherib (705-681) becomes king

701 B.C. Sennacherib attacks Judah and Jerusalem

Two political events dominate the time of First Isaiah. First, around the year 734 B.C. Syria and the northern kingdom of Israel (also called Ephraim) tried to attack Judah. It was at the time of this "Syro-Ephraimite war" that Isaiah spoke his famous "young woman"[2] prophecy to encourage faithless King Ahaz (Isaiah 7-8). The other political event was even larger: the rise of Assyria in Mesopotamia. Assyria eventually dominated the ANE, destroyed Israel and its capital city Samaria, and also threatened Jerusalem for more than three decades (734-701 B.C.).

Isaiah encouraged faithful King Hezekiah during this crucial

---

[2]Here there is an important difference between the Hebrew text and the Septuagint. Isaiah's words to Ahaz in Isa 7:14 are (in Hebrew) "Behold, a *young woman* (Heb: *almah*, עַלְמָה) shall conceive and bear a son." (The Hebrew word for "virgin" is *bethulah*, בְּתוּלָה and is not found here). Five hundred years later, the Septuagint translators translated *almah* as *parthenos* (παρθένος), which, in Greek, means "virgin." Matthew (and the early church) used the Septuagint, of course, and thus we find the word "virgin" in Matt 1:23.

Isaiah's prophecy may originally have been fulfilled in Isa 8:3-4. The name of the child is different there, but note verse 8 and again verse 10. Certainly the prophecy had to have its primary fulfillment in the lifetime of Ahaz and Isaiah (Isa 7:16 shows this). But the decision of the translators of the Septuagint to use the word παρθένος was an important and influential one. Was it just chance? Was it bad translating? Or was it the work of the Holy Spirit? Whatever the case, Matthew and later Christians recognized in this translation a prophecy of the virgin birth of Christ.

period, declaring that the mighty armies of Assyria would not succeed against much weaker Jerusalem. (This dramatic event is described in 2 Kgs 18:13-19:37). Jerusalem was indeed spared, and Isaiah's words were remembered for generations. But this had both positive and negative results. On the positive side, Jerusalem, its people, and its temple were spared, and this was recognized as a deliverance by God. On the negative side, however, this led many to believe that Jerusalem and the temple were inviolable,[3] eternally safe from harm – even if God's people were unfaithful. This "Zion[4] theology" soon stood alongside the Davidic covenant in the minds of many, and it eventually produced an unhealthy, presumptuous and arrogant attitude. The people would one day have to learn that merely saying "This is the temple of the LORD, the temple of the LORD, the temple of the LORD" (Jer 7:4) was not enough.

First Isaiah has several important sections. It begins with a series of prophecies against Judah and Jerusalem. Then, immediately after Isaiah's call (chapter 6) comes his encounter with Ahaz, mentioned above. This is followed by more judgments against Judah, Israel and even Assyria. Prophecies against both foreign and local enemies are found in Isaiah 13-23.

Then comes Isaiah 24-27, which is quite different from anything else. It describes a universal judgment, and includes unusual apocalyptic[5] images. Thus, this section is often called "Isaiah's Apocalypse." Isaiah 28-32 contains a group of oracles which includes warnings against relying upon Egypt for help.

The final chapters of First Isaiah are also rather unique. They contain words of hope and deliverance, and Isaiah 35 sounds very much like Second Isaiah (below). In fact, as noted at the beginning of the chapter, the end of Isaiah 35 would fit very well with the beginning of Isaiah 40 and perhaps belongs with it. However, the insertion of a section of historical material at this point (Isaiah 36-39[6]) creates the appearance of a break which may not have been there originally.

---

[3]Something which is "inviolable" is something which cannot be violated, harmed or destroyed.

[4]Mt Zion is the high area of Jerusalem on which the temple was built. Thus, "Zion" refers either to Jerusalem or to the temple area.

[5]See the introduction to Daniel (p. 193) for a discussion of apocalyptic.

[6]These chapters (except for Isa 38:9-20) seem to have been copied to or from 2 Kgs 18:13; 18:17-20:19.

Second Isaiah (Isaiah 40-55)

When we turn to Isaiah 40, we move forward 150-200 years and find ourselves among the exiles in Babylon. First Isaiah was concerned with eighth century moral and ethical issues; Second Isaiah is concerned with a sixth century theological crisis. Around the year 600 B.C., Babylon triumphed over Judah and Jerusalem. The city and its temple were destroyed, and the house of David and the other leadership of Judah were taken to Babylon. What had happened to God's promises?

Some time before 538 B.C., God answered that question by calling a prophet and giving him a message of comfort. The message: the period of exile was almost over; the people should prepare to return to Judah and Jerusalem (Isa 40:1ff). The name of this prophet is unknown, although many think that he was an even greater prophet than Isaiah of Jerusalem (1 Isaiah). His words (Isaiah 40-55) are dependent upon the words of 1 Isaiah (Isaiah 1-39), and so they have been placed after those words. Therefore we call him 2 Isaiah. Twice he mentions the name of Cyrus of Persia (Isa 44:28; 45:1) as the one God will use to send his people back from Babylon.

And there is something else: throughout 2 Isaiah a "servant" is mentioned. God speaks through him, and through him even forgiveness of sins may come. We will say more about this Servant in the "Message" section, below.

Third Isaiah (Isaiah 56-66)

The words of Third Isaiah are very similar to those of Second Isaiah, but the situation is quite different. It appears that the people have now returned and are living in Judah and Jerusalem. But they are again somewhat discouraged, since things have not happened as they were expecting. The wealthy and powerful are once again beginning to oppress the poor and the weak. And the people are returning to some of the false worship practices of the past.

Third Isaiah may be the same person as Second Isaiah, writing a couple of decades later (the rebuilding of the temple has already begun). Or he may be a disciple of Second Isaiah who writes in his style. He encourages the righteous, and tells them that God's plans for them will be fulfilled. Others will soon return from exile, the wealth of the nations will be brought to Jerusalem, and the temple "shall be called a house of prayer for all peoples" (Isa 56:7).

Outline

I. Isaiah 1-39 ("First Isaiah") Isaiah of Jerusalem, who prophesied to Judah and Israel in the eighth century B.C.
   A. Isaiah's oracles against Israel and Judah – and his call (1-12)
   B. Oracles against foreign and domestic enemies (13-23)
   C. Isaiah's "Apocalypse": the Day of the LORD[7] (24-27)
   D. Oracles including warnings against alliance with Egypt (28-32)
   E. Later prophecies; some are similar to 2nd Isaiah (33-35)
   F. Historical appendix, cf. 2 Kgs 18:13-20:19 (36-39)

II. Isaiah 40-55 ("Second Isaiah") about 150-200 years later, while the people were in Babylon

III. Isaiah 56-66 ("Third Isaiah") some time later, when the people have returned to Jerusalem

Message

The book of Isaiah is important for many reasons. Like other prophets, Isaiah brought strong words from a holy God. He condemned oppression of the poor and weak, as well as worship of false gods. He warned against putting trust in Egypt, rather than in the God of Israel.

When Syria and Israel (Ephraim) threatened Judah, Isaiah predicted that God would save Jerusalem. This promise came in his "young woman" prophecy of Isaiah 7. His prophecy proved true. More than seven centuries later, because of the way the word for "young woman" was translated in the Septuagint, early Christians recognized in Isa 7:14 a prophecy of the virgin birth of Christ.[8]

When the huge army of Assyria came up against Jerusalem, Isaiah again prophesied that God would deliver Jerusalem. Again he was right, and his words were remembered, and collected, and treasured.

Isaiah ridicules idolatry (Isa 40:19-20; 41:7). In Isa 44:9-20, he shakes his head at the foolishness of those who use one piece of wood to make both an idol and also firewood. Such false gods cannot begin to stand before the God of Israel who created the world and all that is in it (Isa 45:5-7, 18).[9]

---

[7]The day of the LORD is discussed on p. 209.

[8]See the discussion of this matter in footnote 2 on p. 173.

[9]As noted above on p. 28, there is an infinite distinction between the Creator and his creation. God created the world, but is not the same as the world. Those who make idols confuse created things with the Creator.

For Christians, Isaiah's messianic passages are the most well-known. Actually, the word "messiah"[10] appears only once in Isaiah: he says that Cyrus of Persia is God's messiah (Isa 45:1), since Cyrus is God's chosen instrument to bring his people back to Jerusalem. But there are other passages which, although they do not use the word "messiah," do refer to God's promise to send a future "child" or "son" or "prince" or "shoot from the stump of Jesse" (see Isa 9:6-7; 11:1-16). In addition, there are Isaiah's famous "servant songs" (Isa 42:1-9; 49:1-7; 50:4-11 and 52:13-53:12). The identity of Isaiah's "servant" is one of the great puzzles of the Old Testament. Some think (Second) Isaiah may have been thinking of Hezekiah, Jeremiah or even of himself. Others think he considered the nation Israel to have been the "suffering servant."[11] But the texts (especially the fourth song) seem to go beyond any human or historical figures of Isaiah's time, and Christians see complete fulfillment only in Jesus Christ.

Isaiah was remembered for his prophecies which guaranteed the safety of Jerusalem (against the attacks of Syria, Israel and Assyria). What would happen a century later when those words were remembered at a time when another prophet – Jeremiah – was prophesying that God would *not* save Jerusalem?

Some important texts: Isaiah's call (Isa 6:1-13); the "young woman" prophecy (Isa 7:1-17); "unto us a child is born" (Isa 9:1-7); "a shoot from the stump of Jesse" (Isa 11:1-9); "comfort my people" (Isa 40:1-11); the four "servant songs" (Isa 42:1-9; 49:1-7; 50:4-11; 52:13-53:12); "I am the LORD, and there is no other" (Isa 45:5-7); "new heavens and new earth" (Isa 65:17-25).

Verses for memory: Isa 7:14; 40:1-5; 45:5,7

---

[10]The Hebrew word is *mashiach* (מָשִׁיחַ), but the RSV and NRSV never translate the word as "messiah." Rather, they use the word "anointed." Thus, in Isa 45:1 we read "Thus says the LORD to his anointed (*mashiach*), to Cyrus...." For more information on *mashiach*, see p. 9, footnote 10.

[11]This is because Isaiah seemed to know who the servant was, since he often speaks of him in the past tense. Isaiah 53 is particularly interesting because the servant dies and yet Isaiah speaks of him in the past, present and future tenses.

Jeremiah

❧

Overview

The times. The prophet Jeremiah lived through the most dramatic and traumatic period of Judah's history: the last quarter of the seventh century and the first 15 years or so of the sixth. That is, his ministry covered the period 627-586 B.C., just over 40 years. This period saw the collapse of Assyria (which had destroyed Israel and its capital, Samaria) and the rise of Babylon (which would destroy Judah, its capital, Jerusalem, and its temple). Note the following sequence of events, which shows how stressful the period of Jeremiah was:

The Final Years of Judah (627-586 B.C.)

(Review the map on p. 93)

627 B.C. Ashurbanipal, Assyria's last powerful king, dies.
Judah and other nations revolt against Assyria.
Reforms of King Josiah begin.
The Call of Jeremiah

622 B.C. An early edition of Deuteronomy is discovered in the temple.

614 B.C. The Medes destroy Asshur (a major city in Assyria).

612 B.C. The Medes destroy Nineveh, capital city of Assyria.

609 B.C. Babylon challenges weakened Assyria for control of Mesopotamia.
Pharaoh Neco marches north out of Egypt to help Assyria.
King Josiah (who wants Assyria to collapse) tries to stop Neco and is killed at Megiddo.

605 B.C. The army of Babylon destroys the army of Egypt at Carchemish.
Babylon conquers most of the Ancient Near East.

598 B.C. King Jehoiakim rebels against Babylon and is killed.

597 B.C. The first group of exiles is taken from Jerusalem to Babylon.

587 B.C. King Zedekiah rebels against Babylon, is blinded and taken to Babylon.

586 B.C. Babylon destroys Jerusalem and the temple and takes Judah's leadership to Babylon.

Jeremiah remains in Jerusalem to help the survivors.

The survivors rebel one more time and must flee to Egypt. They take Jeremiah with them.

Jeremiah's life. Jeremiah came from a family of priests, but he did not enjoy close relationships with kings as did Isaiah. He was young when he was called (Jer 1:7), and he served as a prophet for more than 40 years. He began to prophesy in the thirteenth year of Josiah (Jer 1:2). Five years later, during the reforms of Josiah, the "book of the law" (most likely an early version of Deuteronomy and its covenant) was discovered in the temple (2 Kgs 22:8, see p. 63), encouraging further reforms.

Jeremiah soon became an "evangelist" of the Deuteronomistic covenant, calling the people of Judah and the city of Jerusalem to obedience (Jer 11:1-8). Later, he became discouraged with their superficial response and, therefore, proclaimed the need for a *new* covenant (Jer 31:31-34). Jeremiah expected that this new covenant would still be based upon the law, but that it would not be written upon stone. Rather, it would be written "upon their hearts"[1] and thus "they shall all know me ... says the LORD" (vv. 33-34).

The book of Jeremiah gives a clear picture of his life. He suffered much, and sometimes became discouraged and complained to God (Jer 20:7-18). He was put in stocks (Jer 20:1-6), his written words were burned (Jer 36:21-25) and then he himself was thrown into a muddy pit to die (Jer 38:4-6), though he was later rescued. He wept for his people (Jer 8:18-9:3), and so he is sometimes called "the weeping prophet."

Throughout the book, Jeremiah uses common objects and images as powerful visual examples: underwear(!) (Jer 13:1-11), a potter (Jer 18:1-11), the shattering of a clay pot (Jeremiah 19), the buying of a field (a rare sign of hope, Jer 32:6-44).

His suffering during the final days of Jerusalem is recorded in detail in Jeremiah 37-44 (cf. Jer 21:1-10; 32; 34). Jeremiah 45 brings a short and sharp word to Jeremiah's secretary Baruch who had expected better things for himself. Finally, the Babylonians destroyed Jerusalem and took its leadership to Babylon. Jeremiah chose to stay behind and helped the Jerusalem survivors (Jer 40:1-6). However, some of the people tried to rebel again against Babylon and, when the rebellion failed, they fled to Egypt. Although this was against Jeremiah's advice,

---

[1]In Hebrew, the "heart" generally refers to a person's mind and thoughts, not to their emotions. Thus, Jeremiah's expectation is that people will simply *know* the law and will not have to learn it.

they not only fled but also took Jeremiah and Baruch with them (Jer 43:1-7). Even in Egypt, the people refused to listen to Jeremiah (Jer 44:15-19); it is assumed that he died there.

The text. Prophets generally spoke their words, and others wrote them down. But Jeremiah often wrote his own words or else dictated them to Baruch, his secretary. One reason he did so was because, at least at one point, he was barred from entering the temple (Jer 36:5).

Apparently, the words of Jeremiah ended up on several scrolls, and as a result the present book is not clearly organized. It has been compared to a library with books scattered around on tables rather than organized on shelves. The LXX version is shorter than the Hebrew and is in a different order. It may have come from an older Hebrew edition which we no longer have today. It has been suggested that the LXX may represent the copy taken by Jeremiah and Baruch to Egypt, and the Hebrew may represent the copy taken by the exiles to Babylon.

If you are using the LXX, you will find a chapter by chapter comparison in J R Lundbom "Jeremiah, Book of" in *ABD* 3:708.

Outline

The book does not outline especially well, but it has a generally concentric structure with the "Book of Consolations" (words of hope) at the center (see below). That is, its order is not chronological; instead, it is according to type of literature or sometimes type of audience. In addition, the major set of oracles against Judah (section B) is framed by visions at the beginning and end:

- The visions of the almond[2] rod and the boiling pot (Jer 1:11-14)
- The vision of the basket of summer fruit (Jeremiah 24)

A **Jeremiah's Call** (Jer 1:1-10)
- B **Oracles** against Judah (Jer 1:11-24:10)(note framing above)
  - C **Narratives** (Jeremiah 25-29)
    - D **Book of Consolations** (hope) (Jeremiah 30-33)
  - C' **Narratives** (Jeremiah 34-45)(compare Jer 39 to 2 Kgs 25)
- B' **Oracles** against foreign nations (Jeremiah 46-51)

A' **Historical conclusion** (Jeremiah 52)(compare to 2 Kgs 24:18-25:30)

---

[2]Visions sometimes involve a play on words. The word for "almond" is *shaqed* (שָׁקֵד), and God uses it because he is "watching" (*shoqed*, שֹׁקֵד) over Israel. See the footnotes in the RSV and NRSV. See also p. 215 footnote 4.

Message

The tension of two covenants. Jeremiah was a southerner, but he lived near the border with the north and his theology shows this. He was influenced by the prophet Hosea who had spoken to Israel a century earlier. Another important influence upon Jeremiah's basic theology was the discovery of the early edition of Deuteronomy with its conditional Mosaic covenant.[3] The people's possession of the land depended upon obedience to this covenant. However, this understanding led to tension with the (southern) Davidic covenant and with temple (Zion[4]) theology. Deuteronomy's theology had conditions, but Davidic and Zion theology were unconditional. This tension can be seen in Jeremiah's famous temple sermon.[5] Jer 7:9-10 says that having the temple does not guarantee God's blessing and protection if

> you steal, murder, commit adultery, swear falsely, burn incense to Baal, and go after other gods that you have not known, and then come and stand before me in this house, which is called by my name, and say, 'We are delivered!' – only to go on doing all these abominations.

The people were taking the temple and the Davidic covenant for granted, and so Jeremiah cried out against idolatry (Jer 2:8-13, 26-28; 11:12; 14:22) and issues of injustice (Jer 5:1-5, 26-29). God is a righteous judge (Jer 11:20) and he will not ignore these things. Repentance is possible (Jer 18:7-8); yet "the heart is deceitful above all things"(Jer 17:9) and people cannot change themselves (Jer 8:4-7; 13:23).

True and false prophets. A major and serious question in Jeremiah's day was, "Who speaks for God?" The people remembered that God had promised through Isaiah, a century before, that Jerusalem would not be destroyed. But now God was saying something different through Jeremiah. Jeremiah said God was using Babylon to punish Jerusalem, and that the city and the temple *would* be destroyed. Who should the people believe? The false prophets were preaching "Peace, peace where there is no peace" (Jer 6:14; 8:11). See especially the dramatic confrontation between Jeremiah and Hananiah in Jeremiah 28

---

[3]As already mentioned, this "book of the law" was found in the temple during Josiah's reforms (2 Kgs 22:8-11). It helped shape and direct those reforms and seems to have had a great impact upon Jeremiah.

[4]See p. 174 for "Zion theology."

[5]Jeremiah 7 has the sermon and Jeremiah 26 has the details of what happened.

– where at one point even Jeremiah is unsure who is right and goes home (Jer 28:10-11). But Jeremiah continued to warn of the approaching "foe from the north,"[6] and he even recommended surrender to Babylon (Jer 38:17-23). The people and their leaders may try to resist this message, but God's word had tremendous power (Jer 1:12; 4:28), it was like a fire and a hammer (Jer 23:29), and it would come to pass.

Major themes. Jeremiah is remembered for

- Prophecies that Judah, Jerusalem and the temple would be destroyed and the people exiled to Babylon (Jer 5:15-17; 7:11-15; 13:1-14; 20:3-6; 24:4-10);
- Prophecies that Judah would then return from exile after seventy years (25:11-12; 29:10). Daniel later picks up on this: Dan 9:2,24;
- Encouraging the people to settle in and pray for Babylon until their time of exile is complete and they return (29:1-14, cf 24:4-7);
- Weeping for his people (8:18-9:3);
- Complaining to God (20:7-18).

But he is also remembered for his words of hope in the "book of consolations" (Jeremiah 30-33) – especially for his conviction that the old Deuteronomistic covenant was now broken and a "new covenant" was needed (31:31-34). The new covenant would still be based on law, however. The major difference Jeremiah expects, between the old and new covenants, is that the new covenant would now be written on human hearts. That is, it would be written within us, rather than on stone tablets. Thus, it will be known by all God's people and will not have to be taught. It will be more effective because it will be a matter of internal conviction rather than external enforcement.

But again, this new covenant will still be based upon the law. Jeremiah remains with the tension between the old (and now broken) covenant of Deuteronomy, and the remaining covenant with David (Jer 33:21). He does not yet foresee how the coming of the New Covenant will take shape as the Gospel through Jesus Christ. That day would arrive much later, as we noted on the first page of this book, and would

---

[6]Jer 1:13-17; 4:6; 6:1,22; 10:22; 13:20; etc. Mesopotamia and Babylon were, of course, to the east, not to the north. But traders and armies followed the Fertile Crescent, and thus were always seen coming from the north. Review the maps found on pp. 10 and 93.

give rise to the names Old and New Testament.[7]

Some important texts: temple sermon (Jeremiah 7; 26); weeping for his people (Jer 8:18-9:3); "seventy years" prophecies (Jer 25:11-12; 29:10-14); conflict with Hananiah (Jeremiah 28); New Covenant (Jer 31:31-34)

Verses for memory: Jer 29:11; Jer 31:31-34

---

[7]The names Old and New *Testament* come about through the Latin translation of the Bible known as the Vulgate. In the Vulgate, the words "new covenant" are translated "foedus novum" in Jer 31:31, but when this verse is then quoted in Heb 8:8 the words "new covenant" are translated "testamentum novum" or "new testament." And, indeed, the writings which came about as a result of the life, death and resurrection of Jesus – the Gospels, the book of Acts, and the letters which follow – were recognized by the early church as the very "new covenant/testament" Jeremiah had predicted.

Lamentations

❧

Overview

The book of Lamentations is a five-chapter poem of lament, written by someone who witnessed the Babylonian destruction of Jerusalem. The writer grieves and does not fully understand, though he does confess that he and his people have sinned and also expresses faith and hope in God.

The translators of the LXX felt that Jeremiah wrote Lamentations because Jeremiah also at times expressed grief (Jer 8:18-9:3), and so they placed Lamentations immediately after Jeremiah. The Hebrew Scriptures do not place Lamentations after Jeremiah, however. Furthermore, while the writer of Lamentations recognizes that the people's sin lay behind the destruction, he still seems to be somewhat puzzled about what has taken place. Therefore it seems unlikely that Jeremiah wrote Lamentations, since Jeremiah had no doubt about why God destroyed Jerusalem. Also, the references in Lamentations to the sins of the people are not as specific as they are in Jeremiah.

Chapter 1	**Chapter 2**	**Chapter 3**	**Chapter 4**	**Chapter 5**
22 acrostic verses Community lament	22 acrostic verses Community lament	66 acrostic verses Individual lament	22 acrostic verses Community lament	22 verses Community lament
		Words of hope in the center: "Great is thy faithfulness" vv. 22-27		

The five chapters are carefully structured. Chapters 1, 2, 4 and 5 each have 22 verses, and the central chapter, chapter 3, has 66 verses.

All chapters except chapter 5 are acrostic poems.[1] In chapters 1, 2 and 4, each verse begins with the corresponding letter of the Hebrew alphabet (verse 1 begins with an *aleph* (א), verse two with *beth* (ב), etc.). In chapter 3, groups of three verses start with corresponding letters (verses 1-3 each start with *aleph*, verses 4-6 each start with *beth*, etc.).

The poet clearly and graphically describes both the suffering of the people due to famine and also their shame due to the jeering and mocking of their enemies. Chapters 1, 3 and 4 end with calls for vengeance upon those enemies. Again, however, as we have seen several times, the center is important.[2] Chapter 3, the middle chapter, is clearly the heart of the book (see the diagram above and the outline below). Furthermore, very near the center of chapter 3 itself, the poet suddenly rises from lament to a declaration of faith, similar to what we see at the center of Job.[3] In Lam 3:19-26, the poet writes:

> Remember my affliction and my bitterness, the wormwood and the gall!
> My soul continually thinks of it and is bowed down within me.
> But this I call to mind, and therefore I have hope:
> The steadfast love of the LORD never ceases, his mercies never come to an end;
> they are new every morning; great is thy faithfulness.
> "The LORD is my portion," says my soul, "therefore I will hope in him."
> The LORD is good to those who wait for him, to the soul that seeks him.
> It is good that one should wait quietly for the salvation of the LORD.

Lamentations is one of the Festival Scrolls of Israel. It is read each year on the Ninth of Ab,[4] the saddest day in the Jewish year. This festival recalls the destruction of the temple in 70 A.D. by Roman Emperor Titus, as well as other tragedies in Jewish history.

Outline

The five chapters of Lamentations contain five poems, all acrostic except the last one. Chapters 1, 2, 4 and 5 are community laments, describing the destruction of the city of Jerusalem (personified as a

---

[1]See p. 126 for acrostics.

[2]See the discussion of centers and concentric patterns on p. 99.

[3]Job 19:25-27, see p. 142.

[4]Ab is the fifth month of the Jewish religious calendar, and comes around July or August. See p. 278 for the Hebrew calendar.

woman in chapters 1 and 2[5]). Chapter 3, the heart of the book, is three times as long as each of the other chapters, and is a lament of an individual – though it calls the entire community to repentance.

I. **Community lament:** General description of fallen Jerusalem (Lamentations 1)
II. **Community lament:** The LORD did it in his anger; details of the destruction (Lamentations 2)
III. **Individual lament:** Lament and confessions (of faith and of sin) (Lamentations 3)
IV. **Community lament:** The LORD did it in his anger; details of the destruction (Lamentations 3)
V. **Community lament:** General description of fallen Jerusalem (Lamentations 1)

Message

Lamentations is addressed to those who survived the destruction of Jerusalem and its temple in 586 B.C. The poet tries to help the survivors deal with and understand what has happened to them. The poet accepts the message of the pre-exilic prophets such as Jeremiah who had said that the people had sinned and that God would allow Jerusalem to be destroyed. However, accepting the fact that God himself had been behind the event was still theologically troubling. How could God allow a pagan nation to conquer his people? The poet answers: God did this because of the people's sin. But the poet is still uneasy.

Chapter three is the theological core as well as the physical center of the book. Like the other chapters, it begins and ends in lament. But it is much longer than the other chapters, and in the middle it makes several strong faith statements. Lam 3:19-26 and Lam 3:32-33 contain confessions of trust and hope in God. Between these two confessions the poet affirms his belief that God's wrath is limited (3:31). Thus, the people are called to repent of their sin in Lam 3:40-42.

The last chapter ends on a plaintive, questioning note, asking God, "Have you utterly rejected us? Are you exceedingly angry with us?" (Lam 5:20-22). In a sense, the question is still unresolved. However, the center of the book provides the theological anchor. There it is

---

[5]See p. 131, footnote 6, for "personification." In Proverbs, it is Wisdom which is personified as a woman (p. 153).

recognized that God's *chesed* (חֶ֫סֶד)[6] and mercy are without limit (3:22), but his wrath does come to an end.

Some important texts: "Is it nothing to you?" (Lam 1:12); "Great is thy faithfulness" (Lam 3:21-25)

Verses for memory: Lam 3:22-24

---

[6]See p. 78 for a discussion of this word.

Ezekiel

❧

Overview

Like Isaiah and Jeremiah, Ezekiel came from a family of priests (Ezek 1:3). He was among the first exiles taken to Babylon in 597 B.C., and he lived with them in Tel Abib, southeast of Babylon, on the river Cheber which feeds into the Euphrates. He received his call in 593, and he prophesied until 571. Throughout the book, God calls him "son of man." This phrase occurs 93 times in Ezekiel and simply means "human being." (It is not related to Dan 7:13-15 or to Jesus' use of the term in the New Testament.)

Ezekiel is known for his very unusual (some would say strange) visions. Indeed, at one point Jews were prohibited from reading Ezekiel until they were thirty years old![1] The book of Ezekiel begins with a dramatic vision of the glory of the LORD in a fiery flying throne surrounded by four living creatures. Two of the most dramatic moments in the book are

(1) when the glory of the LORD leaves the temple and Jerusalem and goes to be with the exiles in Babylon[2] (Ezekiel 10-11), and then
(2) when it returns again in Ezekiel's vision of a future restored temple (Ezek 43:1-5).[3]

---

[1]Mentioned in St. Jerome's letter (number 53) to Paulinus.

[2]This is a very significant moment. The LORD declares that he has not abandoned those who have gone into exile, but rather that he will be "a sanctuary to them for awhile" (Ezek 11:16). Thus, although there is no longer a temple in Jerusalem, there will be a "sanctuary" of the LORD in Babylon.

[3]Later rabbis (after the exile) sometimes referred to the glory of the LORD as the *shekinah.* The word is not found in the Bible, but is sometimes mentioned in popular Bible studies. The word has no special meaning and is just a form of the Hebrew verb *shakan* (שָׁכַן) which means to dwell. The word *mishkan* (מִשְׁכָּן, tabernacle) also comes from *shakan.* Thus, *shekinah* simply refers to the presence of God dwelling or living among his people.

Ezekiel is also known for his use of allegory[4] and a dozen symbolic acts (for instance, building a model of Jerusalem to demonstrate the siege, lying on his left side for 390 days, etc.). The most painful and difficult sign was when God caused Ezekiel's wife to die as a sign of the destruction of the temple (Ezek 24:15-24).

Ezekiel prophesied in Babylon at the same time that Jeremiah (who was probably older) prophesied in Jerusalem. Their messages were at times similar, and they may have known (or known of) each other. Both warned against rebellion against Babylon; both spoke against using the "sour grapes" proverb (Jer 31:29-30 and Ezek 18:2), because this proverb blamed the exile on previous generations and did not accept personal responsibility.

But Ezekiel did not merely teach the people to accept Babylon's power. Rather, he encouraged faithful religious practice, ethical living and loyalty to God even while in Babylon. This was important because God is holy, and the exile had happened because people had profaned God's "holy name." The "holy name" of God and "the glory of the LORD" are important phrases in Ezekiel because they represent the actual presence of God in the midst of the people.

Outline

It was while Ezekiel was in Babylon that Jerusalem was finally destroyed by the Babylonian armies in 586 B.C. The news reached Ezekiel on January 19, 585 B.C. and this is noted in Ezek 33:21-22. This becomes a major turning point in the book. Before this point, words of judgment are spoken; after it, Ezekiel speaks of the future restoration of Judah. Thus, in the outline below, I have referred to Ezekiel 33 as "the present," the chapters before Ezekiel 33 as "the past" and the chapters after Ezekiel 33 as "the future."

I. **The Past (before 586 B.C.)** (Ezekiel 1-32)
    A. Ezekiel's visions and first call (Ezekiel 1-3)
    B. Oracles against Judah and Jerusalem (Ezekiel 4-24)
    C. Oracles against foreign nations (Ezekiel 25-32)
II. **The Present (586 B.C.)** (Ezekiel 33)
    A. Ezekiel's second call (Ezek 33:1-20)
    B. The fall of Jerusalem (Ezek 33:21-22)

---

[4]See p. 162, footnote 5, for the meaning of allegory.

C. Concerning the survivors in Judah and in Babylon (Ezek 33:23-33)

III. The Future (after 586 B.C.) (Ezekiel 34-48)

A. Restoring the people and the land (Ezekiel 34-37)

B. Destruction of Gog of Magog[5] (Ezekiel 38-39)

C. Restoring the temple and the cult (Ezekiel 40-48)

Message

Ezekiel was called to be a watchman for Israel (Ezek 3:16-21; 33:1-9), warning the wicked to turn from their wickedness. But his complete message was broader than that.

First, he had to explain to the exiles why God had sent them to Babylon. He explains that it was because they had been disloyal to God, worshiping other gods at the high places and profaning the Sabbath. Israel is described as a prostitute in Ezekiel 16 and 23 (similar to the imagery of Jeremiah and, earlier, Hosea). Ezekiel 8 gives a graphic description of the false worship taking place in the temple itself. This caused the "glory of the LORD" to leave Jerusalem and go to Babylon in Ezekiel 10-11. Clearly, this showed that God's presence was not tied to the temple. On the one hand, this marked the disintegration of Zion theology (the people's belief that the presence of the temple guaranteed the inviolability of Jerusalem[6]). On the other hand, it encouraged the exiles in Babylon where the glory of the LORD became "a sanctuary to them for awhile" (Ezek 11:16). Ezekiel also agreed with Jeremiah that Nebuchadnezzar had been God's servant when he destroyed Jerusalem (Ezek 29:19-20).

---

[5]"Gog, of the land of Magog, the chief prince of Meshech and Tubal" may originally have been King Gyges of Lydia (today south-central Turkey). But Gyges lived more than 1000 years before Ezekiel. Thus, Ezekiel is apparently using the name symbolically as an almost mythological or even apocalyptic figure who marches from the north to attack Israel before being destroyed by God. In the book of Revelation, Gog *of* Magog becomes two different figures, Gog *and* Magog (Rev 20:8). Modern popular writers have produced several strange interpretations of these names. One of the most common is to identify Meshech with Moscow and to identify Gog and Megog with an invasion of Israel by a military alliance led by Russia. Such interpretations are highly speculative and very doubtful.

[6]See p. 174. Something which is "inviolable" is something that cannot be violated, harmed or destroyed.

Second, Ezekiel brings a message of hope which is grounded only in God himself, and this message comes in a very interesting way. Ezekiel begins by bringing us the strongest message concerning *individual responsibility* found in the Old Testament. In Ezekiel 18 and Ezek 33:10-20 we read that a good child shall not die for the sin of his father, nor shall a bad child be saved by the righteousness of his father. Rather, "the soul that sins shall die" (Ezek 18:4,20). Furthermore, "if a wicked man turns away from all his sins ...; he shall not die" (Ezek 18:21). But here there was a problem. God was eager to forgive people who repented,[7] but the people refused to repent.

Ezekiel, therefore, finds *hope only in God* who – with or without the people's repentance – will finally act out of concern for his holy name. In other words, although the people refuse to repent, God will yet restore them so that his name "should not be profaned in the sight of the nations among whom they dwelt,"[8] and so that all shall know that "I am the LORD."[9] Clearly, Ezekiel has a very high view of the holiness of God, and he uses the exalted name "the Lord GOD"[10] 217 times.

But the people were not merely rebellious; their hope had also died because of the exile. In Ezekiel 37, God gives Ezekiel a vision of a valley filled with dry bones. The dry bones represent the dead hopes of the people, and Ezekiel is told to preach to them. As he does, God restores their flesh and brings them back to life. In a similar way, Ezekiel says, God will put a new spirit within the people; he will take out their hearts of stone and give them hearts of flesh (Ezek 11:19-20; 36:26-27; 37:14). The image is similar to that of Jeremiah's new covenant (Jer 31:31-34), and is again based on law "that they may walk in my statutes and keep my ordinances and obey them" (Ezek 11:20). Like Jeremiah, Ezekiel has a distant vision of what God will eventually do in Christ, but the vision he holds is not yet complete.

Ezekiel's hope for the future is that God himself will become the good shepherd of his people (Ezekiel 34), and that they will return to a

---

[7]"Why will you die, O house of Israel? ... turn, and live," Ezek 18:31-32.

[8]Ezek 20:9, 14, 22, 39; 36:20-23; 39:7, 25; 43:7,8.

[9]Ezek 6:7-14 and about 60 times altogether.

[10]Note the capitalization of GOD here. In Hebrew, the phrase is *adonay Yahweh* (אֲדֹנָי יְהוִה), and GOD represents the name *Yahweh* (which in this case has been given the vowel points (vowels) from *Elohim* (אֱלֹהִים, God)). See the discussion of these names on p. 34.

restored land (Ezek 37:20-28). Ezekiel thus offers a complete program of reform, including a detailed (though only two dimensional) plan for a new temple with a restored cult (Ezekiel 40-46). When this is accomplished, the glory of the LORD will return to Jerusalem (Ezek 43:1-5; 44:4).

Some important texts: Vision of the throne of God (Ezek 1:1-28); the glory of the LORD leaves Jerusalem (Ezek 10:1-11:25); fall of Jerusalem (Ezek 33:21-22); new spirit and hearts of flesh (Ezek 11:19-20; 36:26-27; 37:14); valley of dry bones (Ezek 37:1-14); a future day in which the glory of the LORD will return to the temple (Ezek 43:1-5)

Verses for memory: Ezek 37:11-13

DANIEL

❧

Overview

The book of Daniel is included among the prophets in the Old Testament but not in the Hebrew Scriptures.[1] The Hebrew Scriptures place Daniel among The Writings. One reason for this may be that the style of Daniel is quite different from that of the other prophets. But there is also a question of date. Some think Daniel may have been written many years after the other books of prophecy were written and collected. If so, this would be another reason why Daniel was placed in the later collection called The Writings. More will be said about this below.

The book of Daniel tells the story of four young men, "Daniel, Hananiah, Mishael, and Azariah of the tribe of Judah" (Dan 1:6). They were taken to Babylon when Nebuchadnezzar destroyed Jerusalem, and they were renamed Belteshazzar, Shadrach, Meshach and Abednego. However, throughout the book the name Daniel is used far more often than Belteshazzar. Since the four young men were "endowed with knowledge, understanding learning, and competent to serve in the king's palace" (Dan 1:4), they were given training and became advisors to the king. Later, they all became rulers over provinces.

The rest of the first six chapters of the book describes their lives in Babylon, where they remained faithful to God and refused to worship other gods. They (especially Daniel) are also successful in interpreting dreams. This causes jealousy among the king's other advisors, and they made plots against Daniel, Shadrach, Meshach and Abednego. In Daniel 3, Daniel's three friends are thrown into a fiery furnace from which God delivers them. In chapter 6, Daniel is thrown into a den of lions and he also is saved by God. Throughout the first six chapters, the kings again and again recognize and praise the God of Israel.

---

[1]See pp. 3-6 for a discussion of the Old Testament and its relationship to the Hebrew Scriptures.

In chapter 7, things change dramatically. We enter a different literary world. Chapters 1-6 were narrative, and the type of advice which Daniel offered to the kings is known as mantic wisdom. In other words, in chapters 1-6 Daniel had the ability to interpret dreams, like Joseph in Genesis 37-50. The ability was not his own; God had given it to him as a gift, and the kings recognized this by praising God. However, chapters 7-12 are not narrative and they do not contain any mantic wisdom. Rather, their content is apocalyptic and Daniel does not interpret dreams. Furthermore, in these chapters the kings are not friendly.

Apocalyptic Literature

The prophets expected God to bring justice and destroy wickedness. If situations became extremely bad, God might use foreign nations to punish his people. He could even destroy Jerusalem and the temple. These were all historical events. In the prophets, God works and brings justice within history. But what if the world becomes so bad that even God is not able to repair things within history? This may sound like a very strange question, but there came a time when some felt that this had happened. In such a case, God would have to use supernatural methods to destroy the wicked. This could also mean a change in the created order and even the creation of a new heaven and a new earth.

This viewpoint, known as *apocalyptic*, produced a particular type of literature: the *apocalypse.* An apocalypse is generally

- A *narrative*, in which
- a *human seer or prophet* receives
- a *revelation* which reveals
- *future events* from God through
- a heavenly *mediator.* Sometimes there is
- a "*heavenly journey*," in which the seer is transported to heaven and is shown many things. This does not happen in Daniel, but in the book of Revelation, this occurs in chapter 4. In other apocalypses, the "heavenly journey" is much more elaborate than Revelation 4. In an apocalypse, there is also
- *mythological imagery* (chaos, sea, beasts, etc.) and often
- an *admonition* or warning, as seen in Rev 1:3. Finally, there is
- *judgment* of the wicked and *salvation* of the elect.

Many apocalypses were written between the third century B.C. and the first or second century A.D. Only two are found in the Bible: the last half of Daniel (chapters 7-12) and the book of Revelation in the New Testament, although apocalyptic elements are found in a few other books, as well.

Again, the difference between Daniel 1-6 and Daniel 7-12 is very great. Daniel 1-6 tells of events which are set in the sixth century B.C. (that is, after 600 B.C., when the Babylonians took the exiles to Babylon). But Daniel 7-12 seems to describe events around 165 B.C.[2] To understand this difference, we need to look briefly at what happened in the post-exilic period.

Post-exilic and Intertestamental Period (538-64 B.C.)

As discussed above (p. 103), in 538 B.C. Babylon was defeated by the Persians who then let the exiles of Israel return to their homes. This was the "post-exilic" period during which the temple and Jerusalem were rebuilt. By the year 400 B.C. the Old Testament was essentially finished. Thus, the years between 400 B.C. and the writing of the books of the New Testament are called the "intertestamental ('between the testaments') period." The book of Daniel, however, is unusual because it may have been written during this period. So a few words are needed here about the intertestamental period.

Beginning in the year 335 B.C., Alexander the Great of Greece conquered a huge empire which included Israel (see the map of his empire on p. 6). In 323 B.C., Alexander died at the young age of 32, perhaps of fever in Babylon. His four generals divided his empire, and again the Jews found themselves sitting in a troublesome and dangerous location.

---

[2]There is a further mystery in Daniel. Dan 2:4b-7:28 is written in Aramaic, not in Hebrew. Aramaic is very similar to Hebrew and was used as an official language throughout the ANE. What makes it such a great mystery in Daniel is that the language division (Hebrew and Aramaic) does not match the literary division (narrative vs apocalypse). Daniel 7 is the problem. Its style is apocalyptic, and so it fits with the last half of the book (chapters 7-12); but its language is Aramaic, which makes it fit with chapter 2-6.

One general, Ptolemy, set up the Ptolemaic dynasty in Egypt. Another general, Seleucus, established the Seleucid dynasty in Syria. After some struggle, the Ptolemaic dynasty was victorious and claimed Palestine. Dan 8:5-8, 21-22 seems to describe this rise and fall of Alexander and the four generals who followed him.

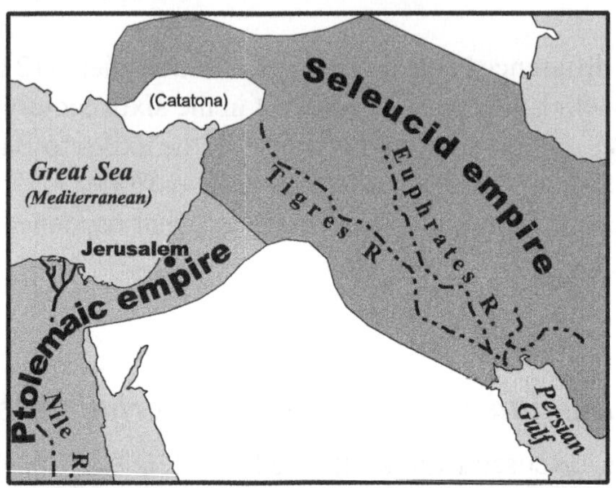

The Ptolemaic and Seleucid Empires, 300 B.C.

The Ptolemies were good rulers, and they ruled Palestine from 320 to 198 B.C. In 198 B.C., however, the Seleucids came down from the north and took over. They ruled the Jews harshly, and tried to bring a strong Greek cultural influence, Greek language, and Greek customs. Life became more difficult. Many leading Jews, and even some of the priests, began to adopt Greek customs. This process of "Hellenization" was opposed by conservative Jews known as the Hasidim.[3]

The worst was yet to come. From 175 to 164 B.C., Antiochus Epiphanes was the Seleucid ruler. His name meant "the visible god" but his enemies called him Antiochus Epimanes, "the crazy one." In 167 B.C., he sent 22,000 troops to attack Jerusalem on the Sabbath. He sought to destroy Jewish traditions by building pagan altars, destroying their scrolls, and by making Sabbath worship and rites such as circumcision illegal. Finally he sacrificed a pig on the temple altar. Dan 8:9-14 and 11:21-45 seem to refer to Antiochus. This desecration

[3]The word Hasidim is related to *chesed* (חֶסֶד, see p. 78), and means "the steadfast and faithful ones." The word appears 34 times in the Old Testament, and is translated in various ways: faithful ones, godly ones, saints, etc.

of the temple is mentioned in Dan 11:31.

This caused an uprising: the Maccabean revolt (169-164 B.C.), led by an elderly Jewish priest names Mattathias and his five sons. When Mattathias died, his third son whom he named Judas Maccabeus ("the hammerer") continued the struggle. Finally, in December 164 B.C., Judas Maccabeus and his forces defeated Antiochus. The temple was rededicated, and the event is celebrated today as Hanukkah. After Judas died, two other brothers led the people. The period of freedom and independence continued for a century until 63 B.C. when Rome took over. This was the longest period that the Jews enjoyed independence after 600 BC.

The second half of Daniel (chapters 7-12) seems to have been written during the period described above, perhaps during the period of the Maccabean revolt. Thus, the date 165 B.C. is often suggested for these chapters. As mentioned above, this late date may explain why the Hebrew Scriptures have placed Daniel in The Writings and not among the Prophets.

But what about the first half of the book? And how does it relate to the second half? More will be said below in the section on "Message."

Outline

- **I. Chapters 1-6: narrative**
  - A. Ch 1: Daniel and his 3 friends are taken to Babylon
  - B. Ch 2: Daniel interprets Nebuchadnezzar's dream of four kingdoms: probably Babylon, Media, Persia, Greece
  - C. Ch 3: The three friends in the fiery furnace
  - D. Ch 4: Daniel interprets a dream of judgment against Nebuchadnezzar
  - E. Ch 5: Daniel interprets the handwriting on the wall (King Belshazzar's feast)
  - F. Ch 6: Daniel in the lion's den (King Darius)
- **II. Chapters 7-12: apocalyptic**
  - A. Ch 7: A four kingdom prophecy; also, the son of man and the Ancient of Days
  - B. Ch 8: The ram (Medes and Persians) and he-goat (Greeks)

C. Ch 9: Jeremiah's seventy-year prophecies (Jer 29:10): seventy weeks of years = 70 x 7 = 490 years
D. Ch 10: Gabriel(?) and Michael fight against the angels ("princes") of Persia and Greece
E. Ch 11: A detailed apocalyptic vision which describes Alexander through Antiochus
F. Ch 12: A time of great trouble; resurrection of the dead

Message

Is it true? The first question which comes up for many is that of the theological integrity of the book of Daniel. The book begins by saying that the events take place while Daniel and the exiles are in Babylon. That would be some time between 600 B.C. and 538 B.C. But then chapters 7-12 seem to come from around the year 165 B.C., some 400 years later. And there are other issues as well: narrative versus apocalyptic, Hebrew versus Aramaic,[4] and the fact that Daniel 1-6 is written in the third person (Daniel is always "he"), but much of Daniel 7-12 is first person ("I, Daniel"). So, if the two parts of the book are really written by two different people at different times, does this mean that the book is untrue? Can we trust it as the word of God?

Many suggestions have been made. One of the most interesting is that of Brevard Childs,[5] who suggested that the original book was just Daniel 1-6, and was written early. Many years later, another writer, living at the time of Antiochus Epiphanes, read this older book and felt that it was describing his own time. He was also impressed by Jeremiah's 70 year prophecies (below). Thus, he wrote Daniel 7-12 as an apocalyptic interpretation of the earlier and older chapters, Daniel 1-6. The major feature, which connects the two parts, is the four-kingdoms dream of Daniel 2 which is then interpreted in the four-kingdoms vision of Daniel 7. It is impossible to prove whether Childs is right or wrong, but his suggestion is worth considering. He is saying that, yes, Daniel is the word of God; but in order to understand it we must understand how it was written.

Daniel is a theology of history. First and foremost, Daniel is saying that God is the author and master of historical events. This is the point

---

[4]See the discussion in footnote 2 on p. 195.

[5]Brevard Childs, *Introduction to the Old Testament as Scripture* (Philadelphia: Fortress Press, 1979) 614-622.

of the four-kingdoms material in chapters 2 and 7. It may not always be clear what God is doing, but his will is ultimately going to be accomplished. At the same time, however, human beings have freedom and responsibility to make decisions. Thus, God's people are called to remain faithful through the ordeals which confront them (fiery furnace, lion's den), and enemies are warned that they will finally bow before the power of God (as do the kings in Daniel 1-6).

Three important texts. Three sections are particularly important for understanding Daniel. In **Dan 7:13-15**, a "son of man" comes with the clouds of heaven and is presented before God ("the Ancient of Days"). He is then "given dominion and glory and kingdom, that all peoples, nations, and languages should serve him." Who is this son of man? If we continue to read the chapter, verse 27 seems to say that the "son of man" represents "the people of the saints of the Most High," that is, Israel.

Daniel assumes that wars between nations on earth are reflections of battles between their angels in heaven. Thus, perhaps the "son of man" in Dan 7:13 originally referred to Michael, Israel's guardian angel, who would conquer the princes of Persia and Greece.[6] Over the centuries, Jewish interpretation of this "son of man" figure developed greatly, and at times it took on surprisingly divine characteristics.[7] The understanding of "the son of man" grows further in the New Testament Gospels, where Jesus tells his hearers that this passage refers to him.[8] And in the book of Revelation, the image appears twice: in Rev 1:7, where it refers to Jesus, and in Rev 14:14-16, where the figure is an angel.

Dan 9:2,24-27 is the second important passage. Here, Daniel considers Jeremiah's prophecies that the Babylonian exile[9] would last

---

[6]See Dan 10:16-21, where the angels are described as "princes."

[7]In the Similitudes of Enoch (first century A.D.), the "son of man" is seen "seated on the throne of glory" (62:5) and is called Messiah (46:1). "Even before the sun and the constellations were created ... his name was named before the Lord of Spirits" (John J. Collins, "Daniel, Book of," *ABD* 2:35). The Jewish development reached its peak much later, in the 4th or 5th century AD, when in 3 Enoch (a mystical work, also called Sepher Hekalot) an angel named Metatron is called "'the little Yahweh,' greater than all princes" (Ibid.).

[8]Mt 24:30; 26:64; Mk 13:26; 14:62; Lk 21:27; 22:69.

[9]Or at least the period between the destruction of the temple in 586 B.C. and its reconstruction and rededication in 515 B.C.

for 70 years (Jer 25:11-12; 29:10). Jeremiah was right, but Daniel sees even more in his prophecy. Dan 9:24 interprets Jeremiah to mean seventy *weeks* of years, that is 70 x 7 = 490 years. Daniel may understand this to be the number of years between the Babylonian exile and his own time (around 165 B.C., just before the Maccabean revolt), although the numbers do not add up precisely.[10]

Dan 12:1-3 is the third important passage. It brings us to the high point and the conclusion of the book of Daniel. Daniel writes at a time of great distress, and he expects to see God's deliverance. But before that happens, "there shall be a time of trouble, such as never has been since there was a nation till that time." Antiochus certainly brought that trouble! Daniel expects that many of his people will die in these last days. But he does not stop there. We have noticed that most of the Old Testament does not know about life after death. Job at one point seems to offer a short glimpse of the hope of eternal life,[11] but here, in Dan 12:1-3, we come face to face with a bold statement of resurrection hope:

> And many of those who sleep in the dust of the earth shall awake, some to everlasting life, and some to shame and everlasting contempt. And those who are wise shall shine like the brightness of the firmament; and those who turn many to righteousness, like the stars for ever and ever.

The book of Daniel leaves us with a number of unanswered questions. But, like the book of Revelation, its central affirmations are clear: the future is in God's hands, there will be salvation for God's people, and death will not have the final word. For those who have suffered unjustly in this life, there is yet hope of future restoration.

Some important texts: the four-kingdoms texts (Dan 2:1-47; 7:1-12, 16-28), the fiery furnace (Dan 3:1-30); Daniel in the lions' den (Dan 6:1-28); the clouds of heaven and son of man (Dan 7:13-15); the resurrection of the dead (Dan 12:1-3).

Verses for memory: Dan 7:13-14; 12:2-3

---

[10]Another number, 3½ years (half of seven years), appears several times in various forms: "a time, two times and half a time" (that is, 3½ "times"), "a thousand two hundred and ninety days" and "the thousand three hundred and thirty-five days" (both about 3½ years). Daniel associates this period of time with the events of the last days.

[11]Job 19:25-27. See *A Final Note* on p. 142.

The Twelve Minor Prophets

The word "minor" is somewhat misleading in this case. The minor prophets are not less important than the other prophets; their books are just shorter than those of the "major" prophets Isaiah (66 chapters), Jeremiah (52 chapters) and Ezekiel (48 chapters).

The order of the minor prophets is generally chronological. Dating is sometimes a bit complicated, but Hosea and Amos are indeed early (eighth century B.C.), and Haggai, Zechariah and Malachi are rather clearly late (sixth and fifth centuries B.C.). See the table on p. 166.

In the Hebrew Scriptures, the twelve Minor Prophets are considered to be a single book. Thus, in the Hebrew Scriptures, the "Latter Prophets" (see p. 3) are Isaiah, Jeremiah, Ezekiel and The Twelve.

Hosea

❧

Overview

Two periods of Israel's history lay under threats from the "north" (that is, from Mesopotamia[1]). First, in the last half of the *eighth* century (roughly 745-722 B.C.[2]), Assyria rose to dominate Mesopotamia. It then expanded to the west and conquered the lands of Palestine, finally destroying the northern kingdom of Israel and its capital, Samaria. Judah also suffered terribly; many villages were destroyed, but Jerusalem itself was saved. A century later, in the last quarter of the *seventh* century (roughly 625-600 B.C.), the threat was from Babylon. This was the period of Jeremiah and Ezekiel.[3]

The prophet Hosea lived during the first of these two periods: the very stressful Assyrian period. During this time, four classical prophets spoke. Isaiah of Jerusalem (First Isaiah) and Micah prophesied in the south (Judah), and Amos and Hosea spoke to the north (Israel). Amos and Hosea thus faced the same historical situations, although their emphases are slightly different. The eighth century B.C. was a time in which the worship of Baal had become so common in Israel that Hosea refers to "the Baals" (Hos 2:13,17; 11:2). Baal was a rain god of Canaan (see p. 273), and so was associated with the land's fertility and crops. Many of the people of Israel had begun to believe that their grain, wine, and other blessings were from Baal and not from the LORD.

The word *baal* (*ba'al*, בַּעַל) also had another, older meaning: "master" or "husband." As we read Hosea, we find that he works with both meanings: Baal as a false god, and *baal* as a "husband." This is a key to understanding the first three chapters of Hosea. Hosea, as a

---

[1]Mesopotamia was, of course, to the east of Israel, not to the north (review the maps found on pp. 10 and 93). But traders and armies followed the Fertile Crescent, and thus were always seen coming from the north.

[2]Assyrian power actually continued for another century, but we note 722 B.C. here because that was the year that the northern kingdom of Israel was destroyed and Hosea's ministry came to an end (if not earlier).

[3]Review "The final Years of Judah" on p. 178.

northerner, has a strong awareness of the conditional Mosaic covenant. Israel's unfaithfulness in following Baal was like that of an unfaithful wife who followed lovers because they gave her food and drink. Thus, in chapters 1-3, we find the story of Hosea and Gomer. Gomer was apparently a prostitute, and God tells Hosea to marry her ("take to yourself a wife of harlotry," Hos 1:2). Both Jews and Christians have had trouble with this idea. Would God really command such a thing? Could it really be true, or was it just a dream or a parable?

The book of Hosea says nothing about the experience being a dream or a parable, and we will not understand the words of Hosea if we get sidetracked with this question. Instead, we must focus on a different question: What was the *point* of Hosea's marriage to Gomer? The point of Hosea 1-3 is simple and very clear: this offensive and unfaithful marriage relationship represents Israel's offensive and unfaithful relationship with the LORD. Hosea is Gomer's real *baal* (husband), but she keeps running off with other *baals* (actually, lovers). And this is the problem with Israel. The LORD is Israel's real husband/*baal*; it is the LORD who has given Israel grain, wine, and oil, as well as silver and gold (Hos 2:8). But Israel forgot this truth, and began following the false god Baal instead.

Hosea and Gomer have three children, and they are given unfortunate names: Jezreel,[4] Not-Pitied, and Not-my-people. The point, of course, is that God is no longer going to have pity on Israel because they are no longer his people. Yet this is not the end of the story. One of the most amazing things about the book of Hosea is the way it shows us both God's judgment and his mercy, both his wrath and his love. No other prophet is able to display this tension as well as Hosea does. Indeed, by the beginning of chapter 2, Hosea is told to give his children new names: "My-people" and "She-has-obtained-pity." Then these children are asked to plead with their mother, Gomer, that she come home and be faithful. Near the end of chapter 2, God hopes that the day will come when Israel "will call me, 'My husband,'[5] and no longer ... call me, 'My Baal.' For I will remove the names of the Baals from her mouth, and they shall be mentioned by name no more" (Hos 2:16-17).

---

[4]Jezreel is name of the place where Jehu murdered the house of King Ahab (2 Kings 9-10).

[5]The Hebrew word here is *ish* (אִישׁ), which can mean "man" or "husband." Thus, Hosea is able to work with two words, *ish* (אִישׁ) and *baal* (בַּעַל), both of which can mean "husband," but only one of which can mean Baal.

The rest of the book is a collection of oracles in which there are words of judgment, not only upon Baal worship (many references) but also upon immoral and unjust relationships between people (Hos 4:1-3; 7:1-4; 12:7-8). At the same time, there are also places in which the tension between God's wrath and his love is stretched almost to the breaking point. More is said below in the section on "Message."

Hosea is not optimistic. He does not think the people are able to change (Hos 5:4), and so his words are generally intended to prepare them for judgment. Yet in spite of this pessimism, the final chapter of the book is one of hope in which Hosea does call the people to return to God in repentance.

Outline

I. Hosea and Gomer (Hosea 1-3)
II. Oracles of warning and judgment (Hosea 4-13)
III. Oracles of hope and calls to return (Hosea 14)

Message

Hosea is the only truly northern prophet found among the classical biblical prophets. Amos prophesied in Israel at the same time as Hosea, but he came from Judah. Thus, in Hosea we hear some of the clearest statements of northern theology. The north (Israel, with its capital Samaria) was focused much more upon the Mosaic covenant than was the south.[6]

Twice in Hosea (Hos 12:9; 13:4) we hear abbreviated reminders of the opening words of the Ten Commandments: "I am the LORD your God from the land of Egypt." And throughout Hosea, we are reminded again and again that God found Israel in Egypt and brought the people out. God remembers those early days in the wilderness as a time of faithfulness; Israel is described as a young wife (Hos 2:14-16) or a son (Hos 11:1). The covenant is mentioned in Hos 6:7; 8:1.

However, things then went very wrong. The people became

---

[6]The south recognized the Mosaic covenant, certainly, but was more interested in the unconditional Davidic covenant and Zion (Jerusalem, temple) theology. However, remember that Jeremiah was influenced by northern theology, and even by Hosea (p. 181, above). So strong, challenging words were also spoken in Judah as well.

unfaithful. The story of Jacob and Esau is recalled, and Jacob[7] is remembered as one who "took his brother by the heel." God "will punish Jacob [that is, the northern kingdom] according to his ways, and requite him according to his deeds" (Hos 12:2-5[8]). Truly, the deeds of the people have been evil. Their worship of Baal and their unjust treatment of each other have been mentioned above. Hosea also notes their misguided dependence upon sacrifice (Hos 6:6; 8:13) and foreign alliances (Hos 5:13; 7:11; 8:9-10; 12:1). Even when they talk about "return" to God, it is superficial and shallow (Hos 6:1-6).[9] Thus, Hosea concludes that the people cannot repent (Hos 5:4). Several times, he says that they are going to "return to Egypt" – and by that he means they will go into exile in Assyria (Hos 8:13; 9:3,6; 11:5).

But then there is Hosea 11. In this astounding chapter, we seem to enter the very heart of God and we witness a tremendous struggle between his wrath and his love, between his judgment and his mercy.

> When Israel was a child, I loved him, and out of Egypt I called my son.
> The more I called them, the more they went from me ....
> Yet it was I who taught Ephraim[10] to walk ....
> They shall return to the land of Egypt, and Assyria shall be their king ....
> How can I give you up, O Ephraim! How can I hand you over, O Israel!
> ....
> I will not execute my fierce anger, I will not again destroy Ephraim; ....
> Ephraim has encompassed me with lies, and the house of Israel with deceit; ....

Read the rest of chapter 11 carefully and note the intensity of this tension within God. Nowhere else in the Bible do we witness this depth of internal divine struggle (though several times the Old Testament

---

[7] In Hosea and elsewhere in the Old Testament, the names Jacob and Ephraim are both often used to refer to the northern kingdom of Israel.

[8]This is the only place in the Bible where it says Jacob wrestled with an "angel." Genesis 32 just mentions "a man."

[9]Here, the RSV and NRSV misunderstand, with the RSV adding the word "saying" at the end of 5:15 and the NRSV adding a colon. These additions have been made in an attempt to connect 5:15 with chapter 6. But these texts should not be connected. See the NAS and NIV which allow verse 15 simply to stand alone as the end of God's speech. The words of the people in 6:1-3 are actually shallow and superficial. They do not take seriously God's words of judgment. 6:4 is God's response to this.

[10]That is, the northern kingdom of Israel. See footnote 7, above.

suggests that God can change his mind or "repent"[11]).

Finally, in spite of Hosea's pessimism expressed elsewhere, the book concludes with a chapter of hope in which Hosea calls the people to return to God in repentance (Hosea 14). In spite of the unfaithfulness of the people, God's love and mercy are expected to win in the end.

Some important texts: Hosea and Gomer (Hos 1:1-3:5); she did not know that it was I (Hos 2:8); my husband and not my Baal (Hos 2:16-17); steadfast love and not sacrifice (Hos 6:6); God's wrath and love (Hos 11:1-12); return to the LORD (Hos 14:1-2). See also the reference to Hos 1:6-2:1 in 1 Pet 2:10.

Verses for memory: Hos 6:6; 14:1-2

---

[11]See the discussion of the golden calf incident, on p. 41. A fuller discussion of the "repentance of God" is found on p. 224 in the section on Jonah.

Joel

❧

Overview

The book of Joel begins with a disastrous plague of locusts, which Joel sees as a sign of the coming day of the LORD[1] (Joel 1:15). Such locust plagues were common in the Middle East before the days of spraying crops with pesticides.[2] The locusts travel close together, consuming every green thing in their path. Joel understands the locusts to be a punishment sent by God, but they are more than that. They are also a sign of a future invasion by a foreign army. Yet it is not clear what nation Joel has in mind.

The book of Joel has two distinct parts. The first part describes the plague of locusts, and Joel calls the people to lament because he sees the locust invasion pointing ahead to the coming day of the LORD. Joel describes cosmic events (the swarm of locusts darkens the skies, Joel 2:2,10-11), and the theme is judgment upon Judah. The second half of the book is quite different from the first and, as was the case with the second half of Daniel, it is apocalyptic[3] in style (Joel 2:30-32; 3:15). Joel sees these events, too, as the day of the LORD. In this case, however, the focus has changed. The judgment will be upon Judah's enemies, and Judah will be restored. Joel sees God's judgment upon the nations taking place in the Valley of Jehoshaphat (Joel 3:2,12), an unknown place, the name of which means "the LORD judged" or "the LORD judges."

When did Joel speak or write about these events? It is difficult to

---

[1]See the discussion of the day of the LORD on p. 209.

[2]These locust invasions can be huge. A 1957 invasion contained 16 billion locusts, and the total weight of the swarm was 50,000 tons. Locusts daily eat their own weight of plants, and so this swarm (which had invaded Somaliland) ate 50,000 tons of crops, trees and grass each day. T. Hiebert, "Joel, Book of," *ABD* 3:876.

[3]See p. 194 for a summary of apocalyptic literature.

answer that question. The book does not mention any dateable events or the names of any kings, and there are no records of a locust invasion which could help us. But there are several other hints. First, the temple is standing, and so we are looking at a period either before the Babylonian destruction of 586 B.C. or after the rebuilding of the temple in 515 B.C. Second, the attitude toward the priests and the cult is positive, and this was not true for the earlier prophets. Third, the influence of apocalyptic theology was not felt until after the exile. So perhaps a fifth century date (500-400 B.C.) is a reasonable suggestion.[4]

Outline

In the outline which follows, there are two structural issues to notice:

- a concentric pattern in Joel 2:1-11 and
- the "turning point" of Joel 2:12-29

Both are discussed after the outline is presented:[5]

I. **Judgment on Judah** (Joel 1:1-2:11)
   A. The locust invasion, and a call to lament (Joel 1:1-20)
   B. The locust invasion as an image of the coming Day of the LORD (Joel 2:1-11 – a concentric pattern, see below)
II. **The turning point:** A call to repentance, and God's response (Joel 2:12-29, see below)
III. **Judgment on the nations**, restoration and prosperity for Judah (Joel 2:30-3:21)
   A. Apocalyptic signs of the day of the LORD (Joel 2:30-32)

---

[4]A number of scholars suggest another possibility: that the first part of Joel, which deals with the plague of locusts, was written earlier, and that only the last (apocalyptic) part is post-exilic. The placement of Joel between Hosea and Amos indicates that the ancient rabbis thought Joel belonged in the eighth century B.C. However, the Septuagint puts Joel with the undated books (Obadiah and Jonah), so the matter is not clear.

[5]Those who study the book in Hebrew should note another point. Chapters 2 and 3 of the Hebrew were combined into a single chapter 2 in the Septuagint and Vulgate (and therefore in the English translations). Chapter 4 in Hebrew is therefore chapter 3 in the Septuagint, Vulgate and English. Thus, if we compare English chapters to Hebrew chapters, we have:

Eng 1 = Heb 1; Eng 2 = Heb 2-3; Eng 3 = Heb 4.

B. Destruction of Judah's enemies (Joel 3:1-16)
C. Restoration of Judah (Joel 3:17-21)

A *concentric pattern*, which places the locust invasion at its center, is found in Joel 2:1-11 as follows:

A The day of the LORD is coming (2:1)
  B Cosmic events (2:2)
    C Description of the locust invasion (2:3-9)
  B' Cosmic events (2:10-11a)
A' The day of the LORD is great (2:11b)

The turning point. The chapter on Ezekiel notes an important turning point at Ezek 33:21-22 when Ezekiel heard the news of the fall of Jerusalem (see p. 189, above). Before the fall of Jerusalem, Ezekiel spoke words of judgment; after the fall of Jerusalem, he spoke words of hope and restoration. The situation is similar in Joel. The actual center of the book is not the locust invasion (above) but rather the "turning point" of Joel 2:12-29. In vv 12-16, there is a call to repentance and fasting. Then in vv. 17-18, the priests cry out for mercy, and the LORD becomes "jealous for his land" and has "pity on his people." Before this turning point, we read of the locust invasion and the approaching day of the LORD as judgment on Judah. After Joel 2:17-18, the focus changes and we read of the day of the LORD as judgment on Judah's enemies and a restoration of Judah.

Message

The Day of the LORD. The dominating theme of Joel is the approach of the "day of the LORD." This day is first mentioned by the eighth century prophet Amos (p. 216, below). It is not the end of the world (which is more of a New Testament apocalyptic theme); rather, it is a day within history on which the LORD will come to bring judgment upon the earth. This, of course, can be either a positive or a negative event. If you are suffering from injustice and oppression, you will look forward to the day of the LORD because God will punish the oppressor. But if you are the oppressor, then the day of the LORD is a day of terror.

Both of these understandings are seen in Joel. In the first half of the book, the locusts are understood by Joel as God's judgment upon Judah, and he calls the people to lament and repent because even darker days are coming. But in the second half of the book – after the turning point of Joel 2:12-29 – the day of the LORD is seen as a day on which God will judge the enemies of Judah and bring salvation and restoration to his people. In this part of Joel, the day of the LORD does take on apocalyptic overtones.

The turning point. As mentioned above, the center of the book and of Joel's message is the turning point of Joel 2:12-29. In this section, there is a call to the people and the priests to repent, and a plea to God for mercy. God does have "pity on his people" and, in the following verses, sends "grain, wine and oil" and promises deliverance. Many of the other prophets speak against the cult because of abuses and misuses of sacrifice and ritual; Joel does not. Although he warns against empty ritualism ("Rend your hearts and not your garments," Joel 2:13), he also appeals to the priests and the cult to lead the people in lament and repentance (Joel 2:15-17).

A puzzling verse. In the midst of this, Joel 2:14 at first seems confusing. In Joel 2:13, after telling the people to "rend your hearts and not your garments," Joel continues with "Return to the LORD, your God, for he is gracious and merciful, slow to anger, and abounding in steadfast love, and repents of evil." He then goes on in verse 14 to say: "Who knows whether he will not turn and repent, and leave a blessing behind him, a cereal offering and a drink offering for the LORD, your God?" I would paraphrase that as follows: "Who knows whether *God* will not turn and *relent*[6] and leave a blessing behind him, [renewal of crops which can then be used for] a grain offering and a drink offering for the LORD, your God." In other words, God's response to lament and repentance will be to relent (change his mind) and restore the crops. These crops can then be used once more for offerings back to God.

Pouring out of God's Spirit. The last part of Joel's prophecy is the apocalyptic section. Here, God promises to destroy Judah's enemies and then restore what the people have lost to both the locusts and their enemies. Just before this section, we find a prophecy which has special importance for Christians. In Joel 2:28-29, God says:

> And it shall come to pass afterward, that I will pour out my spirit on all flesh; your sons and your daughters shall prophesy, your old men shall dream dreams, and your young men shall see visions. Even upon the menservants and maidservants in those days, I will pour out my spirit.

---

[6]That is, change his mind, soften his judgment. See NIV, NASB and NRSV for similar translations of this word. For "repent," see p. 224.

When will this take place? Joel does not tell us, and probably did not know. He just says "afterward," and then moves directly into the apocalyptic section. But the change will be significant! Women and servants are included. Centuries later, Peter pointed to these verses in his Pentecost sermon, and said that "this [coming of the Holy Spirit] is what was spoken through the prophet Joel" (Acts 2:16-21).

Some important texts: rend your hearts and not your garments; return to the LORD your God (Joel 2:13), pouring out of God's spirit (Joel 2:28-29)

Verses for memory: Joel 2:13; 2:28-29

AMOS

❧

Overview

Around 750 B.C., the northern kingdom of Israel reached the peak of its prosperity. Its enemy to the north, Syria, had been defeated by Assyria, so Israel was able to develop freely. And so it did. The rich got richer, and the poor got poorer. The wealthy and powerful mistreated and abused the poor. This was not the way God intended his people to live. Thus, he raised up two prophets: Hosea, who was a citizen of the northern kingdom, and a man named Amos, who came north from the southern kingdom of Judah.

Little is actually known about Amos as a person. His village, Tekoa, was about 10 miles south of Jerusalem in a very desolate area. But when God called Amos and sent him north, he sent him not north to Jerusalem, but further north to Samaria, the capital city of Israel, with all of its wealth and power. "Amos" means "burdensome" or "burden bearer," and Amos indeed became "burdensome." His words were heavy against those rich and powerful people in Israel who lived by oppressing others. He was eventually asked to leave!

One of the challenges which faced Amos was that of the "professional prophets" (see p. 167). These "professionals" were false prophets who worked for the king and the religious establishment, and they always said what the king wanted them to say. They were silent in the face of injustice, when the rich oppressed the poor. Amos was not silent, and this brought him trouble – especially since he was recognized as being a foreigner from the south. One of the most famous confrontations in the Bible is found in Amos 7:10-17 where the (northern) priest Amaziah tells Amos to return "to the land of Judah, and eat bread there, and prophesy there." Amos wanted to deny any possible connection with the false prophets, and so responded:

> I am no prophet, nor a prophet's son; but I am a herdsman, and a dresser of sycamore trees, and the LORD took me from following the flock, and the LORD said to me, 'Go, prophesy to my people Israel.'

> Now therefore hear the word of the LORD ....

And the "word of the LORD" in the verses which follow (Amos 7:16-17) was indeed unpleasant for Amaziah.

As the response of Amos to Amaziah indicated, his background was rural. Thus, his words are filled with pictures from the life of a shepherd or farmer (Amos 3:4; 5:8; 7:1). At the same time, it is clear that he was also familiar with the sights of the city. He knew of

> the overfed, callous plutocrats at ease in their expensive houses, thinking only of how to amuse themselves, the peasant burdened with debts and sold into slavery for the price of a pair of shoes, the sanctuaries crowded with confident worshipers exulting in their good fortune, prophets and priests with no word to speak to a swiftly decaying society.[1]

Amos was fairly sophisticated and understood his times. Although he came from Judah, he knew (northern) Israel's historical, religious and legal traditions, and he knew geography and politics. He was also a skilled poet who used striking imagery (see Amos 2:9; 3:12), and who sometimes wrote with a poetic rhythm which gave a feeling of approaching disaster and doom.[2] Amos was also very skilled in his use of drama and suspense and surprise.

The book opens with two chapters of prophecies against foreign cities and nations (Amos 1-2). In Amos 1:3, he begins: "For three transgressions of Damascus, and for four, I will not revoke the punishment." Then he prophesies against Gaza (1:6); then Tyre (1:9); then Edom (1:11). Look carefully at the path in Fig. 1 on the next page. In Fig. 2, his words create a huge X over ...where? We must wait to find out. His listeners in Israel do not at first realize that he has just created the world's largest "chiasm."[3]

The prophecies continue (Fig. 3): against Ammon (1:13), then against Moab (2:1), then even against Judah (2:4). Perhaps by now the people of Israel were cheering. But suddenly Amos says, "For three

---

[1]J. D. Smart, "Amos" in *IDB* 1:117.

[2]Whether there is meter and rhythm in Hebrew poetry is debated by scholars. Some have noted what they call a "Kinah" meter which has one line with 3 beats followed by an "incomplete" or "broken" line of 2 beats. Thus 3 + 2. The broken or incomplete line gives the sense of being cut off too soon, and was thus used in laments for tragedies such as an early death.

[3]That is, a large letter X over the land. See p. 126 for chiasm.

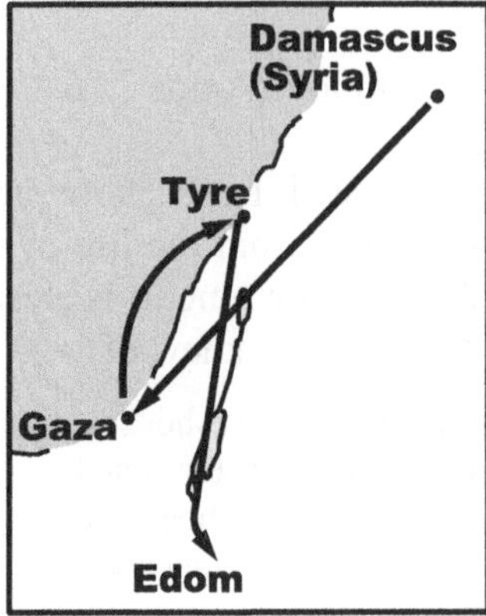

Figure 1

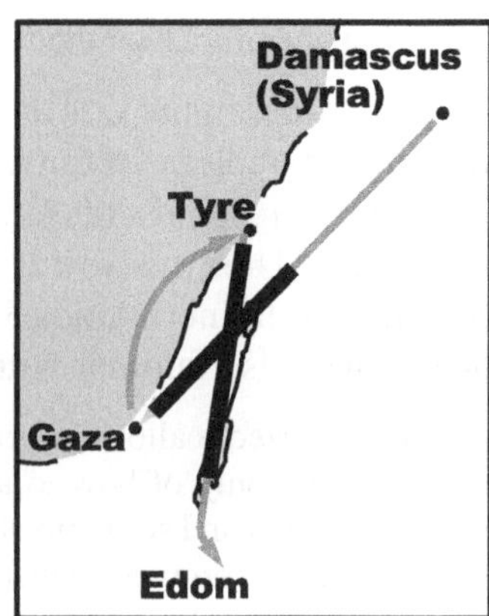

Figure 2

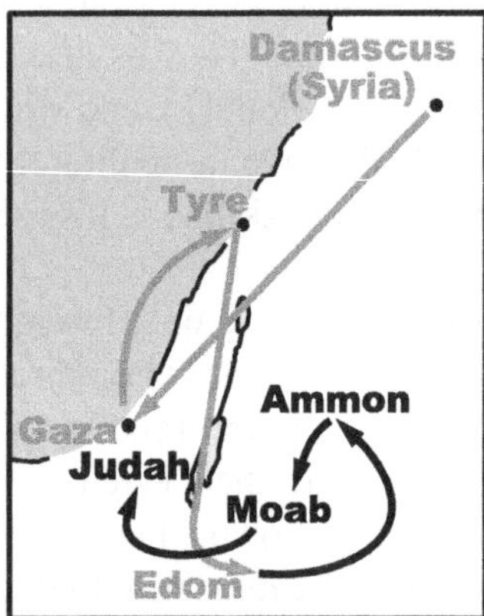

Figure 3

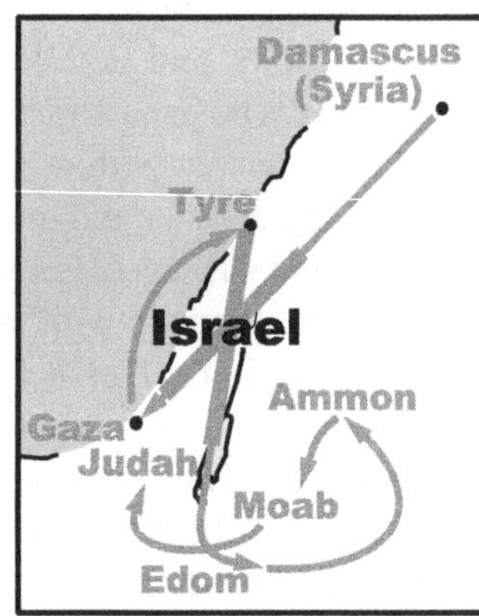

Figure 4

transgressions of **Israel**, and for four, I will not revoke the punishment" (2:6). The people of Israel are shocked. But now it is clear what lies in the center of the "chiasm" (see Fig. 4): Israel! And the rest of Amos 2 – the longest part of the oracle – is a series of prophecies against the people of Israel. His listeners were shocked; but he had their attention.

Outline

I. **Oracles:** against nations – including Israel (Amos 1-2). Note the structure, above

II. **Speeches:** "Hear the word of the LORD" (Amos 3-6).

III. Visions: "The Lord God showed me" (Amos 7-9)[4]

Message

Amos and Hosea. Hosea and Amos are the only two classical prophets who spoke directly to the north, and they spoke during the same period of Israel's history (the eighth century B.C.). They saw the same situations – worship of Baal and the rich oppressing the poor – but their messages were different in tone. Hosea was himself a northerner, and perhaps this is why he seems to experience God's own pain when he speaks words of judgment against his people (see the discussion of Hosea 11 on p. 205, above). His greatest concern was his people's unfaithfulness as they chase after the Baals. Amos comes up from the south, and seems to experience no personal hesitation or pain in delivering his strong message. And he never mentions Baal.[5] For Amos, the major issue is that of social injustice.

God and Israel. The clear and unhesitating message of Amos is that God is supreme, sovereign, and all-powerful. He is creator and sustainer (Amos 4:13; 5:8-9) and he controls both nature (Amos 8:9; 9:5-6) and the destiny of nations (Amos 1-2, discussed above). Most of all, God is righteous, and will not tolerate injustice among his people (Amos 2:8, cf Exod 22:26; Amos 4:1-3; 6:4-7; 8:4-6). Israel is God's people, but this brings responsibility as well as blessing, and can even lead to judgment ("You only have I known of all the families of the earth; therefore I will punish you for all your iniquities," Amos 3:2). Thus, the people have no special status, or religious or national "membership," which will make them right with God. Israel belongs to God, but God does not belong to Israel; there is no "national" God. Note that Amos never calls God the "God of Israel" or "God of Judah."

Cult and sacrifice. Amos also points out that mere sacrifice and cultic practice will not save the people. Joel was fairly positive toward the cult and sacrifice (see p. 210). Amos is not. Amos does not completely reject the temple and sacrifice, but he is very clear that such

---

[4]Visions sometimes involve a play on words. In Amos 8:2, the play is on two words which sound very similar: *qayits* (קָ֫יִץ) and *qets* (קֵץ). We read, "And [the LORD] said, 'Amos, what do you see?' And I said, 'A basket of summer-fruit (*qayits*).' Then the LORD said to me, 'The end (*qets*) has come upon my people Israel ....'" See also p. 180, footnote 2 regarding Jer 1:11-12.

[5]Other gods are mentioned in a few places, e.g., Amos 2:8; 5:26; 8:14.

rituals can become empty and useless. The most famous passage in Amos (5:21-27) begins with the words "I hate, I despise your feasts, and I take no delight in your solemn assemblies. Even though you offer me your burnt offerings and cereal offerings, I will not accept them."[6] Rather, "let justice roll down like waters, and righteousness like an ever-flowing stream" (Amos 5:24).

The Day of the LORD.[7] Amos is the first prophet to mention the day of the LORD, and he speaks against a misunderstanding of it. The day of the LORD refers to a time within history when God will appear and bring judgment against those who practice wickedness.[8] And although this, in general, is a good thing, Amos points out to the people of Israel that *they* had been living in wickedness and injustice. Thus, for them, the day of the LORD was not going to be pleasant. In Amos 5:18-20, he cries out,

> Woe to you who desire the day of the LORD. Why would you have the day of the LORD? It is darkness, and not light; as if a man fled from a lion, and a bear met him; or went into the house and leaned with his hand against the wall, and a serpent bit him. Is not the day of the LORD darkness, and not light, and gloom with no brightness in it?

The people did not realize that the day of the LORD would be a day of suffering for those who lived unjustly. They would not be spared simply because they were "God's chosen people."

Warnings to the wealthy. Amos brings us some of the Bible's strongest criticisms of injustice and misuse of wealth. By the time we finish reading Amos, we may find ourselves asking, "Does God hate wealth? Does God hate those who are wealthy?" And the questions are good and valid ones. Some suggest that God prefers those who are poor, and may even love them more. Jesus came into the world not as a rich

---

[6]In Amos 5:25, God asks the rhetorical question, "Did you bring to me sacrifices and offerings the forty years in the wilderness, O house of Israel?" The implied answer here is No. Like Hosea and Jeremiah, Amos thinks of the period of wilderness wandering as a time of faithfulness, in which the people lived under the law with integrity, and thus did not need sacrifice. See H.W. Wolff, "Joel and Amos," Hermeneia (Philadelphia: Fortress, 1977) 265.

[7]See also the discussion on p. 209, above.

[8]This is different from apocalyptic literature, which waits for God to shatter history itself and perhaps create a new heaven and a new earth. See p. 194.

man but as a poor carpenter's son. Yet, at the same time, wealth is often seen in the Old Testament as a sign of God's blessing. Abraham, Isaac and Jacob are all shown to be wealthy, and this is understood to be a good thing. David became wealthy. But then there was Solomon who became *very* wealthy and eventually went astray in his later years.

The issue, in Amos and in many places in the Bible, is not merely wealth – which, after all, is one of God's many gifts. Rather, the issue is that of privilege and responsibility. Being rich is not a sin in itself. Yet so often – in the Bible, and in the world around us – we see that wealth and power (or the *desire* for wealth and power) can become a great source of temptation. If we are blessed with wealth, it is so that we, in turn, may be a blessing to others. Privilege brings responsibility. This brings us back to Abraham and to that ancient promise where everything began, Gen 12:3: "and all peoples on earth will be blessed through you." Abraham was blessed – and God's people are blessed – *in order to be a blessing.*

But we can soon develop a sense of "entitlement" – that is, we can begin to feel that we deserve (and others do not) what we have. At that point, God may send a prophet like Amos, with words which accuse and burn, to challenge, to bring discomfort and perhaps even to threaten.

Hope? Are there any words of hope and promise in Amos? There are very few. The message of Amos is well summed up in the phrase, "Prepare to meet your God, O Israel" (Amos 4:12). He pleads with the people to repent (Amos 5:14-15), and he pleads with God for Israel (Amos 7:1-6). But finally he expects the northern kingdom to be destroyed; and in 722 B.C. this is what happened.

Yet at the very end of Amos, we do find words of hope – not that Israel will be spared, but rather that the house of David (which, of course, means the southern kingdom of Judah) will be restored (Amos 9:11). This will eventually lead also to "restor[ing] the fortunes of my people Israel" (Amos 9:14-15). But first, Israel must go through the experience of the Assyrian conquest.

Some important texts: Prepare to meet your God (Amos 4:12); the day of the LORD (Amos 5:18-20); let justice roll down like waters (Amos 5:21-24).

Verses for memory: Amos 4:12; 5:24

Obadiah

❧

Overview

The name Obadiah means "servant of Yahweh," and this may be a description rather than the prophet's real name.[1] The book is the shortest book in the Old Testament (just 21 verses[2]), and is a small collection of oracles against Edom,[3] Judah's southeastern neighbor (see the map on p. 13).

Why is Edom the target? Genesis says the people of Edom were descendants of Esau (Gen 25:30; 32:3; 36:1,8-9). Thus, the Edomites were generally looked upon as "brothers."[4] However 2 Sam 8:14 says that David conquered them and made them vassals,[5] and, at one point, David and Joab "slew every male in Edom" (1 Kings 11:15; see also Ps 60:1). So the relationship was not always a friendly one.

When Babylon destroyed Jerusalem and the temple in 586 B.C., some of Judah's near neighbors rejoiced. They may even have taken part in the destruction, or perhaps they betrayed Judah in one way or another. This would certainly not be an unusual attitude among vassal states such as Edom, and in Ps 137:7 we read of the Edomites cheering as Jerusalem was destroyed. This may also be suggested in Lam 4:21-22. And Jer 49:9-10, 14-16 is so similar to Obadiah 1-6 that there may be a relationship between the two.[6]

When did Obadiah speak or write his prophecy? There is no

---

[1]The same is true of the name Malachi, which means "my messenger" and may not be the prophet's actual name.

[2]In the New Testament, only 2 John and 3 John are shorter.

[3]The book of Nahum is similar, but Nahum's target is Assyria.

[4]The Jacob and Esau stories in Genesis 25-35 are one indication of this.

[5]A vassal is a state or a person who is owned or controlled by someone more powerful, and who therefore must serve them, pay taxes, etc.

[6]The whole oracle is Jer 49:7-22. We also find oracles against Edom in Amos 1:11; Isa 34:5-9; 63:1; Ezek 25:12-14; 35:1-15; 36:5; Joel 3:19; Mal 1:4.

information in the book which helps us answer that question, other than the references to Edom. He may have lived soon after the destruction of Jerusalem (during the time of Jeremiah and Ezekiel). Some scholars suggest that he may have lived later, in the fifth century, when Edom faced threats from the Nabataeans.[7] The answer depends in part upon how we translate the prohibitions in verses 12-14. The Hebrew literally says "Do not gloat ...; do not rejoice," etc., which places the situation in the present. But the RSV and NRSV translate "You should not have gloated ...; you should not have rejoiced ...," etc., which places the action in the past.

Outline

I. **Oracles against Edom** (Obadiah 1-10)
II. **Edom's sins** (Obadiah 11-14)
III. **The Day of the Lord** (Obadiah 15-18)
IV. **Restoration of Judah** (Obadiah 19-21)

Message

Obadiah does not bring us the theological weight of Isaiah or Jeremiah, but he is familiar with the prophetic themes which we find there and elsewhere. He speaks against national arrogance and pride (12-14), and looks for a remnant to survive in Israel (17). Beginning in verse 15, he looks for the day of the Lord, when Israel's enemies will be overthrown and Israel will be restored and again possess the land. Therefore he, too, like other prophets, hopes for the overthrow of evil and the ultimate rule of God as king.

---

[7]The Nabateans, like the Edomites, lived generally southeast of the Dead Sea. See the map on p. 13.

JONAH

❧

Overview

The book of Jonah is different from the other prophetic books. It contains only five words of prophecy (in the Hebrew text), it never calls Jonah a prophet, and it is concerned not with Israel or Judah but with the city of Nineveh. So how should we describe the book of Jonah? In many ways, the book of Jonah is more like a large parable than a book of prophecy. And who was Jonah? And where was Nineveh?

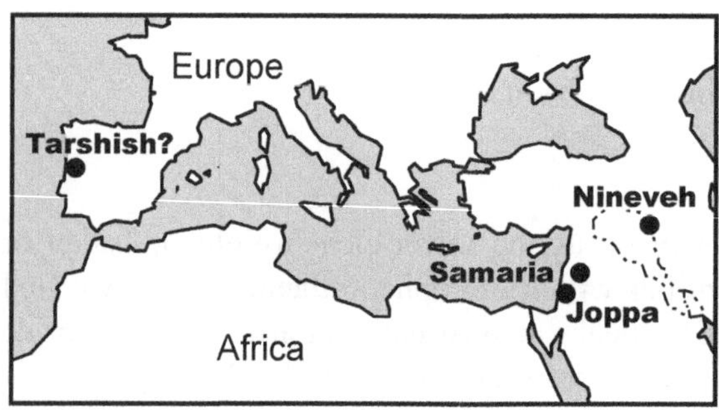

The World of Jonah

We read of "Jonah the son of Amittai, the prophet, who was from Gathhepher" in 2 Kings 14:25. The king of Israel at that time was Jeroboam II (786-746 B.C.). The book of Jonah itself, however, seems to come from a time when the city of Nineveh was hated by the Jews. (Certainly Jonah hates the city!) Nineveh was the capital of Assyria, and Assyria destroyed Samaria in 722 B.C. So, it seems likely that the book of Jonah has these facts in mind. As we shall see in the section on "Message," below, it is even possible that the book of Jonah is really concerned not with Nineveh but with the lives of the later exiles in Babylon. Thus, the book may come out of the period of the Babylonian exile and may represent the many questions raised by that experience.

We assume that Jonah was in Samaria, the capital city of Israel, when God called him. God told him to go to Nineveh (1:2), the capital of Assyria, which was northeast of Israel. Instead, Jonah headed southwest to Joppa and got on a ship going to Tarshish (1:3). Where was

Tarshish? Several suggestions have been made: Egypt, Sidon, Asia Minor, Greece, North Africa. But many think that Tarshish was on the west coast of Spain – as far from Nineveh as Jonah could possibly go in those days. Why did he go there? Because he did not want to go to Nineveh – though we are not yet told why. Furthermore, we read that "Jonah rose to flee to Tarshish *from the presence of the LORD*" (1:3).

Of course, it is really not possible to "flee from the presence of the LORD," and the writer of Jonah knew this, as we shall see. The book of Jonah is a satire,[1] and the writer is attacking the points of view which Jonah represents. We can see something similar in Job, where the three friends represent a point of view which the writer opposed. But Job did not use humor and irony[2] in the same way that we will see in Jonah. Jonah is satire; Job was not.

Jonah tries to flee in a ship, but God sends a storm after him. The gentile sailors pray while Jonah sleeps. Here is another indication that we are reading satire: the "pagan" gentile sailors seem more religious and pious than Jewish Jonah does. The captain of the ship awakens Jonah, and he and the sailors discover why they are having trouble: it is because Jonah is running away from "the LORD, the God of heaven, who made the sea and the dry land" (Jon 1:9). More satire. If Jonah believed that God had created the sea, how could he attempt to flee from him in a ship? Even the gentile sailors recognize that this is foolish, and so now they begin to pray not to their own gods but to the LORD. Again, the gentile sailors seem more pious than Jonah.

Jonah says that they should throw him into the sea, but they refuse at first and try to fight the storm. This shows us two things. First, it shows us that the gentile sailors care for Jonah's life more than Jonah

---

[1]Satire is a type of literature in which the writer uses humor to attack a point of view which he opposes. The writer will exaggerate the truth, or use irony (p. 33, footnote 6) or sarcasm to make his point. The writer of Jonah certainly does not believe that it is possible to flee from God's presence, and he soon shows this with the storm and the big fish. He also does not believe that it is good or right for Jonah (who represents Israel) to hate Nineveh. Satire is not fiction; it is exaggerated truth. It is truth which is stretched or distorted in order to get people to laugh at something which is wrong. Thus, the writer of satire shows his disagreement with someone else's point of view not by directly contradicting it but rather by showing it to be foolish through the use of humor and irony.

[2]See p. 33 footnote 6 for the meaning of irony.

cares for Nineveh; second, it shows us that Jonah's refusal to go to Nineveh was *not* because he hated gentiles. He actually offers to be thrown overboard for the sake of these gentiles. So Jonah hated Nineveh, not merely gentiles.

But there was another reason why Jonah was fleeing God's call. That reason is found in a conversation which took place at the very beginning of Jonah, between Jon 1:2 and Jon 1:3. But the conversation is not written there, and we as readers do not even know that it happened – until it is mentioned and explained at the end of the story. And when we come to the end of the story and read about that conversation, we will suddenly understand the whole book of Jonah! But the writer keeps that conversation well hidden until then.

Eventually, the sailors agree to throw Jonah into the raging sea. The storm then stops, and God "appoints" a fish to bring him back to land. This time, when God tells Jonah to go to Nineveh, Jonah goes. And he preaches a very short message: "In 40 days, Nineveh shall be overthrown." Jonah does not preach for repentance, he just preaches judgment. Yet the people of Nineveh repent anyway. More irony. And when the people of Nineveh repent, so does God (3:10, RSV). We will say more about this below.

This double repentance makes Jonah angry, but he still has hope that God might destroy Nineveh, and so he leaves the city and sits down east of it and builds himself a shelter. There he waits to see what God is going to do. What God does is again "appoint." This time, he appoints a plant, a worm and "a sultry east wind" to try to teach Jonah a lesson. But Jonah is angry and does not want to learn. When the story ends, we are unsure whether Jonah has learned anything. But we as *readers* have learned some things – things discussed after the outline..

Outline

The outline of Jonah is very simple. The story has two parallel sections, chapters 1-2 and chapters 3-4. Both sections start with exactly the same words: "Arise, go to Nineveh the great city and call out (*qara'*, קָרָא)." At that point, however, there is a significant difference in the Hebrew. The first time he is told to call out *against* (*'al*, עַל) Nineveh, and the second time he is told to call out *to* (*'el*, אֶל) Nineveh.

I. Section 1: the disobedient Jonah

A. Jonah is called and runs away (Jonah 1)

B. Jonah before God: in the belly of the fish (Jonah 2)

II. Section 1: the resentful Jonah

A. Jonah is called and goes to Nineveh (Jonah 3)

B. Jonah before God: outside Nineveh (Jonah 4)

Message

Is God just? Whoever wrote the book of Jonah[3] is dealing with some challenging questions.[4] When Assyria destroyed Samaria – and certainly when Babylon destroyed Jerusalem and the temple – the Jews were greatly distressed. Yes, Israel and Judah had sinned before God; but the Assyrians and Babylonians were even worse! So the people began to ask questions like

- "Why do bad things happen to good people?" (Surely the people of Israel and Judah were better people than those of Assyria or Babylon!) And ...
- "Why do good things happen to bad people?" (Why did God give success to Assyria and Babylon?)

Job asks the first question; as we shall see, Jonah seems to be asking the second question.

Jonah's problem. Jonah is not anti-gentile. As we saw above, he had a good relationship with the gentile sailors, and he even volunteered to be thrown into the stormy sea to save them. Jonah's problem was Nineveh, because Nineveh had destroyed Samaria. Thus, he hated Nineveh (as did many of the people of Israel). But Jonah had even a bigger problem than Nineveh. Jonah had a problem with God.

Jonah tries to avoid doing what God called him to do by running away. The writer of the story uses words very carefully, and shows Jonah going down, down, down as he runs away from God. In Jon 1:3, he goes down (*yarad*, יָרַד) to Joppa and finds a ship, and then goes down (*yarad*) into the ship. Then, when the storm comes up, we find that

---

[3]Clearly, Jonah himself did not write the book because (1) the story is written in the third person, not the first person (that is, Jonah is "he" not "I"), and (2) the writer disagrees with Jonah's attitude.

[4]By the time of Jesus, the troubling questions which lie behind Jonah had receded to the background. Thus, Jonah is only described as a "sign" (Matt 12:39-41; 16:4; Luke 11:29-32), and the issues of the book of Jonah are not mentioned.

Jonah had gone further down (*yarad*) into the hold of the ship (Jon 1:5). There, he fell "fast asleep," and here the writer cleverly uses a verb which also sounds like *yarad*: *way**yeradam***.[5] Finally, in the belly of the fish, Jonah cries out, "I descended (*yarad*) to the roots of the mountains" (Jon 2:6, NASB). Here, Jonah has sunk as far as he can go. Now the only way to go is up.

Clearly, Jonah has now learned that it is not possible to "flee from the presence of the LORD." As we noted above, this point is also made again and again as God "appoints" nature to do his will, first appointing the fish, and later the plant, the worm, and the wind.

The repentance of God. In Jonah, however, God does not just appoint. In Jon 3:10, God also repents (RSV) or changes his mind (NRSV). Either translation is difficult and troubling for us. We first learn that God is willing to change his mind in Genesis 18 (p. 32, above), where perhaps Abraham should have argued with God about Sodom a little longer. After that, God actually did change his plans in Exodus 3-4, where he allowed Moses to argue with him at the burning bush. Later, after Aaron and the people made the golden calf, God repented of doing evil to his people when Moses again argued with him (Exodus 32, see p. 41). Now, in Jonah, something similar happens again. When Jonah preaches his very short sermon, the people of Nineveh "turned (*shub*, שׁוּב) from their evil (*ra'*, רַע)[6] way" (Jon 3:10), and at that point "God repented (*nacham*, נָחַם) of the evil (*ra'*, רַע) which he had said he would do to them; and he did not do it." Can God repent of evil (RSV)? Does God even change his mind (NRSV)?

The question is a deep and philosophical one. Monotheists such as Christians, Jews and Muslims must eventually deal with it. If there is only one God, and all things come from him, then it would seem that even evil must also come from God.[7] Yet certainly this does not mean that God is unreliable. In matters of trustworthiness and integrity, "God

---

[5]וַיֵּרָדַם from *radam* רָדַם, "to fall sound asleep."

[6]"Evil" (*ra'*, רַע) is an important theme in Jonah. The book begins by mentioning the "evil" of the Ninevites (Jon 1:2), and of the storm (Jon 1:7,8). Jon 3:8 then mentions the evil from which Nineveh is to repent. Then, when they repent of their evil in Jon 3:10, God repents of his! This repentance of God is then seen by Jonah as a great evil in Jon 4:1.

[7]The Bible suggests this, too. In Isa 45:7, God says "I form light and create darkness, I make weal and create woe (*ra'*, רַע), I am the LORD, who do all these things."

is not man, that he should lie, or a son of man, that he should repent" (*nacham*, נָחַם).[8] This is clear. Yet scripture also has places in which God appears willing to change his plans when confronted by human arguments, actions or requests.

At this point, we can only note what is said in each place where this idea appears. At the burning bush, when God allows Moses to change his (God's) plans, he is trying to encourage Moses and to build trust and a relationship with him. Even in the Garden of Eden, where God asked Adam, "Where are you?" (Gen 3:9), we find God seeking to maintain a damaged relationship. Surely this is one important lesson: God so much wants relationship with us that he is willing to let us argue with him, and perhaps even change his plans. After the people build the golden calf, God's words to Moses (Exod 32:7-10) seem designed to provoke Moses to plead for the people.[9] Indeed, Moses then tells God to repent (RSV; in NRSV Moses tells God to "change his mind")[10] of evil and God does so (Exod 32:11-14). Here, the point seems to be that God desires our prayer and intercession and that he listens to us.

But what about God's repentance in Jon 3:10? God has not been seeking a relationship with Nineveh (as he did with Adam and Moses). Jonah certainly does not pray to God on behalf of Nineveh[11] (as Abraham did for Sodom, or as Moses later did for Israel). Rather, the point seems to be this: *even when God declares that he is going to destroy a city*, he will change his mind ("repent of evil") if the people of

---

[8]Num 23:19, RSV. NRSV says "nor a son of man, that he should change his mind."

[9]Compare to the similar conversation with Abraham in Gen 18:17-33.

[10]The important verb is *nacham* (נָחַם), which has many meanings including "to repent" and "to change one's mind." One very interesting passage is 1 Sam 15:10-35, where in verse 11 God says "I repent (*nacham*) that I made Saul king." Samuel then says that God "will not lie or repent (*nacham*); for he is not a man, that he should repent (*nacham*)" (verse 29). Finally, at the end, "the LORD repented (*nacham*) that he had made Saul king over Israel." In all three cases, the form of the verb is Niphal, as in Jonah 3:9-10. The Bible never fully resolves this tension of God's stability and change. And perhaps it is necessary that this tension be left unresolved (see the similar tension in Hosea 11). Human language always falls short of fully explaining God.

[11]Even the writer may have *some* reserve regarding Nineveh. When the gentile sailors make vows, they pray to "the LORD" (that is, to *Yahweh*, the God of Israel). The people of Nineveh do not; they just pray to "God."

that city repent. Jeremiah also explores this idea (Jer 18:1-10) as does Ezekiel (chapter 18). Even when God threatens judgment, he asks, "Why will you die,..? For I have no pleasure in the death of any one, says the Lord GOD; so turn, and live" (Ezek 18:31-32).

Jonah's anger. Why is Jonah displeased when God changes his mind? Some suggest it is because this change leaves his prophecy unfulfilled and makes him a false prophet! But there is much more to it than that. At the beginning of chapter 4 we are finally told about the earlier conversation, mentioned above, which took place between Jonah and God.[12] Now we learn why Jonah tried to flee in the first place – though the author has kept it a secret until now. In Jon 4:2, Jonah looks up to God and angrily complains:

> O LORD! Is not this what I said while I was still in my own country? That is why I fled to Tarshish at the beginning; for I knew that you are a gracious God and merciful, slow to anger, and abounding in steadfast love, and ready to relent (*nacham*) from punishing. (NRSV)

This is what we did not know in chapter 1: Jonah tried to flee to Tarshish not merely to avoid preaching judgment to Nineveh, but because he knew God was merciful. He knew that if Nineveh repented God would forgive them, and Jonah simply could not accept that idea. Jonah thinks God is too soft, and he tells him so. Fortunately for Jonah, God also has a sense of humor. We first saw this when God used a fish to bring Jonah back. Now God "appoints" a plant, then a worm and then "a sultry east wind" to chide and even tease Jonah a bit. The plant gives Jonah shade, but the worm and the wind make Jonah miserable. God then uses all three to show Jonah how selfish he had been. Jonah had cared about a plant (because it helped *him*!) but he did not care about "more than a hundred and twenty thousand persons who do not know their right hand from their left, and also much cattle" (Jon 4:11).

Again, we must remember that this is satire. But satire can be used in a serious way, and the issues here *are* serious. So now, having finished the basic discussion of Jonah, I want to add some final thoughts which make use of the other material mentioned in this book.

Beyond Jonah: some further reflection.

In exile in Babylon, many Jews were asking questions such as the

---

[12]On p. 222, we noted that a conversation apparently took place between Jon 1:2 and Jon 1:3, and that the reader has been left unaware of it until now.

following:

- How can God be fair and just if he lets an evil nation such as Assyria or Babylon defeat us?
- Can God really be righteous if he forgives sin? (We might ask, "Can a judge be righteous if he frees criminals?")
- If relationships with foreigners caused us to sin before the exile, should we reject all contact with gentiles after we return from Babylon? (Here you can hear the voices of Ezra and Nehemiah.)
- God said he would "visit the iniquity of the fathers upon the children and the children's children, to the third and the fourth generation" (Exod 34:6-7; Num. 14:18). This is now happening to us in Babylon. We are suffering because of the *sins of our parents*. Why should *we* repent?

These were and are serious questions. In seeking to answer them, we need to consider the following.

Jonah himself. In the book of Jonah, Jonah seems very rigid. He does not *want* God to be merciful; he wants God to be righteous. He wants God to destroy Nineveh. But the writer has another point of view. Using gentle satire, the writer is saying to Jonah (and to the reader), "Jonah, God *is* merciful. And that really is good news; it is gospel. Yes, it was good news for Nineveh, but it is also good news for us. For if God immediately had mercy on the repenting sinners in Nineveh, then it may mean that his threat to 'visit the iniquity of the fathers ... to the third and fourth generation' is not his 'final offer.'" Perhaps the writer of Jonah remembered Jer. 18:7-8, where God said:

> "If at any time I declare concerning a nation or a kingdom, that I will pluck up and break down and destroy it, and if that nation, concerning which I have spoken, turns from its evil, I will repent of the evil that I intended to do to it."[13]

To exiles living in Babylon, this was a marvelous word of hope. If they turned to God in repentance, God would restore them immediately – not after three or four generations. Just as their rebellion had brought punishment even after God had promised to bless Israel, so their repentance could lead to forgiveness even after God had brought judgment.

Another tension. Once again, we have a tension. We have seen this

---

[13]See also Ezekiel 18.

many times now (look up "Tension" in the Index at the back of this book). On the one hand, God had warned the first generation at the time of Moses that their sins would affect their descendants "to the third and fourth generation."[14] And this indeed happened. This is an important word of warning to parents: your sins will have horrible effect in the lives of your children and even their children. On the other hand, when the children were indeed suffering many generations later, there was a new word – from Jeremiah, from Ezekiel, and now from Jonah. Some of their suffering was brought on by their own sin. It was *not* all their parents' fault (see Jer 31:29,30; Ezek 18:2). But God is merciful, and God will "repent of evil" when those who are evil repent. Do not blame your parents for your suffering; you have your own sins to account for. Instead, accept personal responsibility and confess your sins before God. Two words: a word to parents, and then a word to children many generations later. These two statements remain in tension for all time. They remain in tension for us today, as well.

Jonah thought God's graciousness and mercy were bad news. He did not realize how good the news really was, for him, for Israel, and for the world.

Some important texts: God's calls to Jonah (Jonah 1:2; 3:2); God's "appointments" in nature (Jonah 1:17; 4:6-8); Jonah's psalm in the belly of the fish (Jonah 2:2-9); Jonah's short sermon (Jonah 3:4); Nineveh's repentance (Jonah 3:5-9); God's repentance (Jonah 3:10).

Verses for memory: Jonah 4:2

---

[14]Exod 20:5; 34:7; Num 14:18; Deut 5:9.

MICAH

❧

Overview

The first verse of the book tells us three things about Micah. First, he came from Moresheth.[1] Second, the word of the LORD came to him during the reigns of Kings Jotham (742-735 B.C.), Ahaz (735-715 B.C.) and Hezekiah (715-687/6 B.C.). Third, he prophesied against both Samaria and Jerusalem.

Thus, Micah spoke at the same time as Isaiah, who was with him in Jerusalem. This was also the time of Amos and Hosea, both of whom prophesied in Israel and Samaria. There must have been a connection between Micah and Isaiah because Mic 4:1-3 and Isa 2:2-4 contain the same words. However, we have no way of knowing whether Micah got the words from Isaiah, or Isaiah from Micah, or whether they each got them from a third source.

All we know about Micah is what we learn from the book of Micah itself – and also from a single very interesting reference in Jeremiah a century later. Jer 26:10-24 mentions a trial, in which the leaders of Judah consider putting Jeremiah to death because he had prophesied against Jerusalem. In Jer 26:18-19, we read that some of the elders spoke on behalf of Jeremiah, saying:

> "Micah of Moresheth prophesied in the days of Hezekiah king of Judah, and said to all the people of Judah: 'Thus says the LORD of hosts, Zion shall be plowed as a field; Jerusalem shall become a heap of ruins, and the mountain of the house a wooded height.' Did Hezekiah king of Judah and all Judah put him to death? Did he not fear the LORD and entreat the favor of the LORD, and did not the LORD repent of the evil which he had pronounced against them? But we are about to bring great evil upon ourselves."

---

[1]This probably means Moresheth-gath (mentioned in Mic 1:14), a small and rural village which lay about 25 miles SW of Jerusalem in the foothills between the coastal plain and the hills of central Judah.

Here, the elders remember words of Micah (Mic 3:12) spoken 100 years earlier, and they use them to defend Jeremiah. (We shall return to Mic 3:12 below, on p. 232.) This passage from Jeremiah is very interesting because it tells of a confrontation between Micah and Hezekiah. We do not read about that in Micah. According to this passage from Jeremiah, however, Hezekiah (who was a good king) repented and prayed to the LORD; and at that point the LORD "repent[ed] of the evil which he had pronounced against them."[2]

Hezekiah. King Hezekiah is remembered as one of Judah's two good kings (in addition to David, of course, who is the model for all of them). The other one was Josiah, Hezekiah's great-grandson. Both Hezekiah and Josiah engaged in religious reforms,[3] and thus both had the support and trust of prophets and priests. Hezekiah centralized worship in Jerusalem, and took down the high places. He also expanded Jerusalem to make room for refugees who came down from Samaria when it was destroyed by the Assyrians. In addition, he strengthened the walls of Jerusalem before the Assyrians themselves came south, and he is most famous for building the 533 meter Siloam tunnel through solid rock to bring water from a spring into Jerusalem during the siege.

Assyria. In 745 B.C., the powerful and assertive Tiglath-Pilesar III became king of Assyria and started expanding his empire toward the west.[4] Israel and its capital city, Samaria, were destroyed in 722 B.C. after which Assyria turned south toward Judah. In the attack of 701 B.C., Tiglath-Pilesar's grandson, Sennacherib, destroyed 46 fortified Judean towns. Finally, Hezekiah paid a ransom, and Jerusalem was spared (2 Kgs 18:13-16).

Reading Micah. The book of Micah is, for the most part, a collection of independent short poems. Thus, each prophecy usually stands alone and is not connected with what comes before or after. This means we cannot depend upon what comes before or after to help us in our understanding. Instead, we must look for clues within the individual

---

[2]See pp. 224-228 and the Index at the back of the book for discussions about the "repentance of God."

[3]It is possible that the early edition of Deuteronomy, which Josiah found in the temple in 622 B.C. (p. 57f), was originally brought south from Israel when Samaria fell in 722 B.C. If so, then it may have inspired the reforms of Hezekiah as well as those of Josiah 100 years later.

[4]See the chronological table on p. 173, and review the maps on pp. 10, 13 and 93.

prophecies themselves.

Furthermore, like other prophets, Micah sometimes uses plays on words. For instance, in Mic 1:10-16, the name of each town sounds like its fate – as if one were to say "London shall be undone; Texas shall pay taxes; there shall be robbery in Nairobi."[5]

Outline

Micah has two sections, and in each section there is movement from judgment to salvation:

I. **First group of prophecies** (Micah 1-5)
   A. Prophecies of judgment (Micah 1-3)
   B. Prophecies of salvation (Micah 4-5)
II. **Second group of prophecies** (Micah 6-7)
   A. Prophecies of judgment (Mic 6:1-7:7)
   B. Prophecies of salvation (Mic 7:8-20)

Mic 7:8-10 may have been written somewhat later, perhaps after the Babylonian victory over Jerusalem. In these verses, it sounds as if Jerusalem has suffered defeat because of God's judgment, and that the city now waits for his deliverance.

Message

General message. Like other eighth and seventh century prophets, Micah announces that God is going to punish the people with military defeat and then exile because of their sin. Later, he will restore them to the land and will give them eternal peace.

The main issues in Micah are ethical. Exploitation and oppression by high officials (including priests, prophets and judges) are mentioned, especially in chapters 2, 3, and 6. Like Amos in the north, Micah insists that the people should be consistent in their religious and social lives. Sacrifice or worship at the temple were empty and meaningless if the

---

[5]Remember also Amos 8:2 (p. 128), where Amos speaks of "summer fruit" (*qayits*, קַ֫יִץ), and "end" (*qets*, קֵץ). Or Isa 5:7 (p. 128), where God looked for "justice" (*mishpat*, מִשְׁפָּט), but found "bloodshed" (*mispach*, מִשְׂפָּח), and for "righteousness" (*tsedaqah*, צְדָקָה), but instead found "a cry" (*tse'aqah*, צְעָקָה). Or Jer 1:11-14 which uses "almond" (*shaqed*, שָׁקֵד), and "watching" (*shoqed*, שֹׁקֵד) (p. 180, footnote 2).

people then acted unjustly and exploited their neighbors. God would use Assyria to punish both Samaria and Jerusalem, since these wealthy cities and their leaders were the heart of the problem.

Traditions of Israel (north) and Judah (south). Micah was a southern prophet, but he was not an advocate of Davidic or Zion traditions. Like Jeremiah who prophesied a century later, he did not believe in the "inviolability of Jerusalem" (that is, that Jerusalem could never be "violated" or destroyed). Rather, Micah was very much aware of the conditional traditions of Moses and Sinai. These were better known in the north and needed to be held in tension with the unconditional Davidic covenant of the south.[6] Thus, Micah shocked the people of Jerusalem when he said, "Zion shall be plowed as a field; Jerusalem shall become a heap of ruins, and the mountain of the house a wooded height" (Mic 3:12). As noted above (p. 229), the people remembered these words a century later during the time of Jeremiah.

Well-known texts. In addition to Micah's "Zion shall be plowed like a field" prophecy, discussed in the previous paragraph, there are two other texts which are particularly well known. In **Mic 5:1-4**, the prophet points to Bethlehem Ephrathah as the future birthplace of one "who is to be ruler in Israel, whose origin is from of old, from ancient days." Under this future leader, people will return to Israel and be reunited, and there will be peace and security. Many years later, Matthew (Matt 2:6) understood this text to be a prophecy of the birth of Christ. A second well-known text is the lawsuit controversy between God and his people in **Mic 6:1-8**. Here, the mountains are called as witnesses, and the accused people cry out, "What do you want from us, God? What shall we bring? More sacrifices? Do you want us to sacrifice our children?!" Micah answers for God: "He has showed you, O man, what is good; and what does the LORD require of you but to do justice, and to love kindness, and to walk humbly with your God?" Again, cultic activity (sacrifice and worship) are meaningless if people are living unjustly with one another.

Words of hope. Each of the two sections of Micah ends with prophecies of salvation (see the outline above). Mic 4:1-3 is essentially the same as Isa 2:2-4, and speaks of a day when "the mountain of the house of the LORD shall be established as the highest of the mountains," and the nations of the world will say, "Come, let us go up to the

---

[6]See the discussion of this matter found in the "Message" section of Jeremiah, pp. 181-183, above.

mountain of the LORD," in order to learn God's ways and walk in his paths. Here, there is great hope that, through the people of Israel and a restored temple (Mount Zion), all people in the world will come to know God. Micah (and Isaiah) looks for a day of peace and justice between people, in which "nation shall not lift up sword against nation, neither shall they learn war any more" (Mic 4:3).

Micah 7 concludes on a similar theme and, as noted above, seems to speak of a day after Jerusalem has suffered tremendously and has then been restored.[7] The chapter describes

- the building of walls (7:11)
- the return of refugees (7:12) and a remnant (7:18)
- the nations' shame at what they have done to Israel (7:16-17)

The last two verses of Micah (7:19-20) conclude with an exalted vision of a day in which God will show mercy and forgive sins:

> He will again have compassion upon us, he will tread our iniquities under foot. Thou wilt cast all our sins into the depths of the sea. Thou wilt show faithfulness to Jacob and steadfast love to Abraham, as thou hast sworn to our fathers from the days of old.

Some important texts: "Zion shall be plowed as a field" (Mic 3:12); the "mountain of the house of the LORD" as "the highest of the mountains" (Mic 4:1-4); "O Bethlehem Ephrathah" (Mic 5:1-4); God's lawsuit with Israel (Mic 6:1-8)

Verses for memory: Mic 5:2; 6:8

---

[7]Thus, many think it was written not by Micah but rather by someone living after Babylon destroyed Jerusalem.

NAHUM

❧

Overview

The prophet. The prophet Nahum came from Elkosh (Nah 1:1), possibly a town in southwest Judah although the actual location is uncertain. And although the name "Nahum" probably means "comfort" or "consolation," we find little of either in this book. Rather, it contains a vivid description of the LORD's judgment against Nineveh, the capital of Assyria. Yet Nahum probably prophesied 100 years after the time when Assyria was threatening Samaria. Thus, he prophesied much later than Amos, Hosea, Isaiah, and Micah ... but when?

The times: two large clues. No kings are mentioned, and so the date of Nahum must be found from other clues within the book. And there are two large clues that tell us when this book was written.

First, Nahum prophesies against Nineveh (Nah 1:1; 2:8; 3:7), and so Nineveh was still standing when Nahum wrote. This means Nahum prophesied before 612 B.C., since that is the year Nineveh was destroyed by the Medes.[1]

The second great clue is found in Nah 3:8-10. Here, Nahum asks Nineveh, "Are you better than Thebes that sat by the Nile...? [S]he was carried away, she went into captivity; ... and all her great men were bound in chains." Thebes was destroyed in 663 B.C. Since Nahum knows about this event, he prophesied after it. Thus, Nahum prophesied sometime after 663 B.C. (when Thebes fell) and before 612 B.C. (when Nineveh fell).

We can therefore say that Nahum prophesied sometime in the period 663-612 B.C.[2]

---

[1]See p. 178 for a chronological table of this period.

[2]***Terminus a quo* and *terminus ad quem*.** You may encounter these Latin phrases in your reading elsewhere. This discussion of the dating of Nahum is a good demonstration of what they mean. *Terminus a quo* is the earliest possible date for something. *Terminus ad quem* is the latest possible date. Thus,

It is possible that the prophecy of Nahum encouraged King Josiah (640-609 B.C.) in his reforms. In 627 B.C., Ashurbanipal, the last great king of Assyria, died. Certainly, this event could have been seen as a sign that Nahum's words were coming true; and the fall of Nineveh in 612 B.C. would have been understood as a fulfillment of his prophecy.

Reading Nahum. Nahum was not only a prophet but also a great poet. He brings us vivid images of the power of God, as well as of the expected fall of Nineveh. Chapters 2 and 3 have been described both as an "ode[3] on the fall of Nineveh" as well as a "taunt song."[4] They give a graphic description of what a military assault on a large city was like in the seventh century B.C. Nahum prophesied at the same time as Habakkuk, whose prophecy should be studied along with that of Nahum.

Outline

Nahum begins with a psalm or hymn which describes the LORD as "slow to anger but great in power" and one who "will by no means clear the guilty" (1:3). But for those who take refuge in him he is "a stronghold in the day of trouble" (1:7). This hymn is often described as a theophany.[5]

I. **Title and Hymn of Theophany** (Nah 1:1-8)
II. **Prophecies of judgment and promise** (Nah 1:9-2:2)
III. **Fall of Nineveh foretold** (the "ode" or "taunt song") (Nah 2:3-3:19)

Message

Many readers find Nahum to be troubling and too nationalistic. Unlike most other prophets, Nahum does not condemn the sins of Israel

---

in the paragraph above, the fall of Thebes in 663 B.C. is the *terminus a quo* for the prophecies of Nahum, and the fall of Nineveh in 612 B.C. is the *terminus ad quem* for his prophecies. We can show this as follows:

Terminus a quo	Nahum's prophecies	Terminus ad quem
663 B.C. |———	———————————	———| 612 B.C.

[3]An ode is a formal poem, usually somewhat long, and often written in a style which can be sung by the poet.

[4]To "taunt" is to mock and insult someone scornfully. "Taunt songs" are often sung at an opposing army or group in order to insult and anger them.

[5]See p. 31, footnote 2, for "theophany."

or Judah; yet he rejoices greatly over the future destruction of Nineveh. This attitude toward Nineveh is quite different from that of the book of Jonah (though not different from the attitude of Jonah himself!), and reading Jonah alongside Nahum can offer some balance.

On the other hand, Nahum does show us several sides of God's nature in the opening psalm. We read that God is the lord of history and commands the fate of nations. He is slow to anger, but his patience will not prevent him from ultimately judging the wicked. Furthermore, God protects those who seek refuge in him.

As mentioned above, possibly one of Nahum's most important contributions was as an inspiration for the important reforms of King Josiah. Although Nahum's words to Nineveh were threatening, his words to the people of Judah brought hope. "Behold, on the mountains the feet of him who brings good tidings, who proclaims peace!" (Nah 1:15; cf. Isa 52:7 and Rom 10:15).

Some important texts: the LORD is slow to anger but punishes the guilty (Nah 1:3); the feet of one bringing good tidings (Nah 1:15); the fall of Thebes (Nah 3:8-10)

Verses for memory: Nah 1:15a

Habakkuk

❧

Overview

Habakkuk prophesied in Judah at about the same time as Jeremiah, Nahum and Zephaniah – perhaps around 625-600 B.C. Like his fellow prophets, he was aware of both the wickedness of the wealthy and powerful as well as the threat from Mesopotamia, where Assyria was crumbling and Babylon was increasing in power. But, whereas Nahum looked at decaying Assyria and prophesied the destruction of Nineveh, Habakkuk was concerned about the approach of Babylon.

Habakkuk begins with a serious question which may remind us of Job: Why do the "wicked surround the righteous?" (Hab 1:4). Habakkuk looks around him and sees nothing but injustice. Why do good people suffer, and evil people seem to succeed? We must begin by asking, who were "the wicked" in the time of Habakkuk? He may have meant either the Babylonians, the weakening Assyrians, or the corrupt leaders of Judah. All were a problem for the righteous. The first two chapters of Habakkuk could be summarized as follows:

Habakkuk:	"O God, why do the wicked succeed and good people suffer?" (1:2-4)
God:	"I am raising up the Chaldeans[1] in your days." (1:5-11)
Habakkuk:	"The Chaldeans??!! To punish the wicked? But they themselves are wicked, too!!" (1:12-2:1)
God:	"This is a time for those who are righteous to live by faith; others will fail." (2:2-5)
Habakkuk:	"Woe to the wicked!" (five woes) (2:6-20)

---

[1]For our purposes, the Chaldeans may be considered to be the same as the Babylonians. Technically, they were an outside group that entered southern Mesopotamia and lived there approximately 1000-600 B.C. They spoke a different language than the Akkadian language of the Assyrians and Babylonians and, for a time, even ruled the Babylonians. After the fall of Babylon in 539 B.C. they were absorbed into the culture.

In Hab 2:1, Habakkuk is so upset about God's plans to raise up the Chaldeans that he says he is going to climb up into a tower and wait there like a watchman until God answers him.[2]

The book then concludes with a hymn or psalm of theophany[3] similar to the one found at the beginning of Nahum. Like many other psalms, it even has instructions for the leader of music. The last three verses of the book present a strong confession of trust in "the God of my salvation."

Outline

I. Title and Habakkuk's complaints to God (Hab 1:1-2:5)

- A. Habakkuk's complaint about the success of the wicked (Hab 1:1-4)
- B. God's response: I am raising up the Chaldeans (Hab 1:5-11)
- C. Habakkuk's complaint about the Chaldeans (Hab 1:12-2:1)
- D. God's response: the righteous will live by faith (Hab 2:2-5)[4]

II. Five woes against the wicked (Hab 2:6-20)

III. Habakkuk's prayer: a hymn of theophany (Hab 3:1-16)

IV. Confession of trust: I will rejoice in ... the God of my salvation (Hab 3:17-19)

Message

"O LORD, how long shall I cry for help, and thou wilt not hear?" (Hab 1:2). The cry of Habakkuk is often heard among God's people. Why does God sometimes seem so distant or silent in the face of trouble? It is actually a sign of faith when people such as Job and

---

[2]In the RSV of Hab 2:1, Habakkuk says that he will wait "to see what he will say to me, and what I will answer concerning my complaint." The "I" does not seem to fit, and so the NRSV has chosen to follow the Syriac translation instead of the Hebrew: "and what **he** will answer concerning my complaint." This is probably a better translation.

[3]See p. 31, footnote 2, for "theophany."

[4]Hab 2:5a, "Moreover wine is treacherous," is somewhat of a puzzle. Indeed, wine can cause a great deal of trouble, but the words do not seem to fit here. NRSV translates "wealth is treacherous," but that is not found in the Hebrew. Perhaps we must simply accept the judgment of the RSV footnote: "The Hebrew of these two lines is obscure."

Habakkuk and the writer of Lamentations cry out and insist that God listen. They do not give up; they are convinced that God is real, that God is faithful, and that God cares, and so they do not let the situation go unnoticed or unmentioned. "O LORD, how long?"

The answer we find in Habakkuk is neither clear nor complete, but it is an answer. God says that he is doing a work in Habakkuk's day that Habakkuk "would not believe if told" (Hab 1:5). The work was a dark work, and it would include the destruction of Jerusalem and its temple. Ultimately, the people of God would survive, and they would return to rebuild Jerusalem and its temple. But in the near future, God tells Habakkuk, "he whose soul is not upright in him shall fail," and only "the righteous shall live by his faith" (Hab 2:4). The day of "the wicked [who] surround the righteous" (Hab 1:4) would soon end.

Many years later, Paul turned to Hab 2:4. In Rom 1:17 and Gal 3:11 he expands upon the thought of Habakkuk and notes that the righteousness of God comes to us through faith, not works of the law. The emphasis is different in Paul, of course. Habakkuk tells residents of Jerusalem that God will use the Babylonians as a scourge against the wicked; the only survivors will be the righteous whose faith will bring them through the trial; surely it will not be those who trust in idols (Hab 2:18-19; cf. Isa 40:19; 44:9-20)! For Paul, it is faith itself which God uses to bring righteousness to those who trust in the work of Christ. In the end, therefore, whether the threat is Babylon, or whether it is sin, death and the power of the devil, "the righteous shall live by his faith."

The last chapter of Habakkuk brings us a concluding prayer which contains a cosmic theophany. Habakkuk is confident that the universe is in God's hands, and thus God will be able to do what he intends to do – whether it is with Judah or with Babylon.

The book ends on a marvelous and strong note of faith. In 3:17-19, Habakkuk, who stood in a tower to wait for God to answer him, now stands before his hearers and confesses that even if crops and herds fail, "yet I will rejoice in the LORD, ... the God of my salvation. GOD, the Lord, is my strength ...."

Some important texts: Habakkuk's complaint: "O LORD, how long?" (Hab 1:3-4); " I will... station myself on the tower" (Hab 2:1); "the righteous shall live by his faith" (Hab 2:4); "yet I will rejoice in the LORD" (Hab 3:17-18)

Verses for memory: Hab 2:4; 3:2; 3:17-18

Zephaniah

❧

Overview

The prophet. Zephaniah prophesied in Judah during the reign of Josiah (640-609 B.C.), just before Jeremiah, Nahum and Habakkuk. He may be reacting strongly against the evils of Manasseh (687/6-642 B.C.) and Amon (642-640 B.C.), who had mixed the worship of foreign gods with the worship of the LORD. At least part of Zephaniah's prophecies seem to have been made before the reforms of Josiah began.

The first verse of Zephaniah (the title or inscription) is unusual; it is the only four-generation genealogy given for a prophet. It goes back to "Hezekiah." Does this mean that Zephaniah was a descendant of the good King Hezekiah? This is not said, and yet the fact that the editors included this long genealogy meant that it was important. So perhaps Zephaniah was indeed a descendant of the king. It has also been suggested that Zephaniah might have been among those who discovered and promoted the early version of the book of Deuteronomy in 622 B.C. during the reign of Josiah. This is because his theology has Deuteronomistic elements.[1]

The message. Zephaniah brings messages similar to those we have heard from other prophets. There are words of judgment upon those who oppress the weak and the poor, upon corrupt officials, and upon others who engage in unjust activity. But there are also words of hope. Judah will be punished, but will then be restored. A righteous remnant, "a people humble and lowly," will be left in the land.[2] In Zephaniah, we find themes also found in Isaiah,[3] and some have suggested that perhaps

[1]J. S. Kselman mentions "the host of heaven" (1:5; cf. Deut 4:19; 17:3; 2 Kgs 17:16; 21:3,5; Jer 8:2), worship "on the rooftops" (1:5; cf. 2 Kgs 23:12; Jer 19:13; 32:29), and the futility curse (1:13; cf. Deut 28:30). *ABD* 6:107.

[2]Zeph 2:3; 3:12-13; cf. Jesus' words, "blessed are the meek," in Matt 5:5.

[3]Compare Zeph 3:1-3 and Isa 1:21-23, as well as the mentions of the day of the LORD in Zeph 1:7,14 and Isa 13:6-11.

he was a disciple of (First) Isaiah.[4]

The book. In Zephaniah 1-2, it seems that the reforms of Josiah have not yet begun to take place. Thus, perhaps these first two chapters are from the approximate period 640-625 B.C. (since Deuteronomy was discovered in the temple in 622 B.C.). Zeph 2:13-15 contains prophesies against Assyria and Nineveh which would have encouraged Josiah in his reforms, just as did the words of Nahum (see p. 234). Zeph 3:1-13 seem somewhat later, since it appears to show disappointment (similar to that of Jeremiah) that the reforms did not produce the results he had hoped for. Near the end (Zeph 3:14-17), there is a joyful concentric pattern. At the center are words of encouragement: Do not fear!

A Sing aloud (Zeph 3:14a)
 B Rejoice and exult (Zeph 3:14b)
  C (God is) king of Israel (Zeph 3:15c)
   D the LORD is in your midst (Zeph 3:15c)
    E **fear ... no more** (Zeph 3:15d)
    E' **do not fear** (Zeph 3:16b)
   D' the LORD is in your midst (Zeph 3:17a)
  C' (God is) a warrior (Zeph 3:17b)
 B' Rejoice, renew and exult (Zeph 3:17c)
A' Loud singing (Zeph 3:17d)

Outline

- **I. Title** (Zeph 1:1)
- **II. Oracles of Judgment** (Zeph 1:2-3:8)
  - A. Judgment announced (Zeph 1:2-2:4)
  - B. Judgment described (Zeph 2:5-3:8)
- **III. Oracles of salvation** (Zeph 3:9-20)

The book may have an *inclusio*[5] at the beginning and end: In Zeph 1:2-4, God will "sweep away" and "cut off" wickedness. Then, at the

---

[4]See p. 171 for "First Isaiah," or "Isaiah of Jerusalem," who lived a century before Zephaniah. He may have developed a following – a group of disciples that continued to study and teach his words for several generations after his death. Perhaps Zephaniah was part of this group, or at least influenced by it, a century later.

[5]An *inclusio* is a literary frame around a text. See p. 29 footnote 12.

end, in Zeph 3:18-19, God "removes" disaster and the oppressor. If this is, indeed, an *inclusio*, it is another example of moving from images of judgment to those of salvation, as seen in the basic outline (above) and as often seen in the prophets in general.

Message

Zephaniah begins by describing God's wrath against all creation and even describes a "reverse creation" in Zeph 1:2-3.[6] Some parts of Zephaniah 1 (1:2-3, 14-18) are almost apocalyptic in their style.[7] At first, the real target is not the whole world, though. Rather, the target is Judah and the corrupt leadership of its capital city, Jerusalem. Zeph 1:4-12 brings us a graphic picture of Jerusalem prior to the reforms of Josiah. And in Zeph 3:3-5, there is a strong contrast between "the *officials* within" Jerusalem, who are "reckless, faithless persons," and "the *LORD* within" Jerusalem, who "does no wrong."

Zephaniah speaks out against sins of idolatry (Zeph 1:4-7), foreign customs (Zeph 1:8), injustice (Zeph 1:9[8]), and a dismissive contemptuous attitude toward God (Zeph 1:12[9]). Zeph 1:10-11 refers to new areas of Jerusalem which had been constructed under Hezekiah (p. 230) or Manasseh; they were thus probably wealthy areas. Because of all this, the day of the LORD (Zeph 1:7-18) is approaching. In the popular mind, the day of the LORD was a day on which all Israel's enemies would be destroyed. However, Zephaniah, like Amos (p. 216) and other prophets, says that punishment will begin with God's own people.[10] Zephaniah gives a more complete description of this day than any other prophet. It starts in Jerusalem (Zeph 1:10-12) but soon extends to the

---

[6]This is similar to what we find in Jer 4:23-26. Compare to the order of creation in Gen 1:20-26.

[7]Zephaniah is probably too early for apocalypticism but may (like Ezekiel) provide some of the imagery that later appears in apocalyptic literature. See p. 194 for a discussion of apocalyptic literature.

[8]"leap[ing] over the threshold" is probably a superstitious, idolatrous practice similar to that mentioned in 1 Sam 5:5.

[9]"thickening upon their lees" (mentioned also in Jer 48:11) refers to the process of making wine. If the grape sediment (the lees) is left too long in the wine before removing it, the wine becomes thick like syrup. Similarly, these men of Jerusalem have become lazy and arrogant, and thus "thick" and ruined.

[10]A similar point is made in the New Testament in 1 Pet 4:17.

whole world (Zeph 1:17-18; 2:4-15).

Zephaniah calls for repentance, since repentance alone brings hope of avoiding the crisis (Zeph 2:1-3). But the people are rebellious and unwilling to listen (Zeph 3:1-4) even when they are confronted by God's law (Zeph 3:4), his faithfulness in nature (Zeph 3:5), and his warning acts of destruction (Zeph 3:6-7). Thus, as Jeremiah also said, the punishment is unavoidable.

But punishment will not be the final word. A remnant (Zeph 2:7,9) of "people humble and lowly" will be left in the midst of Judah (Zeph 3:9-13). Finally, in the midst of this reformed and renewed people, there will be a joyful restoration of Zion (Zeph 3:14-18). This is similar to what we read in Isaiah 2:2-4 (= Mic 4:1-3). There will be rejoicing and singing in which even God will take part (note the concentric pattern on p. 241, above). Even the lame and the outcast will be saved (Zeph 3:19; vs Lev 21:16-23[11]).

Some important texts: I will sweep away everything (Zeph 1:2-3); the day of the LORD (Zeph 1:7-9); woe to faithless leaders (Zeph 3:1-4); sing aloud, O daughter of Zion (Zeph 3:14-15)

Verses for memory: Zeph 3:14-15.

[11]Leviticus excludes the blind and the lame and those with any blemish from offering sacrifices to the LORD. Zephaniah, Jeremiah (Jer 31:8) and Micah (Mic 4:6-7), on the other hand, look for a day in which all *including* the blind and the lame will be invited.

Haggai

❧

Overview

The Prophet. Haggai (and Zechariah) lived and prophesied in Jerusalem approximately 100 years after Jeremiah, Nahum, Habakkuk and Zephaniah. This was after the Babylonian exile, when Cyrus of Persia had let the people return to Judah to rebuild Jerusalem and the temple. Nothing is known about either Haggai or Zechariah except for the words of their prophecies, and two very brief mentions in the book of Ezra (Ezra 5:1; 6:14). Surely they must have known each other, since reconstructed Jerusalem was small at that time and they both encouraged the people to finish rebuilding the temple. Yet, strangely, neither prophet mentions the other one.

The setting. In 586 B.C., the first temple (the temple of Solomon) was destroyed by the Babylonians and the leadership of Judah was taken into exile. They returned in 538 B.C. under the leadership of Sheshbazzar (Ezra 1:11) and Zerubbabel (Ezra 2:2), and it is possible that some work was begun on the temple at that time (Ezra 5:14-16).

However, in 522 B.C. Darius I (Darius the Great, 522-486 B.C.) became king of Persia. Changes of leadership are sometimes an opportunity for vassal states to rebel against the new leader,[1] and Darius indeed had to crush widespread revolts in the Persian empire at that time. This discouraged nationalistic hopes in many places including Judah, and it also affected the rebuilding of the temple. By 520 B.C., very little had been done. Yet surely their "return" from Babylon would not be complete until the temple was again fully rebuilt! A century earlier, Jeremiah had prophesied that the people would "serve the king of Babylon seventy years" (Jer 25:11-12; 29:10). Surely the approach of the year 516 B.C. was significant, since that year would be the seventieth year after the temple fell in 586 B.C. Jeremiah's prophecies had been right once, and they might be right again.

---

[1]For "vassal" see p. 14, footnote 15. See also p. 148 regarding Psalm 2.

Thus, in the year 520 B.C., the prophet Haggai spoke. Judah was now under the joint political and religious rule of a dyarchy.[2] The king of Persia had ultimate authority, of course, but he had appointed a governor (Zerubbabel) and a high priest (Joshua) to rule over Judah. Although Zerubbabel's name sounds foreign, he was actually Jewish and – most significantly – he was a descendant of David.[3] But note that his title was governor,[4] not king. The king was still Darius of Persia!

Post-exile Events: (538-445 B.C.)[5]

538 B.C.	Cyrus lets the exiles return	Ezra 1-6
520 B.C.	Work on the temple is begun	Ezra 1-6
515 B.C.	The temple is completed	Ezra 1-6
458 B.C.	Ezra arrives	Ezra 7-10 (more than 50 years after Ezra 1-6)
445 B.C.	Nehemiah arrives	Nehemiah

Haggai says that harvests have been poor and wages low because the people have not finished rebuilding the temple (Hag 1:5-7). On 29 August, 520 B.C.,[6] Haggai spoke to Zerubbabel, Joshua the high priest, and "the remnant of the people" (Hag 1:1,12; 2:2), encouraging them to return to rebuilding the temple. Within a month, on 21 September, they responded (Hag 1:15). By 17 October (Hag 2:1), enough progress had been made that those who remembered Solomon's temple could see that the new temple appeared to be less glorious than the original. Haggai thus encouraged them further (Hag 2:4-9).

---

[2]"Dyarchy" is the rule of two people together at the same time, just as "monarchy" is the rule of one person.

[3]Zerubbabel was the grandson of King Jehoiachin, and his father was either Shealtiel, Jehoiachin's eldest son (Hag 1:1,12,14; 2:2,23; Ezra 3:2; Matt 1:12; Luke 3:27) or Pedaiah, a younger son (1 Chr 3:19).

[4]The word "governor" appears in Hag 1:1,14; 2:2,21. It has also been found by archeologists on seal impressions of the administrator of the Persian district of Yehud (i.e., Judah) during that period.

[5]This table is also found on p. 112.

[6] We know the precise dates on which Haggai spoke to the leaders and the people because Hag 1:1 and Hag 2:1-2,10 refer to "the second year of Darius the king." And we know that Darius ruled Persia from 522 B.C. to 486 B.C. The "second year of Darius the king" is thus 520 B.C. See R. L. Smith, *Micah-Malachi* (Waco: Word Bible Commentary, 1984) 148.

Hag 2:10-14 uses a cultic example of clean and unclean. The example itself is clear: holiness is not transferred through indirect contact, but uncleanness is. However, what verse 14 means is not clear. Either the people or their offerings are unclean, or the uncompleted (and thus unconsecrated?) temple and altar itself are unclean. But Hag 2:15-19 is clear: now that the temple is being rebuilt, a good future lies ahead. God says, "From this day on I will bless you" (Hag 2:19b).

The end of the book, Hag 2:20-23, has produced a great deal of discussion and speculation. There, we read

> 20The word of the LORD came a second time to Haggai on the twenty-fourth day of the month, 21"Speak to Zerubbabel, governor of Judah, saying, I am about to shake the heavens and the earth 22and to overthrow the throne of kingdoms .... 23On that day, says the LORD of hosts, I will take you, O Zerubbabel my servant, the son of Shealtiel, says the LORD, and make you like a signet ring; for I have chosen you, says the LORD of hosts."

Zerubbabel was a descendant of David, as already mentioned above. Is this text saying that God is now going to restore the Davidic dynasty? There are several things to note in this text:

- Earlier in the book, Zerubbabel's royal ancestry (son of Shealtiel) was mentioned each time (Hag 1:1,12,14; 2:2[7]). But now in Hag 2:21 he is just called "governor of Judah." Is this omission meant to de-emphasize and minimize his royal descent at this point?
- Zerubbabel will not gain military victories as David did. Rather, everything in Hag 2:21-22 will be done by the LORD himself.
- Although Hag 2:23 does then call him "the son of Shealtiel" (actually, "*my servant*, the son of Shealtiel") and says that the LORD has chosen him, it does not mention him becoming king. Rather, God will make him "like a signet ring." A signet ring (or "seal ring") is used to make an impression in a seal. It *represents* the authority of the one who wears it, but it is not the authority itself.

These points may indicate that Zerubbabel is not going to become a king. If this is the case, then Hag 2:20-23 may expect Israel to return to theocracy (God as king, with the people led by charismatic leaders as during the time of the judges; see pp. 74 and 84, above). Zerubbabel would thus become merely a signet ring, an earthly symbol of power which now all belongs to God. Certainly the temple is central in this book, and the temple represents God's presence and power. We will explore this further in Zechariah.

There is no indication that Haggai saw the completion of the temple five years later in 515 B.C. All his prophecies took place before the end

---

[7]Hag 2:4 does not repeat "son of Shealtiel" so soon after Hag 2:2.

of the year 520 B.C. Did he die before then? We do not know.

Outline

I. **The call to rebuild the temple** (Hag 1:1-11)
II. **The people's response: construction begins** (Hag 1:12-15)
III. **God's promises of blessing** (Hag 2:1-19)
   A. Does the new temple lack the first one's glory? God says it shall be greater (Hag 2:1-9)
   B. Sacrifices were not accepted before: God says "Now I will bless you" (Hag 2:10-19)
IV. **Zerubbabel: the signet ring of the LORD** (Hag 2:20-23)

Message

The people who returned from Babylon undoubtedly came with great hopes. And it appears they even began to rebuild the temple. But life was hard back in Judah. The Babylonians had completely destroyed the city of Jerusalem, and that meant not only its temple but also homes and important buildings. So the people soon stopped working on the temple and focused upon restoring other things. This was understandable at first. But as time went on, they never returned to restoring the temple. They continued to improve their own personal situations, building their own houses with fine wood paneling, but the house of God was now forgotten.

Haggai, therefore, brought an important message regarding priorities. "Is it a time for you yourselves to dwell in your paneled houses, while this house lies in ruins?" (Hag 1:4[8]). Times were still difficult, but surely this was because God was withholding his blessing. Return to rebuilding the temple, Haggai tells the people, and God will return to giving his blessing. And the leaders and the people "obeyed the voice of the LORD their God, and the words of Haggai the prophet, as the LORD their God had sent him" (Hag 1:12). And God responded, "I am with you, says the LORD" (Hag 1:13b). So, the message of Haggai was important because it helped turn the eyes of the leaders and the people back to the LORD and to the temple which would become so central to their religious life in years to come.

Haggai needed to encourage the people twice more. At one point, those who remembered the original temple of Solomon became discouraged, since it seemed that the new temple would not be as glorious as the old. Through Haggai, God reminded the people that he owned all the silver and gold in the world (Hag 2:6-8), and thus "the

---

[8]How different their priorities were from those of David in 2 Sam 7:2: "The king said to Nathan the prophet, 'see now, I dwell in a house of cedar, but the ark of God dwells in a tent.'"

glory of this present house will be greater than the glory of the former house" (Hag 2:9, NIV). The other word of encouragement is found in Hag 2:10-14. As mentioned above, the point here is not entirely clear. Most likely, however, God is saying that their sacrifices had been rejected earlier since the temple had not been completed. In the verses which follow, God tells them to "consider what will come to pass from this day onward. ... From this day on I will bless you" (Hag 2:15-19).

The final word of encouragement (Hag 2:20-23) is to Zerubbabel, the governor, who shared power in the dyarchy[9] with Joshua, the high priest. Most of what Haggai has said so far has been focused upon the temple and thus, by implication, upon Joshua. But here at the end of the book he points out that God has not forgotten Zerubbabel. Yet the word is somewhat muted. Zerubbabel is a descendant of David, but we do not read here that God is going to restore Zerubbabel to the throne of David. The "signet ring" imagery gives a picture of importance but of lesser importance. It is not entirely clear what Haggai expects at this point; one possibility is that Israel would return to theocracy, as noted on p. 246, above. Perhaps the family of David is to continue, but with a lesser role. Then again, maybe not. It appears that the Persians later removed Zerubbabel from power.

Some important texts: Consider what has happened (Hag 1:2-7); the leaders and people obey (Hag 1:12-15); Zerubbabel, God's signet ring (Hag 2:20-23)

Verses for memory: Hag 1:13; 2:19

---

[9]See p. 245 footnote 2 for dyarchy.

Zechariah

❧

Overview

The book of Zechariah has two parts. Zechariah 1-8 comes from the same time and setting as Haggai (read the Haggai overview on pp. 244-245 for this background information). Zechariah 9-14, on the other hand, contains two "oracles" (Zechariah 9-11 and Zechariah 12-14) which seem to come from a later time.

The name Zechariah appears only four times in the book, and all four are in the first section (Zech 1:1,7; 7:1,8). Thus, some think that Zechariah 9-14 was written later by someone other than Zechariah.[1]

Zechariah 1-8

As mentioned above, Zechariah 1-8 comes out of the same historical situation as Haggai. Both prophets encouraged Joshua the High Priest and Zerubbabel the governor. Both encouraged the people to rebuild the temple, and the book of Haggai and the two chapters of Zechariah 7-8 are very similar.

All of Haggai's prophecies were made in the year 520 B.C., but Zechariah prophesied from 520 B.C. to 518 B.C.[2] It was Haggai who motivated the people to return to the work; in the time of Zechariah, the reconstruction was already under way. Thus, Zechariah could focus on the meaning and central importance of the temple itself and how it gave legitimacy to the dyarchic[3] rule of Joshua, the high priest, and Zerubbabel, the governor.[4]

Only the opening verses of Zechariah 1 bring words of criticism.

---

[1]In addition, Mt 27:9-10 says that Zech 11:12-13 was written by Jeremiah, as we will note below.

[2]Like Haggai (p. 244), Zechariah dates his prophecies according to the reign of king Darius I of Persia (522-486 B.C.). Thus, Zech 1:1 = Oct or Nov 520 (no day is mentioned); Zech 1:7 = 15 Feb 519; Zech 7:1 = 7 Dec 518. See R. L. Smith, *Micah-Malachi* (Waco: Word Bible Commentary, 1984) 169.

[3]See p. 245 footnote 2 for dyarchy.

[4]As noted above in the section on Haggai, the ultimate power rested with the king of Persia. However, he had appointed Joshua and Zerubbabel to rule together in Judah as high priest and governor respectively.

Otherwise, Zechariah generally brings a message of encouragement and hope for the future.

In Zech 1:12, the angel of the LORD asks, "O LORD of hosts, how long will you have no mercy on Jerusalem and the cities of Judah, against which you have had indignation these seventy years?" This is undoubtedly a reference to Jeremiah's seventy-year prophecies (Jer 25:11-12; 29:10), and God reassures the people that "I am exceedingly jealous for Jerusalem and for Zion" (Zech 1:14).

The core of Zechariah 1-8 is a **group of eight visions** found in Zech 1:7-6:8. Zechariah received them in a two month period during 519 B.C., the year after Haggai's prophecies. These eight visions have a concentric pattern[5] and – except for the first and last visions – are grouped in pairs:

A *Cosmic power of God* (one vision)
 B *Judah's* political *restoration* (two visions)
  C *God and his chosen representatives* (two visions)
 B' *Judah's* spiritual *restoration* (two visions)
A' *Cosmic power of God* (one vision)

The emphasis seems to be upon the central set of visions which deals with Joshua the high priest and Zerubbabel. Below is a more detailed representation of the eight visions:

Cosmic power of God

Vision 1: Four (?) horsemen patrolling the earth (Zech 1:7-17)

Judah's *political* restoration

Vision 2: Punishing the nations (Zech 1:18-21)
Vision 3: Restoring Jerusalem (Zechariah 2)

God and his chosen representatives

Vision 4: Affirmation of High Priest Joshua (Zechariah 3)
Vision 5: Lampstand and two olive trees (Zechariah 4)

Judah's *spiritual* restoration

Vision 6: Curse on thieves and false witnesses (Zech 5:1-4)
Vision 7: Removal of the people's wickedness (Zech 5:5-11)

Cosmic power of God

Vision 8: Four chariots; red, black, white and gray horses (Zech 6:1-8)

The people faced a new situation: a temple without a king's palace. In the past, the king always took responsibility for establishing and maintaining the temple. Would it now be possible to have a temple

[5]See page 99, footnote 12, for concentric patterns.

without a king? Yes it will, Zechariah tells the people. The central visions encourage Joshua the high priest and Zerubbabel, the governor; these visions also show the people that the LORD has chosen them.

Zechariah 3 affirms Joshua in particular. Here we have another appearance of the "*satan*" figure;[6] in this case, he accuses Joshua, the high priest. The LORD defends him, and this may indicate a controversy in the community regarding Joshua's authority. If so, then this vision answers: Yes, Joshua has been chosen and affirmed by the LORD.

Zechariah 4 returns to the image of the dyarchy. The lamp represents God; the two olive trees, which stand on each side of the lamp, represent Joshua and Zerubbabel.

In **Zechariah 5**, visions 6 and 7 represent Judah's spiritual restoration under the covenant (the flying scroll and its curse). This includes the removal of the ephah (basket) of wickedness to Shinar in Babylon.

Zechariah 6 contains the eighth and last vision: the cosmic vision of Zech 6:1-8. After that, there are no more visions. In Zech 6:9-15, the focus returns to the high priest Joshua. A crown[7] is to be made and placed on his head. He is called "the Branch," and he is told that he "shall build the temple of the LORD" (Zech 6:13).

In **Zechariah 7**, the people bring a question regarding fasting, but Zechariah's word from the LORD points out that they are not serious; their fasting "for these seventy years" had been hypocritical (Zech 7:5-6). In Zech 7:9-10, Zechariah gives an answer similar to that of Mic 6:8,[8] but the people appear to reject this advice.

Zechariah 8 is more positive in tone. The people have made progress on the temple, and God will bless them as a result (this section is very similar to Haggai). As a result, "many peoples and strong nations shall come to seek the LORD of hosts in Jerusalem, and to entreat the favor of the LORD" (Zech 8:22).

---

[6]See the discussion of the *satan* in the section on Job, above, p. 135. Here, as in Job, the Hebrew refers not to "Satan" but to "the *satan*" (note the definite article), that is, to "the adversary," one whose office it is to accuse people before God.

[7]Actually, the Hebrew text is plural ("crowns") in Zech 6:11 and Zech 6:14. Some think that originally the text described the crowning of *both* Joshua and Zerubbabel. But at this point Zerubbabel seems to recede. Zech 3:8 referred to "my servant the Branch," and that probably meant Zerubbabel, a descendant of David (cf. Isa 11:1; Jer 23:5; 33:15; cf. also discussion of Zerubbabel, p. 246, above). But here in Zech 6:12 Joshua becomes the Branch.

[8]"He has showed you, O man, what is good; and what does the LORD require of you but to do justice, and to love kindness, and to walk humbly with your God?"

Zechariah 9-14: Two oracles

Zechariah 9-14 is quite different from Zechariah 1-8. The chapters contain two oracles (Zechariah 9-11 and Zechariah 12-14) which seem to be by unknown authors from a later time. (The name Zechariah never appears in these chapters.)

The investigation of these chapters began when people noted that Mt 27:9-10 says that Zech 11:12-13 was written by Jeremiah. Much discussion and debate has followed.[9] Generally, these last six chapters seem to have been written by someone disillusioned with their situation and frustrated with their leaders. Toward the end of the second oracle, the imagery becomes rather apocalyptic.[10] Although Zechariah's authorship may be uncertain, we will continue to refer to the writer as Zechariah in the paragraphs which follow.

First Oracle: Zechariah 9-11:

Zechariah 9 begins with prophecies against other nations, similar to the way Amos began. The LORD is victorious in the last part of the chapter, saving and protecting his people. For Christians, the most well-known text in this chapter is Zech 9:9-10: "Rejoice greatly, O daughter of Zion! ... your king comes ... humble and riding on an ass ..." Amazingly, as this king's weapons decrease, his kingdom increases. Finally, there will be peace to the nations, and the king's dominion will extend to the ends of the earth. This text expresses the hope for a messianic figure who would bring peace not only to Israel but also to the world. Later, the text became important for the Gospel writers as they described Jesus' entry into Jerusalem (Matt 21:2-7; Jn 12:14-15).[11]

Zechariah 10 expresses anger at "the shepherds," that is, the leaders of the people.[12] It is not clear whether these leaders are Israelites or foreigners. In *Zechariah 11* God apparently asks Zechariah to become shepherd (leader) of Judah. In one month, Zechariah destroys "the three shepherds" (Zech 11:8) who also are not named but who must be three unfaithful leaders of the people. But Zechariah's relationship with the

---

[9]Some think that the first oracle comes from Persian period (539-333 B.C.) but the second from the Hellenistic period (333-164 B.C.). Another suggestion is found in the section on Malachi, below (p. 258, footnote 4).

[10]See p. 194 for a discussion of apocalyptic literature.

[11]A note on Zech 9:15: RSV and NRSV translate "they shall drink their blood like wine" (though note RSV footnote). It is better to follow NIV, "They will drink and roar as with wine," or NASB, "they will drink, and be boisterous as with wine." Both may be closer to the Hebrew, which is somewhat unclear, and literally says "and-they-will-drink they-were-boisterous like-wine."

[12]See also Jer 10:21; 12:10; 23:1-4; 25:34-36; 50:6-7; Ezek 34:1-10.

people then seems to go bad. He says he will no longer be their shepherd and he breaks his two staffs named Favor and Unity[13] (Zech 11:10,14). Breaking the staff Unity shows his despair concerning the possibility of reunifying (former) Israel and Judah. In Zech 11:12-13, Zechariah receives his wages and then casts them into the "treasury" (Hebrew "potter").[14] These verses are later quoted in Mt 27:9-10 when Judas returns the money paid to him and it is then used to buy the potter's field. Finally, Zechariah is again called to be a "worthless shepherd" and the chapter ends on a negative note.

Second Oracle: Zechariah 12-14:

Zechariah 12. The first verses of this oracle say that it is "concerning Israel,"[15] though Israel is not mentioned again and the rest is about Judah and Jerusalem. Judah will be avenged against "all the nations of the earth [who] will come together against [Jerusalem]" (Zech 12:3). The house of David will be restored, though its power (and the power of Jerusalem) over the rest of Judah will be limited. Perhaps there had been persecutions by the house of David (Zech 12:10). Because of this, the house of David and all the people will mourn for "him whom they have pierced." Whom have they pierced? Some think the writer refers to himself, and others suggest he is remembering the tragic death of King Josiah. In the New Testament, both Jn 19:37 and Rev 1:7 (where "all the tribes of the earth" mourn) see this prophecy fulfilled in Jesus.

---

[13]**Favor:** the Hebrew is *no'am* (נֹעַם), an unusual word occurring only seven times in the Bible (twice here). It means "beauty, favor, pleasantness," and it is related to the name Naomi (נָעֳמִי). **Unity:** the Hebrew is *chobalim* (חֹבְלִים), another unusual word. It occurs only here in the Bible, but it is related to a more common word (*chabal*, חָבַל) which generally means to bind or pledge.

[14]The Hebrew text has the word "potter" (*yotser*, יוֹצֵר), which does not make sense but which is found in the NIV and NASB translations. The Syriac version and some of the Targums, all of which come from early Hebrew versions of the text, have the word "treasury" (*'otsar* אוֹצָר), and RSV/NRSV uses that word. These two words look and sound very similar, and so many suggest that the Hebrew originally had *'otsar*, "treasury." What is most interesting is that *both* words, "treasury" and "potter," have ended up in the Mt 27:9-10 quotation of this verse.

[15]Or "*against* Israel," since the same Hebrew preposition *'al* (עַל) is used in verse 2 for "*against* Judah also." The point is that the city of Jerusalem is going to be attacked by all those around her. The attackers will include people from the surrounding territory of Judah (Zech 12:2), and so it is possible that people from the former territory of Israel, to the north, might also be involved. If so, "against Israel" would be a good translation here.

Zechariah 13 comes from a later time when classical prophecy was no longer accepted, and anyone claiming to be a prophet would be punished or even put to death. Thus, the parents of such a person "shall pierce him through when he prophesies" (Zech 13:3). If he is beaten and someone asks him about the wounds, he will be ashamed and say, "The wounds I received in the house of my friends" (Zech 13:6). The chapter concludes with an oracle against "my shepherd." The people (the sheep) will be scattered, but a remnant will remain and be refined and will become God's people once again.

In *Zechariah 14*, we enter, or come very close to, the world of apocalypticism. It is a time of stress in which followers of the LORD will suffer (Zech 14:2), and all creation will be affected in the devastating events which follow (Zech 14:4-6). In the end, however, Jerusalem will supply "living water" for the world (Zech 14:8) and the LORD will become "king over all the earth" (Zech 14:9). People from the nations of the world "shall go up year after year to worship the King, the LORD of hosts, and to keep the feast of booths"[16] (Zech 14:16), and "there shall no longer be a trader in the house of the LORD of hosts on that day" (Zech 14:21). It will be a good world but not a perfect world; Zech 14:17-19 suggests that some may refuse to come. The oracle – and the book of Zechariah – ends with a description of a ritually pure Jerusalem in which even the bells on the horses will be inscribed "Holy to the LORD."

Outline

I. **Introduction:** "Return to me and I shall return to you" (Zech 1:1-6)
II. **The visions of Zechariah** (Zech 1:7-6:8)
   A. Four (?) horsemen with red, sorrel (reddish brown) and white horses (Zech 1:7-17)
   B. Four horns and four smiths (Zech 1:18-21)
   C. A man with a measuring line (Zechariah 2)
   D. Joshua the high priest and the *satan* (Zechariah 3)
   E. Lampstand with seven lamps, two olive trees (Zechariah 4)
   F. Flying scroll (Zech 5:1-4)
   G. Ephah (basket) carried by two women (Zech 5:5-11)
   H. Four chariots with red, black, white, and gray horses (Zech 6:1-8)
III. **The messages of Zechariah** (Zech 6:9-8:23)
   A. Joshua the high priest is crowned, and shall build the temple of the LORD (Zech 6:9-15)

[16]Thus the second section of Zechariah (chapters 9-14) ends as did the first (chapters 1-8) with the nations of the world going up to Jerusalem.

B. The people inquire but are not serious (Zechariah 7)
C. Restoring Zion and Jerusalem (Zechariah 8)
1. "I am jealous ... I will return" (Zech 8:1-8)
2. Progress is made on the temple (Zech 8:9-11)
3. God will bless Judah (Zech 8:12-19; cf. Haggai)
4. Nations will come to seek LORD (Zech 8:20-23)

IV. The oracles of Zechariah (Zechariah 9-14)
A. First Oracle (Zechariah 9-11)
B. Second Oracle (Zechariah 12-14)

Message

Here, we must consider the book of Zechariah in its two main parts, chapters 1-8 and chapters 9-14.

Zechariah 1-8. These first eight chapters encourage the people to complete the rebuilding of the temple, and then help them to understand what the temple means. Judah is moving further and further away from being a monarchy. The people's hope of having a king seems to die as Zerubbabel fades and the crown (crowns?[17]) ends up on the head of Joshua the high priest. But the people learn that it is indeed possible to have a temple and to have leadership without having a king. Judah – the new Israel – did eventually develop into a theocracy under Zadokite[18] priests for the rest of the Persian period and then almost to the end of the Hellenistic period (333-164 B.C.).

In Zechariah 5, the basis for the people's new life before God is given. It would be the Mosaic covenant, as represented by the flying scroll. The removal of the ephah basket of wickedness to Shinar (Babylon) may represent the removal of foreign worship practices from the midst of the people (Zech 5:5-11). But not all references to foreigners are negative in Zechariah 1-8. At the end of chapter 8, we find the nations coming "to seek the LORD of hosts in Jerusalem, and to entreat the favor of the LORD."

Over all, the goal in Zechariah 1-8 is to rebuild the temple, to strengthen and encourage Joshua the high priest, and to maintain holiness in Israel so that the glory of God would dwell there. This was necessary, since their economic and political well-being depended upon God's holy Presence.

Zechariah 9-14. The two oracles of this section have concerns which are quite different from chapters 1-8. Here, we find an individual or a group which felt disillusioned, marginalized, and perhaps excluded from power.

The great hope for a society of justice and peace, promised in 2

---

[17]See the discussion on p. 251, footnote 7.

[18]See p. 91 for the background of the Zadokite priesthood.

Isaiah, had not yet appeared. Furthermore, it was becoming clear that it was not going to be brought about merely by a priestly government centered in Jerusalem and its temple. The existing (Zadokite?) leadership is no longer trusted. These shepherds need to be removed, and now we again see hope emerging for a king. But the tone now is clearly moving toward apocalyptic, similar to what we find in Joel 2:28-3:21 and Isaiah 24-27.[19] Israel's hope now lies in a "day of the LORD" in which God will break into history and bring a new world order. The phrase "day of the LORD" or "on that day" is never found in Zechariah 1-8, but it occurs twenty times in Zechariah 9-14. Eighteen of those times are in the second oracle (Zechariah 12-14).

Some important texts: The high priest Joshua before the *satan* (Zech 3:1-5); the two olive trees (Zech 4:1-14); the nations come (Zech 8:20-23); rejoice greatly, O daughter of Zion! (Zech 9:9-10); living water from Jerusalem (Zech 14:8-9)

Verses for memory: Zech 4:6b; 9:9-10

[19]For further discussion of this idea of social marginalization and discouragement and the move toward an apocalyptic world view, see Paul D. Hanson, *The Dawn of Apocalyptic*, Philadelphia: Fortress Press, 1979.

Malachi

❧

Overview

The setting. During the period 520-515 B.C., Haggai and Zechariah encouraged those who had returned from Babylon to rebuild the temple. They said that when the temple was completed, God would restore Judah not only spiritually but economically. Some also hoped that God would restore the Davidic dynasty,[1] and others expected to see a great flow of returning exiles from Assyria and Babylon. But in the decades after the completion of the temple, life did not improve as much as some people thought it should. Indeed, to some people it even seemed that those who were dishonest and who ignored God had more success than the righteous. So the morale of the people began to fall, and some became cynical and apathetic. They felt God was not holding up his end of the bargain, and so worship in the temple began to be neglected.

This is the period during which Malachi lived. Malachi does not mention dates, as Haggai and Zechariah do.[2] But the situations he describes sound very similar to those found in Ezra and Nehemiah.[3] Thus, Malachi may have prophesied some time between the completion of the temple, in 520 B.C., and the arrival of Ezra, in 458 B.C. In fact, he may actually have lived at about the same time as Ezra and Nehemiah, since temple life seems to have degenerated a great deal. For instance, the priests were offering blind, lame, and sick animals (Mal 1:6-10; 3:8-9). Therefore, Malachi seeks ritual and moral reform.

The name Malachi. "Malachi" may or may not be a personal name. The Hebrew word *mal'akiy* (מַלְאָכִי), which is found in Mal 1:1, simply means "my messenger." It is also found in Mal 3:1 where we read, "Behold, I send my messenger [or Malachi?] to prepare the way before me." So Mal 1:1 could be translated "The oracle of the word of the

---

[1]See the discussion of Zerubbabel as God's signet ring (Hag 2:20-23) on p. 246.

[2]See p. 245, footnote 6.

[3]Nehemiah came to Jerusalem in 445 B.C. Ezra's date is less certain, and in this book we are assuming he arrived earlier, in 458 B.C. A table of dates is found on p. 245. See p. 112, footnote 2, for a discussion of the uncertainty concerning the dating of Ezra who may have arrived as late as 398 B.C..

LORD to Israel by my messenger."[4] In the discussion which follows, however, we will assume that Malachi is the prophet's name.

His concern. Like Haggai and Zechariah, Malachi is very interested in the temple and in priestly and sacrificial matters. But his greatest concern is with Israel's covenant[5] relationship with the LORD. Malachi is aware of the blessing and curse formula of Deuteronomy[6] (Mal 2:2; 3:9-12; 4:6), and thus of the danger involved in neglecting the Mosaic covenant. This covenant relationship is now threatened, because the disillusionment and indifference of priests and people has led to careless worship practices (Mal 1:6-10; 3:8-9). Malachi also has a strong sense of God's holiness and of the seriousness of personal sin. This leads him to consider the issue of the wicked versus the righteous (Mal 3:18). Like prophets before him, he speaks against idolatry (Mal 2:11) and social injustice (Mal 3:5). But he speaks specifically against divorce (Mal 2:13-16), and, like Ezra and Nehemiah who came after him, he opposes intermarriage with foreigners (Mal 2:10-16).

The structure of the book. The book of Malachi is made up of six oracles, followed by two appendices (see the outline, below). Each of the oracles begins with a question.

FIRST ORACLE (Mal 1:2-5). "How have you loved us?" God assures the people that he loves them, pointing out that "I have loved Jacob, but I have hated Esau." This refers not to Jacob and Esau in Genesis, but rather to their descendants, the people of Israel and the people of Edom.[7] However, those who remember the Genesis story will recall that Esau despised his birthright (Gen 25:34). Thus, the oracle serves two functions: to say that, yes, God loves Israel, but also to remind of the danger of despising one's heritage.

---

[4]Many scholars also note the two oracles at the end of Zechariah, which come right before Malachi. (See the first paragraph of the Zechariah overview on p. 249, as well as the discussion of Zechariah 9-14 which begins on p. 252.) Some suggest that the editors of the Minor Prophets wanted a total of 12 books in the collection, and that Zechariah 1-8 was the 11th book. But the editors still had three anonymous oracles left. So two of these oracles were added to the end of Zechariah (becoming Zechariah 9-14), and the third was made into the 12th book of the collection. Since the first verse of this third oracle spoke of "my messenger," it was then called the book of *mal'akiy* (מַלְאָכִי), or Malachi.

[5]Malachi mentions several covenants: with Levi (Mal 2:1-9), with "our fathers" (Mal 2:10), and the covenant of marriage (Mal 2:14). He also refers to "the messenger of the covenant" (Mal 3:1).

[6]See p. 61, above.

[7]Malachi refers to a recent invasion of Edom, though we are not told by whom. See also Jer 49:7-22.

SECOND ORACLE (Mal 1:6-2:9). "How have we despised your name?" Here, the priests are condemned for insolence and for offering a double standard in teaching and moral leadership. They have permitted impure sacrifices, and thus have despised the name of the LORD. It would be better if sacrifices were stopped altogether, since even the gentiles are offering better sacrifices.

THIRD ORACLE (Mal 2:10-16). This oracle contains many questions, but the two central ones are "Why does the LORD not regard our offerings?" (Mal 2:13-14) and "What does he desire?" (Mal 2:15). Here, the lay people are criticized for being faithless by marrying foreign women and divorcing their Jewish wives. Undoubtedly Malachi remembered the words of earlier prophets who had compared covenantal faithfulness to marriage: Hosea (especially chapters 1, 2 and 11), Jeremiah (2:1-3; 31:31-32), and Ezekiel (chapter 16). Part of the danger of intermarriage was that it brought in foreign religious practices. But God also says "I hate divorce" (Mal 2:16).

FOURTH ORACLE (Mal 2:17-3:6). "How have we wearied the LORD?" The people have wearied God by saying that God delights in those who do evil, and by asking "Where is the God of justice?" The people ask this last question cynically, in a tone very unlike that of Job. As a result, the LORD will send "my messenger" (*mal'akiy*, מַלְאָכִי), the "messenger of the covenant," who will judge the people and purify the "sons of Levi" (that is, the priests). Who is this messenger? We are not told. Here, it could be Malachi himself, of course, or perhaps he was thinking of an angel or even of God himself. But later in Mal 4:5-6 (the second appendix, below), Elijah is mentioned. Here, in the fourth oracle, the messenger will be like a refiner's fire (Mal 3:2-3), preparing the community for judgment (Mal 3:5) which is then mentioned again in Mal 4:4-6.

FIFTH ORACLE (Mal 3:7-12). "How shall we return to the LORD?" God says "Return to me, and I will return to you," and the people ask "How shall we do this?" God could point to *many* things, since the people have failed in many ways. But here he mentions only one example: the tithe (Mal 3:8-10). The people have been robbing God by not bringing the "full tithe." The real issues in Malachi are much larger than tithing, of course; tithing is just an example. Thus, the call for "full tithes" is an invitation to complete repentance which will involve many changes.

SIXTH ORACLE (Mal 3:13-4:3). "How have we spoken against the LORD?" Some have been cynical, and have said there is no benefit in serving the LORD. Why? Because it seems to them that those who are arrogant and evil are more successful than the righteous. At this point, however, "those who feared the LORD spoke with one another," and the LORD heard them. He says he will make them his special possession (*segullah*, סְגֻלָּה;[8] Mal 3:16-17). The LORD then turns to the cynics, and warns that "the day" is coming, "burning like an oven" to consume the wicked, but that those "who fear my name" will be healed and will rejoice.

THE TWO APPENDICES. After the six oracles, the book concludes with two very short appendices:

- Mal 4:4, a call to remember the law of Moses
- Mal 4:5-6, the promise to send Elijah before "the great and terrible day of the LORD comes."

The language of the second appendix, "Behold, I will send you Elijah the prophet," may remind the reader both of Exod 23:20 ("Behold, I send an angel before you") as well as Deut 18:15-18 ("The LORD your God will raise up for you a prophet like me from among you, from your brethren – him you shall heed"). Elijah the prophet actually lived 400 years before the time of Malachi, of course. Malachi expects that his miraculous return will reunite the people in such a way that the Deuteronomistic curse will not fall upon them. These two appendices are the final words of "the twelve" (see p. 201), and indeed of the whole prophetic section of the Old Testament. More will be said below concerning how these words have spoken to both Christians and Jews.

Outline

I. **Title** (Mal 1:1)
II. **Six Oracles** (Mal 1:2-4:3)
   A. First oracle: "How have you loved us?" (Mal 1:2-5)
   B. Second oracle: "How have we despised your name?" (Mal 1:6-2:9)
   C. Third oracle: "What does the LORD desire?" (Mal 2:10-16)
   D. Fourth oracle: "How have we wearied the LORD?" (Mal 2:17-3:6)
   E. Fifth oracle: "How shall we return to the LORD?" (Mal 3:7-12)
   F. Sixth oracle: "How have we spoken against the LORD?" (Mal 3:13-4:3)
III. **Two Appendices** (Mal 4:4-6)
   A. Remember the law of Moses (Mal 4:4)
   B. The promise to send Elijah (Mal 4:5-6)

Message

Malachi and earlier prophets. Malachi does not bring us either the drama and intensity of Jeremiah or the inspiring hope of Second Isaiah.

---

[8]See p. 36, footnote 14, for this word, found first in Exod 19:5.

This is because Malachi's situation is quite different from that of either Jeremiah (who warned of Babylon's approach) or Second Isaiah (who later brought dramatic words of a promised return to Judah). Yet Malachi does share some of the basic convictions and beliefs we have seen in the earlier "classical" prophets. Covenant traditions and covenant theology are central for Malachi. For instance, he is aware of the conditional nature of covenant theology and of the blessings and curses of Deuteronomy,[9] and therefore he knows the seriousness of a breach of the covenant.

The major points made by Malachi are as follows:

- God is displeased with the careless worship practices of the people
- These practices represent a despising of the covenant relationship with God
- This has also lead to ethical failure including divorce and social injustice
- God is therefore going to send a messenger to judge, purify, and reunite the people

Cultic reform. Like the prophets before him, Malachi is very critical of the priests and of the people's worship life.[10] Unlike earlier prophets, however, Malachi never appears to reject the temple and its sacrifices.[11] Rather, he is very supportive of *proper* temple worship and so he encourages reform.

Moral reform. It is not just a matter of getting the rites right, however. For Malachi, as for other prophets, *internal attitude* is more important than *external form.*[12] His primary concerns, after all, are the covenant and covenantal *relationships*. He is concerned about the moral purity which should be found among covenant people, and so he also seeks ethical reform. One of his strongest statements is in support of the marriage covenant. Husbands are to remain faithful to "the covenant between you and the wife of your youth" (Mal 2:14). Why? Because

---

[9]For the relationship of blessing and curse, see p. 61, above. See also the discussion of the tension between the conditional Mosaic covenant and the unconditional Davidic covenant found on p. 90.

[10]See, for instance, Amos 5:21-24 and Isa 1:11-13.

[11]The other prophets did not actually *reject* the temple and its sacrifices, of course. But at times they seem to come close. When they do, it is because the people were either (1) mixing Canaanite practices with the worship of the LORD, or (2) engaging in empty worship practices while at the same time treating weaker members of society (especially the widow, the orphan and the sojourner) unjustly. Review the discussion of Mic 6:1-8 on p. 232.

[12]Mal 1:9-13; 2:2-3; 3:16-18; cf. Amos 5:12-15, 21-24; Micah 6:6-8.

when fathers are intimately involved in family life it will provide "godly offspring" as God desires (Mal 2:15). Thus, "I hate divorce, says the LORD the God of Israel" (Mal 2:16).

Malachi is concerned with the whole covenantal relationship. It is therefore superficial to overemphasize the issue of the "full tithe" in Mal 3:8-10. Unfortunately, this is the only text from Malachi known by many preachers (apart from the Elijah text at the end), and they immediately turn to it when they want to preach a "stewardship" sermon. But, as we have seen, Malachi is concerned about many kinds of covenantal unfaithfulness, and he uses tithing as only one example.

Transcendence and Immanence. Malachi is presenting us with a balanced view of God who is both *father* (Mal 1:6; 2:10), making covenant and seeking relationship, as well as *master* (Mal 1:6) and *king* (Mal 1:14), demanding obedience. Malachi thus avoids settling for *either* the transcendence (distance, otherness) of God *or* the immanence (nearness, immediacy) of God. Rather, he seeks to preserve the tension between the two. Both are true, both must be understood. God is indeed just and brings judgment (Mal 2:17-3:2a), but his judgment is intended to restore his relationship with his people by refining and purifying them (Mal 3:2b-4), and bringing about repentance (Mal 3:7). Furthermore, his judgment is on behalf of the weak and the oppressed (Mal 3:5). This is the same message brought by earlier prophets; indeed, God does not change (Mal 3:6).

Malachi and the New Testament. Several Malachi texts are important for the New Testament. The book of Malachi begins with God's statement that he has "loved Jacob but hated Esau" (Mal 1:2-5). We noted above (p. 258) that Malachi is here not referring to the two brothers, Jacob and Esau, as found in Genesis, but rather to the nations of Israel/Judah (Jacob) and Edom (Esau). He is responding to the people's accusation that God has not loved them. In Rom 9:13, however, Paul quotes Mal 1:2-3 in order to discuss not the love of God but rather the complex relationship between the justice and the freedom of God.

Mal 3:16 refers to "a book of remembrance" which was written in the presence of God and which contained the names of "those who feared the LORD and thought on his name." Although this verse is never quoted in the New Testament, it may be the foundation for the "book of life" mentioned in Phil 4:3 and six times in the book of Revelation (Rev 3:5; 13:8; 17:8; 20:12, 15; 21:27). Malachi's reference to this "book of remembrance" might also hint at the possibility of life after death.

The coming of Elijah. Of course, it is the last words of Malachi, concerning the sending of "Elijah the prophet before the great and terrible day of the LORD comes," that are most well known to Christians, since the New Testament often connects them to John the Baptist.[13] But these verses were already speaking to an anxious and eagerly waiting Jewish community of faith long before the time of Jesus. The book of Sirach,[14] written just before the time of Daniel, speaks in glowing terms of Elijah (Sir 48:1-14). It looks back hopefully to these final words from Malachi, and, in Sir 48:10-11, the writer speaks to (the memory of?) Elijah:

> You ... are ready at the appointed time, it is written, to calm the wrath of God before it breaks out in fury, to turn the heart of the father to the son, and to restore the tribes of Jacob. Blessed are those who saw you, and those who have been adorned in love; for we also shall surely live.

This hope continues even today for religious Jews. During modern Passover services (which are today held in homes, not in a sanctuary or synagogue), an extra place is always set at the table – for Elijah! – in the hope that *this year* he will appear. And there is a moment in the celebration when one of the children is sent to open the door of the house, to see if Elijah is there and to let him in if he is, because, if Elijah appears, then it is believed that the Messiah will soon come.

These final verses of Malachi are the "last words" of the prophets, since they come at the very end of the Isaiah-Malachi collection. As we noted at the beginning of this book, these words concerning the coming of Elijah thus become the final words of the Old Testament. They have therefore always been seen by Christians as particularly significant. The Hebrew Scriptures, on the other hand, today end with 2 Chronicles; and that gives a different set of "last words" for modern Jews.[15]

But this was not true for the Jewish community of faith at the time

---

[13]Mt 11:10-14; 16:14; 17:10-12; Mk 6:15; 8:27-28; 9:11-13; Lk 1:17; Jn 1:21,25.

[14]The book of Sirach is also known by its full name "The Wisdom (or Book) of Jesus, son of Sirach" and by two other names: Ecclesiasticus (different from Ecclesiastes!), and "The Wisdom (or Book) of ben Sira." (Jesus, son of Sirach, is not related to Jesus in the New Testament). The book was originally written in Hebrew sometime between 200 and 180 B.C. in Jerusalem during the troubled period under the Seleucids. See the discussion of this "post-exilic period" on p. 195, above.

[15] See p. 5, above. There, we noted that the last words of the Hebrew Scriptures are Cyrus' proclamation in 2 Chr 36:22-23 that the Jews should return to rebuild Jerusalem. Thus, today, each Passover meal concludes with the words, "Next year in Jerusalem!" Christians, on the other hand, hear in the last words of Malachi a promise which pointed to John the Baptist who came to announce Jesus.

of Jesus. As we noted earlier, during the Persian, Hellenistic, Maccabean, and Roman periods, the "Bible" for Jews was the "Law and the Prophets." This was true until the Writings were fully canonized. Thus it was "the Law and the Prophets," which end with Malachi's words about the coming of Elijah, that spoke to the hopes of faithful Jews in the first century. Because of this, and because of other texts as well, Jesus was able to turn to this waiting and seeking community of faith and say, "You search the scriptures ... and it is they that bear witness to me" (John 5:39).

Some important texts: "I have loved Jacob but hated Esau" (Mal 1:2-3); be faithful to the wife of your youth (Mal 2:14-15); "I hate divorce, says the LORD" (Mal 2:16); "I will send you Elijah the prophet" (Mal 4:5-6)

Verses for memory: Mal 4:5-6

Appendices

Books of the Hebrew Scriptures and the Old Testament

The Old Testament and the Hebrew Scriptures have a different ordering of books (see the discussion on p. 2). Below are the books listed in the order in which they appear in each canon.

The Hebrew Scriptures		The Old Testament	
Law	***Writings***	***Law***	***Prophets***
Genesis	Psalms	Genesis	Isaiah
Exodus	Job	Exodus	Jeremiah
Leviticus	Proverbs	Leviticus	Lamentations
Numbers	Ruth	Numbers	Ezekiel
Deuteronomy	Song of Songs	Deuteronomy	Daniel
	Ecclesiastes		Hosea
Prophets	Lamentations	***History***	Joel
Joshua	Esther	Joshua	Amos
Judges	Daniel	Judges	Obadiah
1-2 Samuel	Ezra	Ruth	Jonah
1-2 Kings	Nehemiah	1-2 Samuel	Micah
Isaiah	1-2 Chronicles	1-2 Kings	Nahum
Jeremiah		1-2 Chronicles	Habakkuk
Ezekiel		Ezra	Zephaniah
Hosea		Nehemiah	Haggai
Joel		Esther	Zechariah
Amos			Malachi
Obadiah		***Poetry***	
Jonah		Job	
Micah		Psalms	
Nahum		Proverbs	
Habakkuk		Ecclesiastes	
Zephaniah		Song of Songs	
Haggai			
Zechariah			
Malachi			

Hebrew:
The Alphabet and Some Important Words

It is not necessary to know Hebrew in order to study the Old Testament. But since Hebrew words often appear and are discussed in books about the Old Testament, it can be helpful to know the Hebrew alphabet and a few important words.

The Hebrew language is built upon consonants. The vowels were not written in ancient Hebrew, and they are not written in modern Hebrew. (They were added in the Hebrew Bible about one thousand years ago to help the reader pronounce the words.) Thus, one can do quite a bit with Hebrew just by learning the 23 consonants.[1]

The Hebrew Alphabet.

The table on the next page has two columns. In each column, the Hebrew letter is shown on the left (א ב, etc.), its name is given in the middle (*aleph, bet*, etc), and its pronunciation is given on the right. When two forms of a Hebrew letter appear (for instance כ and ך), the second one is used at the end of the word (just like in Greek, where a letter σ at the end of a word is printed ς). Note that **Hebrew is written and read from right to left.**

Sometimes books will use Roman letters (English letters) to represent Hebrew. This is called *transliteration*. For instance, instead of מלך they will write *mlk* (again note that Hebrew goes from right to left). Since Hebrew has two kinds of *h* and several *s* and *t* letters, special marks are used to distinguish these letters. For instance, both ס and שׂ have an *s* sound. Thus, ס is transliterated *s* and שׂ is transliterated *ś*. When the transliteration uses special marks, it is included in parentheses in the third column, below. (In this book, the transliteration has been very informal, and has not used these special marks.)

[1]There were originally 22 consonants, with the letter ש representing both the sound *s* and *sh*. Later, dots were added to the letter to distinguish between the two sounds. Thus, today שׂ represents *s* and שׁ represents *sh*.

א	*aleph*	* (ʾ)	מם	*mem*	m
ב	*bet*	b	נן	*nun*	n
ג	*gimmel*	g	ס	*samek*	s
ד	*dalet*	d	ע	*ayin*	* (ʿ)
ה	*he*	h	פף	*peh*	p
ו	*waw*	w	צץ	*ṣade*	ts (ṣ)
ז	*zayin*	z	ק	*qof*	q
ח	*ḥet*	hard h (ḥ)	ר	*resh*	r
ט	*ṭet*	sharp t (ṭ)	שׂ	*sin*	s (ś)
י	*yod*	y	שׁ	*shin*	sh (š)
כך	*kaf*	k	ת	*tuv*	t
ל	*lamed*	l			

Two of the consonants above are unusual, and their pronunciations are marked with asterisks (*). These letters are א and ע, and you may wish to ask someone who has studied Hebrew about them. You may generally consider them to be silent letters. And note: although א is called *aleph*, it is *not* the letter *a*. Remember, all the letters in the table above are consonants, not vowels. Thus, א is also a consonant.

Vowels are added as "points" below (and sometimes above) the letters. For instance, the vowel *i* is a dot placed under the letter. Thus, *bi* is written בִ. The simplified list below uses the letter ב for placement:

בָ[2] long *a*   בַ short *a*,   בֵ long *e*,   בֶ short *e*,

בִ *i*,   בֹ or בוֹ *o*,   בוּ long *u*   בֻ short *u*

Another letter, called *shewa* (בְ), is often silent (though not always). Thus אַבְרָהָם is pronounced *ab-ra-ham.*

Accent is always on the last syllable of the word unless an accent mark (֫) appears elsewhere. For instance, words which have an *e* in their first syllable, such as חֶ֫סֶד and פֶּ֫סַח, or the word ר֫וּחַ, have the accent on their first syllable.

---

[2]This vowel point (ָ) is sometimes (though seldom) also used for short *o*.

Letters with dots: Six letters ב ג ד כ פ ת have "hard" and "soft" sounds The "hard" sound occurs when they have a dot in them. This dot does not usually affect the meaning of the letter or the word. The sounds of these six letters are as follows:

בּ=*b*, ב=*v*　　גּ=*g*, ג = *gh*　　דּ=*d*, ד=*dh*

כּ=*k*, כ = *kh*　　פּ=*p*, פ=*ph*　　תּ=*t*, ת=*th*

Thus, בָּבֶל is pronounced *ba-VEL*, and אַבְרָהָם is actually pronounced *av-ra-HAM.* In transliteration, the soft pronunciations have a line under them. Thus, בּ=*b* but ב=*ḇ*.

If a dot appears in a letter other than the six above, it causes that letter to be doubled. Thus, מּ=ממ=mm.

The list on the next page gives a selection of important Hebrew words which are often mentioned and discussed in commentaries and other books about the Old Testament.

Some important Hebrew words

אַבְרָהָם	Abraham
אָדוֹן	lord (cf אֲדֹנָי)
אֲדֹנָי	the Lord (see p. 34)
אָדָם	Adam
אֱלֹהִים	God
בָּבֶל	Babylon
בַּעַל	lord, husband; Baal
בָּרָא	to create
בְּרִית	covenant
בֵּרַךְ	to bless
בְּרָכָה	blessing
גּוֹיִם	nations, gentiles
דָּבָר	word; thing
דָּוִד	David
דַּעַת	knowledge
הֵיכָל	temple, palace
חָכָם	wise
חָכְמָה	wisdom
חֶסֶד	faithfulness, loyalty, steadfast love
יְהוּדָה	Judah
יְהוָה	Yahweh, the LORD (see the discussion of this name on p. 34)
יְרוּשָׁלַםִ	Jerusalem
יִשְׂרָאֵל	Israel
יְשׁוּעָה	salvation
כָּבוֹד	glory, honor, weight
כֹּהֵן	priest
מֶלֶךְ	king
מִנְחָה	offering, gift
מִצְוָה	commandment
מֹשֶׁה	Moses
מִשְׁכָּן	tabernacle tent
מִשְׁפָּט	justice, judgment
נָבִיא	prophet
נָשִׂיא	prince, leader
עָבַד	to serve, worship
עֶבֶד	servant
עֲבֹדָה	service, work, worship
עֹלָה	burnt offering
עַם	people
פֶּסַח	Passover
צַדִּיק	just, righteous
צֶדֶק	that which is right, just
צְדָקָה	righteousness
קָדוֹשׁ	holy
רוּחַ	spirit, breath, wind
שְׁאוֹל	Sheol (vs שָׁאוּל = Saul)
שַׁבָּת	Sabbath
שָׁלוֹם	peace, wholeness
שְׁלֹמֹה	Solomon
שְׁמוּאֵל	Samuel
שָׁפַט	to judge
שֹׁפֵט	a judge
תּוֹרָה	instruction, guidance, "law"

Ancient Near Eastern Gods Mentioned in the Old Testament

Following is a list of the ancient Near Eastern (ANE) gods which appear in the Bible. A few which do not appear in the Bible are also included if they are important.[1]

The ANE was polytheistic and believed in a pantheon[2] of gods. This included a divine council with a supreme god as head.[3] There were male and female gods, fertility gods, gods of war, etc., and the names of these gods varied from place to place. The pantheon was especially complex in Egypt.[4]

Like other ANE cultures, Israel may originally have felt that gods were territorial. In other words, Yahweh was just more powerful than the other gods (see, for instance, Num 33:4b). Later Israel became theologically more confident and denied the reality and existence of these other "gods." Isaiah laughed at idols made by human hands (see p. 176, above). In the Deuteronomistic History, there are several places where the word "god" was simply replaced by the word "abomination."[5]

Unlike other ANE cultures, the Israelites did not associate the name

---

[1]The actual ANE stories of these gods may be found in J. Pritchard, *Ancient Near Eastern Texts* (*ANET*), third edition with supplement (Princeton University Press, 1969). See also dictionary articles such as M. Rose, "Names of God in the Old Testament" (section D., "Foreign Divine Names") in *ABD* 4:1009-1010; R. K. Harrison, "Gods" in *ISBE* 2:516-519. The series of articles on "Religions of the Biblical World" in *ISBE* 4:79-107, 123-129 is particularly helpful.

[2]A pantheon is the whole group of a nation's gods.

[3]Remnants of this idea can still be seen in the "prehistory" (see p. 23) and poetic sections of the Old Testament. See, for instance, the "divine council" in Ps 82:1; the "sons of God" in Gen 6:2,4; Deut 32:8 and Job 1:6; 2:1; 38:7; and the "us" of Gen 1:26; 3:22. Note the further discussion of this on p. 134.

[4]These general characteristics are sometimes called the "common theology" of the ANE. See Morton Smith, "The Common Theology of the Ancient Near East," *JBL* 7 (1952), 35-47; and the discussion of this article in Walter Brueggemann, *Old Testament Theology: Essays on Structure, Theme, and Text* (Minneapolis: Fortress Press, 1992) 5-10.

[5]For instance, "Milcom the abomination of the Ammonites," 1 Kgs 11:5. See also 1 Kgs 11:7 and 2 Kgs 23:13.

of Yahweh with the names of other ANE gods. This is in contrast to the Babylonians, for instance, who had 50 names for Merodach (Marduk), many of which were attempts to make correlations and links to older Sumerian divine names.

Amon. Egyptian god of wind and air; his temple (Karnak) was in Thebes. Amon eventually became the state god of Egypt, and he was then considered the "king of gods." He was described in ways very similar to **Re**, the sun god, and eventually was called Amon-Re. Pharaoh Akenaten (Amenophis IV, 1377-1360 B.C.) eliminated the Amon-Re cult for awhile, in his attempt to establish monotheism, but it returned after his death. The name Amon is mentioned as the Egyptian god only once[6] in the Old Testament (Jer 46:25), though it appears 17 other times referring to the king of Judah or to a governor.

Anat/Anath. Canaanite goddess of fertility; very violent and blood-thirsty; daughter of the high god El (whom she threatens and intimidates). She is sometimes described as Baal's wife, sometimes as his sister. In the Bible, her name is found only in place names (Beth-anath = House/temple of Anath, Josh 19:38; Judg 1:33; Anathoth 20 times) and in personal names (Judg 3:31, 5:6). Anat was also known by several other names: Astarte, Ishtar, Asherah, Ashtoreth.

Asherah. This name has many mixed traditions. Sometimes the Bible mentions "the Asherah" and sometimes it just uses the name "Asherah." In some texts (the) Asherah is a cultic object (perhaps a tree) found in or near a high place or temple. But she/it can also have an image (2 Kgs 21:7). As a goddess, Asherah was connected with the sea, and she had a helper who was a fisherman. She was the wife of either El (in Canaanite tradition) or Baal (in Palestine). She was very important in Tyre, and her presence in Israel was blamed on Jezebel (1 Kgs 18:19) who came from Sidon, very near Tyre. There was sometimes also confusion between Asherah and the goddesses Anat and Astarte. Exod 34:13; Deut 7:5; 12:3; 16:21; Judg 6:25-30; 1 Kgs 15:13; 16:33; 18:19; 2 Kgs 13:6; 17:10,16; 18:4; 21:3,7; 23:4-7,14-15; 2 Chr 14:3; 15:16; 17:6; 19:3; 24:18; 31:1; 33:3,19; 34:3-7; Isa 17:8; 27:9.

Ashur. God of Assyria. Ashur is not mentioned in the Old Testament, though is found in several names: Ashurbanipal, Ashur-nasirpal. Ishtar, goddess of war, was sometimes placed on the same

---

[6]Twice, if the reference to *no-amon* in Nah 3:8 is counted. The phrase is usually simply translated Thebes.

level as Ashur.

Astarte. Only the plural form of this name, Ashtaroth, is found in the Old Testament. Often it is a place name (Deut 1:4; Josh 9:10; 12:4; 13:12,31; 1 Chr 6:71). Other times, reference is to "the Ashtaroth" as if referring to a type of idol (Judg 2:13; 10:6; 1 Sam 7:3,4; 12:10; 31:10). It may be another form of "Asherah."

Baal. Canaanite god of rain and thunderstorm, and thus a god of fertility. Baal was part of El's council of gods, though in some Ugaritic (Canaanite language) literature Baal is considered the high god or perhaps at times even in competition with El. Anath (called Astarte or Asherah in Palestine) is sometimes described as his wife, sometimes as his sister. The word *baal* means *lord*, *husband* or *owner*, and at times in the Bible it is not clear whether the word should be translated as "lord" or as the divine name Baal. Hos 2:16-17 plays upon this double meaning. Sometimes, when the Bible speaks of "the baals," the word just means *idols*. Baal worship became a major challenge to the faith of Israel in the ninth century B.C., and the prophets provided strong opposition.

Baal-Zebub. Philistine god worshiped at Ekron (2 Kgs 1:2-16). The original name was probably Baal-Zebul (perhaps "lord of exalted dwelling") but was changed by the Jews to the insulting name Baal-Zebub ("lord of flies"!). Later the name appears in the New Testament as "Beelzebul the prince of demons."

Behemoth. Not actually a god. Behemoth is mentioned only once in the Bible (Job 40:15). The word may originally have referred to the hippopotamus, but later it gained mythological significance. The description of Behemoth in Job 40:15 is similar to that of Leviathan in Job 41:1.

Bel. The word means "lord" (cf. Baal) and it was used as an alternate name for Merodach/Marduk.

Chemosh. National god of Moab (Num 21:29; Judg 11:24; 1 Kgs 11:7,33; 2 Kgs 23:13; Jer 48:7,13,46). Little is known about this god, though Moabite theology and cult were apparently similar to that of Israel.

Dagon. National god of the Philistines; worshiped much earlier in northern Mesopotamia. Dagon was also considered to be the father of Baal, and like Baal he was considered to be a god of rain and fertility. Not surprisingly, the name Dagon is related to the Hebrew word *dagan* (דָּגָן), *grain*. Judg 16:23; 1 Sam 5:2-7; 1 Chr 10:10.

El. Chief god of the Canaanites. The word *el* (אֵל) can mean either "god" or the name El. It is found in many names; for instance, "Elijah" means "my god (is) Yah(weh)." Although El was considered to be the high god, and chief of the council of the gods, he was not particularly strong. His fierce daughter Anat intimidated him, and at times Baal is seen as a competitor, challenger or even as the high god himself. In the Bible, the name El is often used in combination with other words to mean Yahweh, the God of Israel. For instance, *El Elyon* is often translated "God Most High" and is associated with Jerusalem. *El Shaddai* is translated "God Almighty." Hagar calls God *El Roi*, "God of seeing." Jacob worships *El Bethel*, "God of Bethel" (literally "God of the-house-of-God").

Image of jealousy. This is mentioned only in Ezek 8:3,5 and it probably refers to an idol whose presence in the temple area made God jealous. (See p. 163 footnote 7 regarding the jealousy of God.)

Ishtar. Mesopotamian goddess of war and fertility, found particularly at Nineveh in Assyria. She was the daughter of the moon god and her brother was the sun god. She herself was associated with the planet Venus and sometimes with the goddess Inanna. Tammuz was sometimes considered to be her lover. Ishtar is not mentioned in the Bible, although some think the name Esther is a form of Ishtar.

Kaiwan. See Sakkuth and Kaiwan.

Leviathan. An ancient monster in Ugaritic (Canaanite) mythology representing chaos. It joined with Mot (Death) to fight against Baal, but it was defeated, and the waters of chaos flowed out from its pierced body. The body was then cut into two parts and the heavens and the earth were formed from them, separating the waters of chaos above and below. Shadows of this imagery may possibly be seen in the "firmament" (RSV) or "dome" (NRSV) of Genesis 1. In poetic portions of the Bible, the imagery of Leviathan has been used to speak of God's power over all of creation, including monsters at sea. Job 3:8; 41:1; Ps 74:14; 104:26; Isa 27:1. The "fleeing serpent" of Job 26:13 and Isa 27:1 also refer to Leviathan. See also Rahab.

Marduk. See Merodach.

Merodach. Chief god of Babylon and eventually of Babylonia as a whole. (The name is sometimes spelled "Marduk.") In the Bible, Merodach is sometimes called Bel (Isa 46:1; Jer 50:2; 51:44). Merodach was a high god who ruled with full authority and without needing the agreement of a divine council. The Babylonian creation epic, *Enuma Elish*, describes his ascent to the position of sole authority. The name is also found in names such as Merodach-Baladan, Berodach-Baladan, Evil-Merodach. Some suggest a connection between the name Merodach (Marduk) and the name Mordecai in the book of Esther.

Milcom. Ammonite version of Baal. The name is from the root *mlk* (מלך), "to rule." 1 Kgs 11:5,33; 2 Kgs 23:13; Jer 49:1,3; Zep 1:5. Probably also 1 Chr 20:2 (see NRSV vs RSV).

Molech. A god to whom children were offered by fire. Perhaps originally Phoenician. The name comes from the root *mlk* (מלך), "to rule." Possibly the name Molech was originally pronounced Melech, the same as the Hebrew word for "king" (מֶלֶךְ) but the vowels were changed to rhyme with the word *bosheth* (בֹּשֶׁת) "shame." Lev 18:21; 20:2-5; 1 Kgs 11:7; 2 Kgs 23:10; Isa 57:9; Jer 32:35.

Nebo. Usually Nebo is a location in Moab or a personal name. But in Isa 46:1 it refers to Nabu, son of Merodach (Marduk). The name Nebuchadnezzar means "Nabu protect my boundary stone."

Pharaoh. Egyptians considered their king to be divine, being the son of Re (the sun god) and the Queen Mother. While he was alive, Pharaoh was considered to be the falcon god Horus. When he died, he became Osiris and joined the other gods of the Egyptian pantheon.

Queen of heaven. This name is mentioned five times in Jeremiah (Jer 7:18; 44:17-19,25) and it probably refers to Ishtar (see above).

Rahab. An ancient mythological monster representing chaos. See also Leviathan. The name appears in two forms in the Bible, *rāḥāḇ* (רָחָב) and *raḥaḇ* (רַהַב), and, though spelled the same in English, they have different meanings. The first spelling refers to the prostitute Rahab in Jericho who hid the Israelite spies in Joshua 2 and 6. The second spelling refers four times to the ancient monster of ANE mythology who was defeated at creation (Job 9:13; 26:12; Ps 89:10; Isa 51:9). Two other times, the name is used to refer to Egypt (Ps 87:4; Isa 30:7).

Sakkuth and Kaiwan. Probably both refer to Saturn, the most distant planet visible to the Mesopotamians. It moved slowly and steadily, and so it was revered and worshiped for its stability. Amos 5:26.

Tammuz. This name is mentioned only once in the Old Testament (Ezek 8:14). Tammuz is the Hebrew version of Dumuzi, a Sumerian god who was a shepherd and the lover of Ishtar/Inanna (daughter of Nanna the moon goddess). There is a story of Inanna's descent to the under world, and scholars debate whether Tammuz also went to the world of the dead and was a "dying and rising god" of vegetation. His annual death was mourned because (in northern climates) his death represented the death of the earth's vegetation. Thus, the weeping for Tammuz (Ezek 8:14) was intended to bring the return of spring and vegetation.

Weights and Measures

Length

Measures of length are based upon measurements of the human body, and so they are not precise. The most basic unit is the cubit, which is the length of the forearm, from the elbow to the end of the fingers.

Unit	Definition	Comparisons	Metric*
cubit	elbow to finger tips	-	50 cm
span	thumb to little finger of outstretched hand	1/2 cubit	25 cm
palm	width of the four fingers of the hand	1/3 span, 1/6 cubit	8 cm
finger	width of the finger	1/4 palm, 1/24 cubit	2 cm

*Metric equivalents are very approximate.

Weight

The basic unit of weight was the shekel. Beyond that, things become rather complex. For general purposes, however, the following chart may be used. See the comments which follow, however.

Unit	Comparisons	Metric*	
		Heavy	Light
gerah	1/20 shekel	1 g.	1/2 g.
shekel	-	16 g.	8 g.
mina	50 shekels	800 g.	400 g.
talent	50 minas, 250 shekels	40 kg.	20 kg.

*Metric equivalents are very approximate.

Early "money" was not coins but rather pieces of precious metal such as silver. These had to be weighed to determine their value, and so the word *shekel* eventually came to mean both a weight and a coin.

The Bible nowhere defines any of the weights listed above in grams or kilograms, of course. Five times, the Old Testament says that one shekel is 20 gerahs. Once it says that a mina is 50 shekels. Otherwise, we must rely upon archeology, and archeology has found that there was a rather wide variety of weights in the ANE. The system above is based primarily upon 50 (50 shekels per mina, 50 minas per talent) but, especially in Mesopotamia, a base of 60 was also used. And then there were both a "heavy standard" and a "light standard," as shown above. For more detail, consult the various Bible dictionaries. Do not expect to find simplicity or consistency.

Volume

Volumes are also somewhat variable. The following should be used only as an approximation

Unit	Alternate Name	Comparisons	Metric*
homer	cor	-	225 liters
lethech		1/2 homer	112 liters
ephah	bath	1/10 homer	23 liters
omer		1/10 ephah, 1/100 homer	2 liters
hin		-	½-3½ liters
kab		-	1.5 liters
log		1/4 kab	0.4 liter

*Metric equivalents are very approximate.

The Hebrew Calendar

The Hebrew calendar is lunar, but it also followed the harvest seasons, and those, of course, are solar (following a year of 365¼ days). Since a lunar month has only 29 or 30 days, a lunar calendar will have approximately 360 days and will slowly fall behind a solar calendar. Thus, every third year or so, it was necessary to add an extra month of Adar at the end of the year to catch up.

Because of this, the months of the Jewish calendar will not exactly match the months of the modern calendar. But we can say that Nisan, for instance, fell somewhere in March or April each year.

Not all of the names below are found in the Bible. Some are found in external archeological sources.

Number of month	Name of Month	Approximate modern month
1	Abib or Nisan	March-April
2	Iyyar or Ziv	April-May
3	Sivan	May-June
4	Tammuz	June-July
5	Ab	July-August
6	Elul	August-September
7	Ethanim or Tishri	September-October
8	Bul or Marchesvan	October-November
9	Chislev	November-December
10	Tebeth	December-January
11	Shebat	January-February
12	Adar	February-March

Feasts and Festivals

(see p. 37 for details)

The three major annual feasts, at which all Israelite males were expected to appear at the sanctuary, occurred as follows:

Feast or Festival	Hebrew Month	Approximate Modern month
Passover/ Unleavened bread	Abib	March-April
Weeks/ Pentecost	Tammuz or Ab	midsummer
Ingathering or Booths	Ethanim	September-October

Index of Scripture References

Subject Index

Lightning Source UK Ltd.
Milton Keynes UK
UKOW06f1905080116

266080UK00007B/187/P